Lawrence H. Hammer
Oklahoma State University

William K. Carter
University of Virginia

Milton F. Usry
University of West Florida

STUDY GUIDE

Cost Accounting

PREPARED BY EDWARD J. VANDERBECK

11TH EDITION

COLLEGE DIVISION South-Western Publishing Co.

Cincinnati Ohio

Sponsoring Editor: David L. Shaut
Developmental Editor: Mary H. Draper
Production Editor: Peggy A. Williams
Production House: CompuText Productions, Inc.
Cover Designer: Michael Lindsay/Hulefeld Assoc., Inc.
Cover Photographer: Michael Wilson
Marketing Manager: Sharon C. Oblinger

AE88KD

Copyright © 1994

by SOUTH-WESTERN PUBLISHING CO.

Cincinnati, Ohio

ISBN: 0-538-82809-9

1 2 3 4 5 6 7 8 9 EB 1 0 9 8 7 6 5 4 3

Printed in the United States of America

I(T)P
International Thomson Publishing
South-Western Publishing Co. is an ITP Company. The ITP trademark is used under license.

Material from the Certified Internal Auditor Examination, by The Institute of Internal Auditors, Copyright © 1985-1987, by The Institute of Internal Auditors, Inc., 249 Maitland Avenue, Altamonte Springs, Florida 32701 U.S.A. Reprinted with permission.

Materials from the Certificate in Management Accounting Examinations, Copyright © 1985, 1986, and 1987 by the National Association of Accountants are reprinted (or adapted) with permission.

Material from the Uniform CPA Examination Questions and Unofficial Answers, Copyright © 1980-1983 and 1985-1987 by the American Institute of Certified Public Accountants, Inc., is reprinted (or adapted) with permission.

Contents

Management, the Controller, and Cost Accounting

REVIEW SUMMARY

I. Purpose of the Chapter

This chapter describes the environment of cost accounting from internal and external perspectives. It presents Cost Accounting as part of the management function and discusses the roles of the controller and the cost department. Last, it examines the certification movement, the ethical expectations, and other private and governmental influences on cost accounting.

II. The Three Basic Management Functions

The three basic management functions are planning, organizing, and controlling. **Planning** refers to the construction of a detailed operating program for all phases of operations; and it is the process of sensing external opportunities, determining objectives, and employing resources to accomplish these objectives. The three kinds of plans identifiable in business entities are: *strategic plans* that are formulated at the highest level of management and determine the nature of the firm, its products, and its customers; *short-range plans* or *budgets* that are prepared through a systematized process, are expressed in financial terms, and are for periods of one year or less; and *long-range plans* that are usually prepared for three to five years in advance and are an intermediate step between strategic plans and short-term plans.

Organizing is the establishment of the framework within which required activities are performed. Organizing involves the establishment of functional divisions, departments, sections, or branches.

Controlling is management's systematic effort to compare performance to plans. Actual results are measured against plans; if significant differences are noted, remedial action is taken.

III. Authority, Responsibility, and Accountability

The larger the business organization the greater the problems of planning, and the process of controlling the activities of individual units scattered throughout the world are more involved. Authority and responsibility are assigned to middle and operating management to assure the success and control of management's plans. **Authority** originates with executive management, which delegates it to the various managerial levels. **Responsibility** originates in the superior-subordinate relationship because the superior has the authority to require specified work from the subordinates. Another aspect of responsibility is **accountability**—reporting results achieved back to higher authority.

IV. The Organization Chart

An **organization chart** illustrates each principal management position and helps to define authority, responsibility, and accountability. It is essential to the development of a cost system and cost reports that parallel the responsibility of individuals for implementing management plans. An organization chart based on the *line-staff concept* categorizes all positions as to either "line" or "staff." An organization chart based on the *functional-teamwork concept* categorizes positions as resources, processes, and human interrelations functions.

V. The Controller's Participation in Planning and Control

The **controller** is the executive manager who is responsible for a company's accounting function. The controller coordinates management's participation in the planning and controlling functions, in determining the effectiveness of policies, and in creating organizational structures and procedures. The controller also aids in the control of business operations by issuing performance reports that advise management of activities that require corrective action. Concentrating on the activities that deviate significantly from the plan is called **management by exception**.

VI. The Cost Department and the Role of Cost Accounting

The **Cost Department**, under the direction of the controller, is responsible for keeping records of

1

a company's manufacturing and nonmanufacturing activities. It must issue significant control reports and other decision-making data to those managers who assist in controlling and improving costs and operations. The collection, presentation, and analysis of cost data help management accomplish the following: (1) creating and executing plans and budgets for operating under expected competitive and economic conditions; (2) establishing costing methods and procedures that permit control of activities, reductions of cost, or improvements in quality; (3) creating inventory values for costing and pricing purposes; (4) determining company costs and profit for an accounting period; and (5) choosing from among two or more alternatives that might increase revenues or decrease costs.

A.   Budgeting

The **budget** is the quantified, written expression of management's plans. A workable budget promotes coordination of people, clarification of policies, and crystallization of plans. Budgeting plays an important role in influencing individual and group behavior at all stages of the management process.

B.   Controlling Costs

Responsibility accounting systems limit each manager's responsibility to the costs that are controllable by that manager. To aid in controlling costs, the cost accountant may use predetermined cost amounts called *standard costs*. The cost of *non-value-added activities* result from the complexity that becomes embedded in production settings rather than from the production of the goods and services themselves.

C.   Pricing and Determining Profits

Management's pricing policy should assume long-run recovery of all costs and a profit. In determining profit, total fixed costs may be assigned to a period and matched with revenues of the period, called **direct costing** or **variable costing**; or, the fixed manufacturing costs may be matched with the units of product produced and charged against revenues only when the units are sold, called **absorption costing**.

D.   Cost Accounting and Manufacturing Technology

Technology is changing the nature of costs, for example, lower inventory levels, less use of labor, and increasing levels of fixed costs. In this new environment, cost accounting systems are evolving and taking on increasing importance.

VII.   Certification and Ethics

The **Certified Management Accountant (CMA)** is the professional certification that recognizes professional competence and educational achievement in the field of management accounting. The **Standards of Ethical Conduct for Management Accountants** presents fifteen responsibilities of the management accountant, grouped under the headings of competence, confidentiality, integrity, and objectivity. The standards also outline procedures for management accountants to follow if they have knowledge of, or think they are being asked to do, something unethical.

VIII.   The Influence of Private and Governmental Organizations

In the public sector, financial reporting has been influenced significantly by the Securities and Exchange Commission (SEC), the Internal Revenue Service (IRS), and the Cost Accounting Standards Board (CASB). In the private sector, financial reporting has been influenced by the American Institute of Certified Public Accountants (AICPA), which sponsored the formation of the Financial Accounting Standards Board (FASB); the Institute of Management Accountants (IMA); the American Accounting Association (AAA); the Financial Executives Institute (FEI); and the International Accounting Standards Committee (IASC).

IRS regulations influence financial reporting and cost accounting methods, since income tax consequences of various alternatives are weighed heavily in the decision-making process. The Cost Accounting Standards Board promulgated the cost and profit requirements to be followed by businesses in connection with government contracts.

Part 1 ■ True/False

Instructions: *Indicate whether each of the following statements is **True** or **False**.*

True/False

1. Strategic planning is basically a top-management responsibility. . . . .   _____

2. In practice, planning and control are interrelated functions that are not easily separated. . . . .   _____

3. Participation in the budgeting process has been shown to have negative effects on managers' attitudes toward their jobs. . . . .   _____

4. The accounting function should plan and act independently of the management function. . . . .   _____

5. Examples of non-value-added activities in a factory are moving materials, holding inventories, and reworking defective units. . . . .   _____

6. Nonmanufacturing costs are assigned first to the units manufactured and then matched with revenue when these units are sold. . . . .   _____

7. Executive management delegates authority to the various managerial levels. . .   _____

8. Accountability is the act of reporting results achieved by individual managers back to executive management. . . . .   _____

9. An organization chart is necessary for the development of an effective cost system.   _____

10. In automating a manufacturing process, employee involvement and motivation are the first step. . . . .   _____

11. The resources, processes, and human interrelations functions are position categories under the line-staff concept of management. . . . .   _____

12. The controller's most important contribution to planning is to coordinate information for management's use. . . . .   _____

13. The control phase of cost accounting consists of comparing performance to plans and taking action to correct major differences. . . . .   _____

14. Cost accounting is applicable only to manufacturing operations. . . . .   _____

15. All levels of management should be involved in creating the budget program.   _____

Part 2 ■ Matching

Instructions: *On the line at the left of each of the following items, place the letter from the columns below that identifies the term that best matches the statement. No letter should be used more than once.*

_____ 1. The process of sensing external opportunities and threats, determining desirable objectives, and employing resources to accomplish these objectives.

_____ 2. The process of establishing the framework within which required activities are to be performed.

_____ 3. Originates with executive management, which delegates it to the various managerial levels.

_____ 4. Originates in the superior-subordinate relationship but cannot be delegated.

_____ 5. Reporting results achieved back to higher authority.

_____ 6. Decisions that determine the future nature of the firm, its products, and its customers.

_____ 7. Typically extends three to five years into the future and culminates in a highly summarized set of financial statements.

_____ 8. Sets forth each principal management position and helps to define authority, responsibility, and accountability.

_____ 9. A quantified, written expression of management's plans.

_____ 10. An organizational concept that groups business functions around resources, processes, and human interrelations.

_____ 11. Management's systematic effort to achieve objectives by comparing performance to plans and taking corrective action, if necessary.

_____ 12. Predetermined costs for direct materials, direct labor, and factory overhead that are established by using information accumulated from past experience and from scientific research.

_____ 13. Established by the IMA in response to the need to have a formal means to recognize professional competence in management accounting.

_____ 14. Responsible for the functions of planning and decision processes, special managerial cost analysis, cost accounting, and general accounting.

_____ 15. Often called budgets and are sufficiently detailed to permit preparation of budgeted financial statements.

_____ 16. An approach to accounting and reporting that emphasizes the coordinated development of a company's organization with the cost and budgetary system.

_____ 17. Address issues related to competence, confidentiality, integrity, and objectivity, as well as outline procedures to follow in resolving ethical conflicts.

_____ 18. Limits each manager's responsibility to the costs that are controllable by the manager.

_____ 19. Directs the company's efforts in relation to the behavior of people outside and inside the organization.

_____ 20. Generally result from the complexities that become embedded in production settings rather than from the production of goods.

a.	planning	l.	responsibility accounting system
b.	controller	m.	accountability
c.	strategic plans	n.	responsibility
d.	short-range plans	o.	authority
e.	long-range plans	p.	organizing
f.	responsibility accounting	q.	*Standards of Ethical Conduct for Management Accountants*
g.	budget	r.	non-value-added activities
h.	organization chart	s.	functional-teamwork concept
i.	control	t.	human interrelations function
j.	CMA		
k.	standard costs		

Part 3 ■ Multiple Choice

Instructions: *On the line at the left of each of the following items, place the letter of the choice that most correctly completes each item.*

_____ 1. Examples of these include materials handling, expediting, and reworking defective units:

     a. value-added activities   **c.** variable costs

     b. fixed costs   **d.** non-value-added activities

_____ 2. The facet of responsibility that compares actual performance with predetermined plans and measures the extent to which objectives were reached is:

     a. accountability   **d.** authority

     b. obligation   **e.** securing results

     c. delegation

_____ 3. The organizational group that makes decisions and performs the true management functions is the:

     a. staff   **d.** line

     b. function   **e.** team

     c. executive management

_____ 4. In the functional-teamwork concept of management, the business function that directs the company's effort toward the behavior of people inside and outside the company is the:

     a. executive function   **d.** resources function

     b. staff   **e.** human interrelations function

     c. processes function

_____ 5. The level of management that most requires data for purposes of strategic planning is:

     a. executive management   **d.** scientific management

     b. middle management   **e.** management by exception

     c. operating management

_____ 6. The group that promulgated the cost and profit requirements to be followed by businesses in connection with federal government contracts is the:

     a. Cost Accounting Standards Board

     b. Financial Accounting Standards Board

     c. Financial Executives Institute

     d. Securities and Exchange Commission

     e. Federal Trade Commission

_____ 7. A term associated with changes in manufacturing technology is:

     a. flexible manufacturing system (FMS)

     b. just-in-time production (JIT)

     c. computer-integrated manufacturing (CIM)

     d. optimized production technology (OPT)

     e. all of the above

_____ 8. The professional designation for management accountants is:

     a. Certified Public Accountant (CPA)

     b. Chartered Accountant (CA)

     c. Certified Management Accountant (CMA)

     d. Certified Internal Accountant (CIA)

_____ **9.** Predetermined costs that are established by using information accumulated from past experience and scientific research are:

    a. budgets   **c.** normal costs

    b. actual costs   **d.** standard costs

_____ **10.** A quantified, written expression of management's plans for the future is a(n):

    a. organization chart   **c.** charter

    b. performance report   **d.** budget

Part 4 ■ Problem

Instructions: *Define, describe, or explain each of the following:*

1. The five tasks that the collection, presentation, and analysis of cost data should help management accomplish.

_____

_____

_____

_____

_____

_____

_____

_____

_____

2. The four Cost Accounting Standards that have the potential for impact far beyond the government contracting area.

_____

_____

_____

_____

_____

3. The line-staff concept of management.

_____

_____

_____

_____

_____

_____

4. The differences among strategic plans, short-range plans, and long-range plans.

_____

_____

_____

_____

_____

_____

_____

_____

5. The five ways that budgeting plays an important role in influencing individual and group behavior at all stages of the management process.

_____

_____

_____

_____

_____

_____

_____

_____

6. The procedures that an accountant is to follow in resolving an ethical conduct problem according to the _Standards of Ethical Conduct for Management Accountants._

_____

_____

_____

_____

_____

_____

_____

_____

Cost Concepts and the Cost Accounting Information System

REVIEW SUMMARY

I. Purpose of the Chapter

This chapter presents the fundamental concepts of cost accounting and introduces cost accounting as an information system. It describes several different degrees of cost traceability, states the considerations involved in creating a cost accounting information system, and explains why increased attention is being given to nonfinancial performance measures.

II. The Cost Concept

It is important to distinguish between the terms "cost" and "expense," particularly since they are often used interchangeably. **Cost** is an exchange price, a forgoing, a sacrifice made to secure benefit. **Expense** is the measured overflow of goods and services that is matched with revenue to determine income. A request for cost data must be accompanied by a description of the situation in which the data are to be used. In planning, for example, the accountant must often abandon recorded past costs and deal with future, imputed, differential, or opportunity costs.

A. Cost Objects and Traceability of Costs

A **cost object** is any item or activity where costs are accumulated and measured. Examples of cost objects are units of products, customers' orders, departments, divisions, and projects. Once a cost object is selected, measurement of costs depends heavily on the **traceability of costs** to the cost object. A common way of characterizing costs is to label them as either direct or indirect costs of a particular cost object, as if there were only two degrees of traceability. In fact, degrees of traceability exist along a continuum, with costs that can be physically or contractually identified with the cost object at one extreme and costs that can be identified with the cost object only by the most arbitrary allocations at the other extreme. The traceability of costs is as important for decision making in service businesses as it is in manufacturing, regardless of whether there is a need to determine the cost of inventories for external reporting.

III. The Cost Accounting Information System

A **cost accounting information system** must correspond to an organization's division of authority so that an individual manager can be held accountable for the departmental cost incurred. The information system must reflect the manufacturing and administrative processes of the company for which it was designed, and it should provide prompt and meaningful cost reports to management. In determining the degree of sophistication needed, the cost of the system should be compared to its prospective value to management.

A. The Chart of Accounts

The prerequisite for efficiently collecting, identifying, and coding data for recording in journals and posting to ledger accounts is a well-designed **chart of accounts**. A company's chart of accounts is divided into (1) balance sheet accounts for assets, liabilities, and capital and (2) income statement accounts for sales, cost of goods sold, marketing and administrative expenses, and other income and expenses. Account coding in the form of numbers, letters, and other symbols is essential to facilitate the processing of information.

B. Electronic Data Processing

Data processing is the accumulation, classification, analysis, and summary reporting of large quantities of information. **Electronic data processing** is a system for recording repetitive data. *Programming* involves the analysis of the job to be converted to electronic data processing, the preparation of flowcharts, the instruction coding for the computer, the debugging process, and trial runs.

C. Sensitivity to Changing Methods and Nonfinancial Performance Measures

It is vital that cost accounting systems be in harmony with the manufacturing methods in current usage. Robotics, just-in-time inventory systems, intensified competition, and other changes in the manufacturing environment have created a need to broaden the range of information that accountants deal with and have led to increased attention to **nonfinancial performance measures**. Nonfinancial performance measures use simple physical data rather than allocated accounting data, are not connected to the general financial accounting system, and are selected to measure one specific aspect of performance rather than to be "all things for all purposes."

Some nonfinancial performance measures, such as the number of good units or defective units produced, measure the efficiency or inefficiency of a production process; others, such as the average number of units in process, have arisen in JIT environments; and a third type, such as the number of times a unit is handled in the factory, measures the success in simplifying a process.

IV.   Costs May Be Classified in Many Different Ways

A.   In Relation to Phases of Business Operation

Costs are classified by the nature of the cost element.   **Manufacturing costs** consist of direct materials, direct labor, and factory overhead.   **Commercial expenses** consist of marketing expenses and administrative expenses.   *Marketing expenses* are the expenses of making sales and delivering products.   *Administrative expenses* are incurred in the direction, control, and administration of the organization.

B.   In Relation to the Product

Costs are classified by their relation to the product.   **Direct materials** are all materials that form an integral part of the finished product.   **Direct labor** is labor applied directly to the materials composing the finished product.   **Factory overhead** includes all manufacturing costs except direct materials and direct labor.   **Indirect materials** are the materials that either do not become part of the finished product or are too insufficient to identify with the product.   **Indirect labor** consists of factory workers who do not physically convert the raw materials to finished product.

C.   In Relation to Volume of Production

Costs are classified by their tendency to vary with volume or activity.   **Variable costs** vary directly in relation to changes in the volume of production, remain constant on a per-unit basis within a relevant range, are reasonably easy to assign to operating departments, and are the responsibility of the supervisor of the department in which the costs were incurred.   **Fixed costs** are fixed in amount within a relevant range, decrease on a per-unit basis when output is increased, and are often assigned to departments by arbitrary methods; in most cases, management is responsible for incurring them.   **Semivariable costs** contain both fixed and variable elements.

D.   In Relation to Manufacturing Departments

Costs are classified by their relation to manufacturing departments.   For product costing, the factory is divided into departments, cost centers, or cost pools.   **Producing departments** are those whose costs may be charged to the product because they contribute directly to its production.   **Service departments** are not directly engaged in production but render services for the benefit of other departments.   Factory overhead cost is considered a *direct cost* to a specific department if it is readily identifiable with that department.   It is classified as an *indirect cost* if it is incurred for the benefit of several departments and must be allocated to those departments.

Costs are classified as to their nature as common or joint costs.   *Common costs* are costs of facilities or services employed by two or more operations, commodities, or services.   *Joint costs* occur when the production of one product is possible only if one or more other products are manufactured at the same time.

E.   In Relation to an Accounting Period

Costs are classified with respect to the accounting period in which they apply.   A **capital expenditure** is expected to benefit future periods and is classified as an asset.   A **revenue expenditure** benefits the current period and is termed an expense.

Part 1 ■ True/False

Instructions: *Indicate whether each of the following statements is **True** or **False**.*

True/False

1. "Cost" is the measured outflow of goods and services that is matched with revenue to determine income. . . . .   _____

2. The accountant primarily uses estimates of future costs for planning purposes. . . . . .   _____

3. Indirect materials would include factory supplies and lubricants. . . . .   _____

4. Direct labor would include the wages of assemblers and finishers. . . . .   _____

5. Variable factory overhead would include fuel costs and receiving costs. . . . .   _____

6. Fixed factory overhead would include straight-line depreciation and property taxes. . .   _____

7. Factory overhead includes all manufacturing costs except direct materials and direct labor.   _____

8. Units of production, customer orders, departments, and divisions could all be cost objects.   _____

9. The allocation of joint costs to joint products is a very precise process. . . . .   _____

10. A common way of characterizing costs is to label them as direct or indirect as to a particular cost object, because there are only two degrees of traceability. . . . .   _____

11. Electronic data processing is a system for recording and processing information without rerecording repetitive data. . . . .   _____

12. A manufacturing process that heavily utilizes robotics would be more apt to use direct labor hours than machine hours as a base for allocating factory overhead. . . . .   _____

13. The traceability of costs is as important for decision making in service businesses as it is in manufacturing. . . . .   _____

14. Fixed costs are thought of as the costs of being in business, whereas variable costs are the costs of doing business. . . . .   _____

15. Cost accounting information should be restricted to information that is measured in dollars. . . . .   _____

Part 2 ■ Matching

Instructions: *On the line at the left of each of the following items, place the letter from the columns below that identifies the term that best matches the statement. No letter should be used more than once.*

_____   1. A product, job order, contract, project, or department for which an arrangement is made to accumulate and measure cost.

_____   2. Composed of direct materials, direct labor, and factory overhead.

_____   3. Costs of making sales and delivering products.

_____   4. A trend toward relying on this as the most important basis for classifying and understanding costs.

_____   5. Consists of direct materials plus direct labor.

_____   6. Consists of direct labor plus factory overhead.

_____   7. Remains constant on a per-unit basis within a relevant range.

_____   8. Decreases on a per-unit basis when output is increased.

_____   9. Contains both fixed and variable elements.

_____   10. Includes all materials that form an integral part of the finished product.

_____   11. Includes all manufacturing costs except direct materials and direct labor.

_____   12. Performs manual or machine operations directly upon the product.

_____   13. Does not directly engage in production; but costs are a part of factory overhead.

_____   14. A cost traceable to the department in which it originates.

_____   15. Examples include number of defective units produced, hours of machine downtime, and weight of scrap materials produced.

_____   16. A prerequisite for efficiently collecting, identifying, and coding data for recording in journals and posting to ledger accounts.

_____   17. A cost shared by several departments that benefit from its incurrence.

_____   18. The consumption is so minimal or so complex that attempting to identify them with individual products would be futile.

_____   19. Factory labor that does not directly affect the construction or the composition of the finished product.

_____   20. Work applied directly to the materials composing the finished product.

a.	direct labor	k.	traceability
b.	direct materials	l.	prime cost
c.	indirect labor	m.	direct departmental cost
d.	semivariable cost	n.	nonfinancial performance measures
e.	indirect materials	o.	service department
f.	fixed cost	p.	marketing expenses
g.	indirect departmental cost	q.	producing department
h.	variable cost	r.	manufacturing cost
i.	chart of accounts	s.	factory overhead
j.	conversion cost	t.	cost object

Part 3 ■ Multiple Choice

Instructions: *On the line at the left of each of the following items, place the letter of the choice that most correctly completes each item.*

_____ 1. Factory overhead includes:

    a. all manufacturing costs
    b. all manufacturing costs, except direct materials and direct labor
    c. indirect materials but not indirect labor
    d. indirect labor but not indirect materials
    e. none of the above   *(AICPA adapted)*

_____ 2. The term "fixed costs" refers to:

    a. all costs that are likely to respond to the amount of attention devoted to them by a specified manager
    b. all costs that are associated with marketing, shipping, warehousing, and billing activities
    c. all costs that do not change in total for a given period of time and relevant range, but become progressively smaller on a per-unit basis as volume increases
    d. all costs that fluctuate in total in response to small changes in the rate of utilization of capacity
    e. none of the above   *(ICMA adapted)*

_____ 3. Reasons for the increased attention being given to nonfinancial performance measures include:

    a. dissatisfaction with financial matters
    b. dissatisfaction with the slow pace of a company's accounting and processing departments
    c. dissatisfaction with financial measures of plant utilization
    d. dissatisfaction with financial measures of processing efficiency
    e. all of the above

_____ 4. The term "conversion cost" refers to:

    a. manufacturing cost incurred to produce units of output
    b. all costs associated with manufacturing, other than direct labor and raw materials
    c. the sum of direct labor and all factory overhead
    d. the sum of direct materials and direct labor
    e. none of the above   *(ICMA adapted)*

_____ 5. From the following, the best example of a fixed cost is:

    a. property taxes   **d.** straight-line depreciation
    b. interest charges   **e.** all of the above
    c. corporate president's salary   *(ICMA adapted)*

_____ 6. From the following, the best example of a variable cost is:

    a. inspection   **d.** fuel
    b. salaries of production executives   **e.** none of the above
    c. maintenance and repair

_____ 7. A typical indirect factory overhead cost is:

    a. postage   **d.** freight out
    b. power   **e.** all of the above
    c. stationery and printing

_____ **8.** From the following, the best example of a semivariable cost is:
    a. maintenance and repairs of machinery and equipment
    b. property tax
    c. straight-line depreciation
    d. insurance
    e. none of the above

_____ **9.** A typical administrative expense is:
    a. freight and cartage out
    b. advertising
    c. sales salaries
    d. auditing expenses
    e. all of the above

_____ **10.** A typical marketing expense is:
    a. legal expenses
    b. entertainment
    c. uncollectible accounts
    d. office salaries
    e. all of the above

Part 4 ■ Problem

Instructions: *Place a check mark in the appropriate column to indicate whether the following costs are variable, fixed, or semivariable.*

Item	Variable	Fixed	Semivariable
1. Direct materials..........................			
2. Factory supplies			
3. Property tax			
4. Small tools			
5. Payroll taxes			
6. Direct labor............................			
7. Fuel...................................			
8. Heat, light, and power.................			
9. Rent...................................			
10. Salaries of production executives			
11. Health and accident insurance			
12. Inspection			
13. Wages of security guards...............			
14. Property insurance			
15. Straight-line depreciation			
16. Receiving costs			
17. Royalties			
18. Overtime premium			
19. Patent amortization....................			
20. Machinery maintenance			

Part 5 ■ Problem

Instructions: *Place a check mark in the appropriate column to indicate the proper classification of each of the following costs.*

Item	Indirect Materials	Indirect Labor	Other Indirect Factory Costs	Marketing Expenses	Administrative Expenses
1. Salary of vice-president of personnel					
2. Fire and liability insurance on factory buildings					
3. Lubricants					
4. Salary of vice-president of manufacturing					
5. Office salaries					
6. Uncollectible accounts expense					
7. Freight out					
8. Samples					
9. Payroll taxes on factory wage					
10. Small tools					
11. Overtime premium for factory workers					
12. Experimental work by engineers					
13. Glue and nails in finished product					
14. Cleaning compound for factory					
15. Sales commissions					
16. Entertainment of clients . .					
17. Audit fees					
18. Employer payroll taxes on president's salary					
19. Inspection					
20. Idle time due to assembly line breakdown					

Part 6 ■ Problem

The estimated unit costs for Monarch Machine Tools, when operating at a production and sales level of 5,000 units, are as follows:

Cost Item	Estimated Unit Cost
Direct material	$25
Direct labor	6
Variable factory overhead	9
Fixed factory overhead	15
Variable marketing	3
Fixed marketing	5

Instructions:

1. Calculate the estimated conversion cost per unit.

2. Calculate the estimated prime cost per unit.

3. Calculate the estimated variable manufacturing cost per unit.

4. Calculate the estimated total variable cost per unit.

5. Calculate the total cost that would be incurred in a month that had a production level of 5,000 units and a sales level of 4,500 units.

6. Calculate the total cost that would be incurred in a month that had a production level of 5,000 units and a sales level of 5,500 units.

CHAPTER 3

Cost Behavior Analysis

REVIEW SUMMARY

I. Purpose of the Chapter

This chapter discusses the effect of changes in business activity on costs and classifies costs as fixed, variable, or semivariable. It lists reasons for separating fixed and variable costs and illustrates three techniques used to segregate the fixed and variable components of costs. It illustrates techniques used to determine the degree of correlation among variables.

II. Classifying Cost

A **fixed cost** remains the same in total as activity increases or decreases. However, *programmed fixed costs* may change in the short run due to changes in operations. A *committed fixed cost*, such as depreciation, commits management to the allocation of resources for a much longer period of time. A **variable cost** increases proportionately with an increase in activity and decreases proportionately with a decrease in activity. A measure of activity, such as direct labor hours or machine hours, must be selected as an independent variable for use in estimating the variable cost, the dependent variable, at specified levels of activity. A **semivariable cost** displays both fixed and variable characteristics because items such as maintenance or power require a minimum of organization or quantity in order to maintain readiness to operate, and beyond this minimum, additional cost varies with volume. The *relevant range* is the range of activity over which the calculated amount of fixed cost and the variable cost rate remain unchanged.

III. Separating Fixed and Variable Costs

The **high and low points method** of determining the fixed and variable elements of a semivariable cost selects data points that are the periods of highest and lowest activity levels. In the **scattergraph method**, actual costs for several periods are plotted on a two-dimensional graph, with cost on the vertical axis and activity on the horizontal axis. Fixed cost and the variable rate are determined by visually fitting a line through the data points. For a more exact determination of cost behavior, the **method of least squares** determines mathematically a line of best fit or a linear regression line drawn through a set of plotted points so that the sum of the squared deviations of each actual plotted point from the point directly above or below it on the regression line is at a minimum.

A. Correlation Analysis

The **standard error of the estimate** is the standard deviation about the regression line and can be used to develop a confidence interval to decide whether a given level of expense requires management action. **Correlation** is a measure of the covariance between two variables, i.e., the independent variable and the dependent variable. The **coefficient of correlation** (r) is a measure of the extent to which two variables are related linearly. The **coefficient of determination** (r^2), obtained by squaring the coefficient of correlation, represents the percentage of variance in the dependent variable explained by the independent variable.

B. Distributions of the Observations

After computing the fixed and variable components of cost using the method of least squares, it is useful to plot the regression line against the sample data so that the pattern of deviations of the actual observations from the corresponding estimates on the regression line can be inspected. If the distribution of observations around the regression line is uniform for all values of the independent variable, it is referred to as **homoscedastic**. If the variance differs at different points on the regression line (known as **heteroscedastic**) or the observations around the regression line appear to be correlated with one another (**serial correlation** or **autocorrelation**), the standard error of the estimate and the confidence intervals based on the standard error are unreliable measures.

C. Multiple Regression Analysis

If more than one independent variable is required to describe cost behavior, then **multiple regression analysis** should be used. An assumption is that the independent variables are not correlated with one another. The presence of **multicollinearity** (related independent variables) would not affect the estimate of cost unless one or more important independent variables were omitted. Omitting important independent variables from the multiple regression model is known as **specification error**. If the behavior of a group of costs is being observed, costs may be grouped and classified in sufficient detail so that costs in a particular group are all largely related to one independent variable, thus avoiding multiple regression analysis.

Part 1 ■ True/False

Instructions: *Indicate whether each of the following statements is **True** or **False**.*

True/False

1. Examples of discretionary fixed expenses include advertising and training costs. _____

2. In estimating expenses, an example of a dependent variable would be electricity cost; whereas, an independent variable would be machine hours............ _____

3. The relevant range is the range of activity over which the amount of fixed expense and the rate of variability remain unchanged. .... _____

4. In the high and low points method, if the periods having the highest and lowest activity levels are not the same as those having the highest or lowest expense being analyzed, the highest and lowest expense levels should be used. .... _____

5. The disadvantage of the high and low points method is that it uses only two data points to determine cost behavior. .... _____

6. Generally, there should be as many data points above as below the trend line on a statistical scattergraph. .... _____

7. A more exact trend line than is possible by using the method of least squares may be computed by using the statistical scattergraph method. .... _____

8. If more than one independent variable is required to describe cost behavior, multiple regression analysis should be used. .... _____

9. Levels of expenditures that are determined by management rather than being directly related to sales or production activity, such as recruiting new employees, are known as committed fixed expenses. .... _____

10. In reality, the relationship between a business activity and the related variable cost is usually perfectly linear over the entire range of activity. .... _____

11. Examples of semivariable costs include utilities, maintenance, indirect labor, and travel and entertainment. .... _____

12. The coefficient of correlation and the coefficient of determination establish a cause-and-effect relationship between the dependent variable and the independent variable. .... _____

13. The standard error of the estimate is used by management in developing a confidence interval for deciding whether a given level of expense requires management action. .... _____

14. In multiple regression analysis, the cost relationships are shown on a two-dimensional graph. .... _____

15. When the degree of multicollinearity is low, the relationship between one or more of the independent variables and the dependent variable may be obscured. ... _____

Part 2 ■ Matching

Instructions: *On the line at the left of each of the following items, place the letter from the columns below that identifies the term that best matches the statement. No letter should be used more than once.*

_____ 1. When the observations around the regression line appear to be correlated with one another.

_____ 2. Term used to describe the situation where the variance differs at different points on the regression line.

_____ 3. Increases in total proportionately with an increase in activity and decreases proportionately with a decrease in activity.

_____ 4. Another term for semivariable cost.

_____ 5. Remains the same in total as activity increases or decreases within a relevant range.

_____ 6. When the distribution of observations around the regression line is uniform for all values of the independent variable.

_____ 7. Occurs when important variables are omitted from the multiple regression model.

_____ 8. May change because of changes in management's goals or changes in the number of salaries of the management group.

_____ 9. Examples include installment purchases and long-term lease agreements.

_____ 10. Displays both fixed and variable characteristics.

_____ 11. Range of activity over which the amount of fixed expense and the rate of variability remain unchanged.

_____ 12. Because this method uses only two data points, it may not yield answers that are as accurate as those derived by other methods of estimating cost behavior.

_____ 13. Method of estimating cost behavior that determines mathematically a line of best fit drawn through a set of plotted points.

_____ 14. Defined as the standard deviation about the regression line.

_____ 15. A measure of the extent two variables are related linearly.

_____ 16. Computed by squaring the coefficient of correlation and represents the percentage of explained variance in the dependent variable.

_____ 17. A further application of the method of least squares, permitting the consideration of more than one independent variable.

_____ 18. A measure of the covariation between any independent variable and a dependent variable.

_____ 19. Fixed cost and the variable rate are determined from a two-dimensional graphic analysis.

_____ 20. When the degree of this is high, the relationship between one or more of the independent variables and the dependent variable may be obscured.

a.	discretionary fixed expenses	k.	coefficient of determination
b.	variable cost	l.	committed fixed expenses
c.	standard error of the estimate	m.	specification error
d.	fixed cost	n.	high and low points method
e.	correlation	o.	homoscedastic
f.	scattergraph method	p.	coefficient of correlation
g.	relevant range	q.	heteroscedastic
h.	multicollinearity	r.	serial correlation
i.	mixed cost	s.	method of least squares
j.	multiple regression analysis	t.	semivariable cost

Part 3 ■ Multiple Choice

Instructions: *On the line at the left of each of the following items, place the letter of the choice that most correctly completes each item.*

_____ 1. The term "fixed costs" refers to:

    a. all costs that are associated with marketing, shipping, warehousing, and billing activities

    b. all costs that do not change in total for a given period and relevant range but become progressively smaller on a per-unit basis as volume increases

    c. all manufacturing costs incurred to produce units of output

    d. all costs that fluctuate in total in response to changes in the rate of utilization of capacity

    e. none of the above   *(ICMA adapted)*

_____ 2. A procedure that can be used to determine the fixed and variable elements of a semivariable cost is:

    a. the scattergraph method   **d.** the Program Evaluation

    b. linear programming   and Review Technique

    c. input-output analysis   **e.** all of the above   *(AICPA adapted)*

_____ 3. Within a relevant range, the amount of variable cost per unit:

    a. differs at each production level   **c.** increases as production increases

    b. remains constant at each   **d.** decreases as production increases

         production level   **e.** none of the above   *(AICPA adapted)*

_____ 4. The method of least squares involves the use of:

    a. one variable   **d.** more than three variables

    b. two variables   **e.** none of the above

    c. three variables   *(AICPA adapted)*

_____ 5. A measure that represents the percentage of variance in the dependent variable explained by the independent variable is referred to as:

    a. coefficient of determination   **d.** confidence interval

    b. coefficient of correlation   **e.** none of the above

    c. scattergraph   *(AICPA adapted)*

_____ 6. Aaron wished to determine the fixed portion of its maintenance expense as measured against machine hours for the past year using the high and low points method. The high point was 5,200 machine hours and $2,252 of maintenance expense; whereas, the low point was 4,300 machine hours and $2,000 of maintenance. The fixed portion of the maintenance expense rounded to the nearest dollar was:

    a. $796   **d.** $2,778

    b. $252   **e.** none of the above

    c. $2,000

_____ 7. If the coefficient of correlation between two variables is negative, a scatter diagram of these variables would appear as:

    a. random points

    b. regression line that slopes up to the right

    c. regression line that slopes down to the right

    d. a curvilinear function

    e. none of the above   *(AICPA adapted)*

_____ **8.** Ray Corporation has developed the following formula for annual indirect labor cost: $480 + $.50 per machine hour. The operating budget for the current month is based on 20,000 hours of planned machine time. Indirect labor cost included in this planning budget would be:

    a. $14,800   **d.** $10,400

    b. $10,000   **e.** none of the above

    c. $14,400   *(AICPA adapted)*

_____ **9.** The term "committed fixed costs" refers to:

    a. fixed costs that management decides to incur in the current period to enable the company to achieve objectives other than the filling of customers' orders

    b. fixed costs likely to respond to the amount of attention devoted to them by a specified manager

    c. expenditures that require a series of payments over a long-term period

    d. fixed costs that fluctuate in total in response to small changes in the rate of capacity utilization

    e. none of the above   *(ICMA adapted)*

_____ **10.** Which of the following quantitative methods will separate a semivariable cost into its fixed and variable components with the least degree of precision?

    a. high and low points method   **d.** scattergraph method

    b. multiple regression analysis   **e.** none of the above

    c. least squares method   *(AICPA adapted)*

Part 4 ■ Problem

Semola Company developed the following relationships to indicate cost at various activity levels:

$$
\begin{aligned}
\text{Direct labor} &= \$25 \text{ per unit} \\
\text{Materials} &= \$30 \text{ per unit} \\
\text{Supervision} &= \$40,000 \\
\text{Power} &= \$1,000 + \$1 \text{ per unit} + \$2 \text{ per machine hour} \\
\text{Factory supplies} &= \$1,750 + \$.50 \text{ per unit} \\
\text{Depreciation equipment} &= \$7 \text{ per machine hour} \\
\text{Depreciation—building} &= \$80,000
\end{aligned}
$$

During the next period, the company anticipates production of 10,000 units and usage of 1,000 machine hours.

Instructions:

Determine the production costs to be incurred during the next period.

Production costs:
Direct labor . . . . $
Direct materials . . . .
Overhead to be incurred:
Supervision . . . . $
Power . . . .
Factory supplies . . . .
Depreciation—equipment . . . .
Depreciation—building . . . .   _____   _____
Total production cost . . . . $

Part 5 ■ Problem

A controller is interested in an analysis of the fixed and variable costs of machine repairs and maintenance as related to machine hours.   The following data have been accumulated:

Month	Repairs and Maintenance	Machine Hours
January	$1,548	297
February	1,667	350
March	1,405	241
April	1,534	280
May	1,600	274
June	1,600	266
July	1,613	285
August	1,635	301

Instructions:

1. Determine the variable rate and the amount of fixed overhead using:

   (a) The high and low points method

	Cost	Activity Level
High	$	
Low		
Difference	$	

Variable rate (rounded to three decimal places)

	High	Low
Total repairs and maintenance	$	$
Variable cost		
Fixed cost (rounded to the nearest whole dollar)	$	$

(b) A scattergraph with trend line fitted by inspection

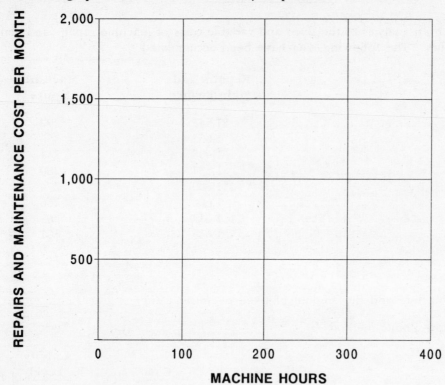

Average monthly cost . . . . $

Less fixed cost . . . .

Average monthly variable cost . . . . $

Variable cost per machine hour
(rounded to three decimal places) . . . .

(c) The method of least squares

Month	(1) Repairs and Maintenance Costs	(2) Difference from Average Cost	(3) Machine Hours	(4) Difference from Average Hours	(5) (4)²	(6) (4) x (2)	(7) (2)²
January	$	$				$	$
February							
March							
April							
May							
June							
July							
August							
Total	$	$				$	$

Average machine hours (x):

Average repairs and maintenance cost (y):

Variable rate (b) (rounded to three decimal places):

Fixed cost per month:

2. Determine the standard error of the estimate. (Round to two decimal places.)

Month	(1) Machine Hours	(2) Factory Repairs and Maintenance Cost	(3) Predicted Repairs and Maintenance Cost	(4) Prediction Error (2) - (3)	(5) Prediction Error² [(4)²]
January		$	$		
February					
March					
April					
May					
June					
July					
August					
Total		$	$	$	$

3. Determine the confidence interval at 90% (Table Factor 1.943) if the actual activity level for the period is 300 machine hours resulting in budgeted repairs and maintenance cost of $1,600.

4. Determine the coefficient of correlation (r) and the coefficient of determination (r^2). (Round to four decimal places.)

Cost Systems and Cost Accumulation

REVIEW SUMMARY

I.   The Purpose of the Chapter

The purpose of this chapter is to introduce and compare several different cost accumulation methods that are used in practice. Before these cost systems are presented, the flow of costs through an accounting system is introduced.

II.   Flow of Manufacturing Costs

Cost accounting records and measures cost elements as resources flow through the productive process. General ledger accounts such as Materials, Work in Process, Finished Goods, and Cost of Goods Sold are used to recognize and measure the flow of manufacturing costs. Each general ledger account or **controlling account** is supported by a number of **subsidiary accounts** or **subsidiary records**, (i.e., a separate materials subsidiary account would be used for each type of material). The flow of costs to these ledger accounts is based on information in source documents such as purchase invoices and materials requisitions.

A.   Journal Entries for Manufacturing Costs

A knowledge of a flow of products through the various productive steps determines the nature of the cost accumulation procedures to be used. Direct materials, direct labor, and factory overhead are charged to Work in Process during the accounting period. The total cost of goods completed is transferred from the work in process account to the finished goods account. The cost of goods sold during that period is transferred from the finished goods account to the cost of goods sold account. Financial statements are prepared from the information in the ledger accounts, including a supplementary schedule of cost of goods sold.

III. Cost Systems

Costs may be accumulated using an **actual** or **historical cost system** or a **standard cost system**. In an actual cost system, the job or the process is charged with the actual costs of material used and labor expended. In a standard cost system, products or processes are costed based on predetermined quantities of resources to be used and predetermined prices of these resources, while the actual costs are also being recorded; and any differences between standard and actual costs are recorded in variance accounts. Costs allocated to units of production may include all manufacturing costs (**full absorption costing**) or only the variable manufacturing costs (**direct** or **variable costing**). Generally accepted accounting principles require that full absorption costing be used for external financial reporting.

IV.   Job Order vs. Process Costing

In a **job order cost system**, the costs of various jobs or contracts are kept separate during their manufacture or construction. The system is used in industry when it is possible to physically identify the jobs produced and to charge each with its own cost. **Process costing** is used in industries when units are not distinguishable from one another during the manufacturing process. Many companies use both the job order and the process cost method (for example, where different units have very different direct material costs, but all units undergo identical conversion in large quantities).

V.   Flexible Manufacturing Systems

Flexible Manufacturing Systems (FMS) consist of an integrated collection of automated production processes, automated materials movement, and computerized systems controls to efficiently manufacture a highly flexible variety of products. FMS impacts upon many of the factors that management should consider in evaluating a system, such as the planning and the control of materials and of work in process inventories. Although an FMS may seem attractive, there is the need to consider the substantial capital investment and the knowledgeable personnel required to run such systems.

VI.   Backflush Costing

In recent years, some manufacturing facilities have so successfully increased their processing times that their average elapsed time between receipt of raw materials and production of finished work has been reduced to a matter of hours. This results in a very small amount of work in process inventory at any given time and makes the tracking of production costs to work in process unimportant.

Backflush costing is a way to accumulate manufacturing costs in a factory in which processing systems are fast. The purpose of backflush costing is to reduce the number of cost accounting entries that must be made. The inventory accounts are not adjusted throughout the accounting period to reflect all of the costs of units in process, but rather their balances are corrected by means of end-of-period adjusting entries, and no subsidiary records are kept for work in process.

Part 1 ■ True/False

Instructions: *Indicate whether each of the following statements is **True** or **False**.*

True/False

1. In practice, there is really only one cost accumulation method that is used with any frequency. . . . . _____

2. The manufacturing process, the physical arrangement of the factory, and the decision-making needs of the managers are the basis for determining how costs will be accumulated. . . . . _____

3. In full absorption costing, all manufacturing costs (whether fixed or variable) flow through the work in process and finished goods accounts. . . . . _____

4. In the ledger, each subsidiary account is supported by a number of controlling accounts. . . . . _____

5. In a standard cost system, any differences between standard and actual costs are recorded in variance accounts. . . . . _____

6. Process cost systems are most frequently used in industries such as breweries and flour mills. . . . . _____

7. Job order costing is used in industries where it is physically impossible to identify individual jobs. . . . . _____

8. For tax reporting, the Tax Reform Act of 1986 requires certain purchasing and storage costs to be allocated to inventory. . . . . _____

9. Process costing is applicable to service businesses (such as accounting and architectural firms) that have only a small number of engagements underway at one time. . . . . _____

10. In flexible manufacturing systems, manufacturing changes can be made more efficiently than in labor-intensive systems. . . . . _____

11. A company cannot use both the job order and the process cost accumulation systems in the same factory. . . . . _____

12. In flexible manufacturing systems, a group of related machines is coordinated by a computer. . . . . _____

13. In a firm that has significantly increased its processing speed, the accurate assignment of costs to work in process inventory is more important than ever. _____

14. In backflush costing, all of the cost accumulation is done prior to the completion of production for the period. . . . . _____

15. Some manufacturers have so successfully increased their processing speed that the average elapsed time from receipt of raw materials to production of finished goods has been reduced to a matter of hours. . . . . _____

Part 2 ■ Matching

Instructions: *On the line at the left of each of the following items, place the letter from the columns below that identifies the term that best matches the statement. No letter should be used more than once.*

_____ 1. A general ledger account that is supported by a number of subsidiary accounts or records.

_____ 2. Term that is synonymous with historical cost system.

_____ 3. Prepared using data from the income statement and balance sheet and from elsewhere in the company records.

_____ 4. Collects costs as they occur but delays the presentation of results until manufacturing operations have been performed.

_____ 5. System in which unit costs are predetermined in advance of production.

_____ 6. System that presupposes the possibility of physically identifying the lots produced and charging each with its own cost.

_____ 7. System used when units are not distinguishable from one another during one or more of the manufacturing processes.

_____ 8. Source documents used to track materials costs.

_____ 9. The requirement for tax reporting that certain purchasing and storage costs be allocated to inventory.

_____ 10. An integrated collection of automated production processes, automated materials movement, and computerized system controls to manufacture products effectively.

_____ 11. Designed to reduce the number of cost accounting entries that must be measured and routinely recorded in a factory where processing speeds are extremely fast.

_____ 12. Provides supporting documentation of the control account.

_____ 13. System that allocates all manufacturing costs to units of production.

_____ 14. Source documents used to track labor costs.

_____ 15. System that charges only the variable manufacturing costs to the units of production.

a.	historical cost system	**i.**	controlling account
b.	full absorption costing	**j.**	flexible manufacturing systems
c.	actual cost system	**k.**	standard cost system
d.	process cost system	**l.**	purchase invoices
e.	time tickets	**m.**	backflush costing
f.	statement of cash flows	**n.**	super absorption
g.	direct costing	**o.**	job order cost system
h.	subsidiary account		

Part 3 ■ Multiple Choice

Instructions: *On the line at the left of each of the following items, place the letter of the choice that most correctly completes each item.*

_____ 1. The best accumulation costing procedure to use when there is continuous mass production of like units is:

   a. actual
   b. historical
   c. job order

   d. process
   e. none of the above

   (AICPA adapted)

_____ 2. Of the following production operations, the most likely to employ job cost manufacturing is:

   a. soft-drink manufacturing
   b. printing
   c. crude oil refining

   d. candy manufacturing
   e. none of the above

   (AICPA adapted)

_____ 3. Which would not be used in job order costing?

   a. standard costing
   b. averaging of direct labor
   and material rates

   c. direct costing
   d. historical costs
   e. none of the above   *(AICPA adapted)*

_____ 4. One feature of a historical cost system is that:

   a. the presentation of results is delayed until all manufacturing operations have been performed
   b. unit costs are predetermined in advance of production
   c. differences between actual and standard costs are collected in separate accounts
   d. products, operations, and processes are costed using standards for both quantity and dollar amounts
   e. none of the above

_____ 5. An industry that would most likely use process costing is:

   a. office equipment
   b. musical instrument manufacturing
   c. aircraft manufacturing

   d. pharmaceuticals
   e. none of the above

_____ 6. The best cost accumulation costing procedure to use when products manufactured within a department or cost center are heterogeneous is:

   a. backflush
   b. standard
   c. job order

   d. process
   e. none of the above

_____ 7. The system that consists of an integrated collection of automated production procedures, automated materials movement, and computerized systems controls used to effectively manufacture products is a:

   a. flexible manufacturing system
   b. just-in-time inventory system
   c. absorption costing system

   d. direct costing system
   e. none of the above

_____ 8. The system that is characterized by one kind of product, a large range of viable production volumes, and tightly constrained production qualities is:

   a. manual system
   b. fixed automation system
   c. flexible manufacturing system

   d. historical cost system
   e. job order cost system

_____ **9.** A system characterized by many kinds of products, a substantial learning curve effect, and long lead times is:

    a. manual system   **d.** process cost system

    b. fixed automation system   **e.** none of the above

    c. flexible manufacturing system

_____ **10.** The cost accumulation method that is characterized by no detailed accounting for work in process inventories is:

    a. job order   **d.** backflush

    b. blended   **e.** historical

    c. process

Part 4 ■ Problem

During the past month, the Berberich Company incurred these costs: direct labor, $180,000; factory overhead, $90,000; and direct materials purchases, $75,000.   Inventories were costed as follows:

	Beginning	Ending
Finished goods	$30,000	$25,000
Work in process	55,000	45,000
Materials	20,000	17,000

Instructions:

1. Calculate the total manufacturing cost.

2. Calculate the cost of goods manufactured.

3. Calculate the cost of goods sold.

Part 5 ■ Problem

Selected transactions of the Grant Company for a recent month are as follows:

a. Materials purchased and received on account: $70,000.

b. Materials requisitioned: $52,000 for production and $6,300 for factory supplies.

c. Total gross payroll of $180,000 was accrued and paid.

d. The payroll was distributed as follows: direct labor, $75,000; indirect factory labor, $40,000; marketing salaries, $30,000; administrative salaries, $35,000.

e. Depreciation of $25,000 and expired insurance of $2,500 related to factory operations were recorded.

f. Other factory overhead costs of $12,500 were recorded as a liability.

g. Accounts payable of $76,000 were paid.

h. Amounts received from customers in payment of their accounts totaled $315,000.

i. Work completed and transferred to finished goods, $151,000.

j. Finished goods costing $140,000 were sold on account for $285,000.

Instructions: *Using the ruled form on page 32, prepare journal entries to record these transactions.*

JOURNAL

PAGE

	DESCRIPTION	DEBIT	CREDIT	
1				1
2				2
3				3
4				4
5				5
6				6
7				7
8				8
9				9
10				10
11				11
12				12
13				13
14				14
15				15
16				16
17				17
18				18
19				19
20				20
21				21
22				22
23				23
24				24
25				25
26				26
27				27
28				28
29				29
30				30
31				31
32				32

Job Order Costing

REVIEW SUMMARY

I. Purpose of the Chapter

This chapter illustrates job order costing in detail. It identifies the eight basic cost accounting entries, illustrates preparation of a job order cost sheet and the use of predetermined factory overhead rates. Further, it explains the application of job order costing to service businesses and manufacturers.

II. Overview of Job Order Costing

In **job order costing**, costs are accumulated for each separate customer order or item. To use job costing, jobs should be separately identifiable, and there should be important differences in unit costs among jobs. In addition, the cost of each order produced or the cost of each lot to be placed in stock is recorded on a **job order cost sheet**. The cost sheet indicates the materials, labor, and factory overhead applied to each order or lot. Cost sheets are subsidiary records and are controlled by the work in process account.

III. Accounting for Materials

When materials are purchased, the account debited is Materials or Materials Inventory. Additionally, each purchase is also recorded on an individual *materials ledger card*. Materials necessary for production are issued to the factory on the basis of **materials requisitions**, prepared by production scheduling clerks. Each requisition of direct materials results in a debit to Work in Process and a credit to Materials, as well as an entry to the materials section of the appropriate cost sheet. When indirect materials are issued, the requisitions are charged to the factory overhead control account and are also recorded on a **factory overhead analysis sheet**.

IV. Accounting for Labor

To compute the direct labor cost of a given order, the time spent on each job during a day must be recorded on each worker's **time ticket**. At regular intervals, the labor time and the labor cost for each job are entered on the job order cost sheets. Indirect labor is also accounted for through the use of time tickets and is entered on factory overhead analysis sheets. The general journal entry to record the payroll includes a debit to the temporary account, Payroll, and a credit to the liability account, Accrued Payroll. When the payroll is distributed to the cost accounts, Work in Process and Factory Overhead Control are debited for the cost of the direct and indirect labor respectively, and Payroll is credited.

V. Accounting for Factory Overhead

Actual factory overhead is charged to Factory Overhead Control and to the factory overhead analysis sheets as the actual expenses become known. Factory overhead is entered on the job cost sheets on the basis of a **predetermined overhead rate**. A causal relationship between two factors such as activity in machine hours and factory overhead cost is used as a basis for charging factory overhead to jobs. The activity chosen is called the **overhead allocation base**. An applied factory overhead account is often used to keep applied costs and actual costs in separate accounts, resulting in a debit to Work in Process and a credit to Applied Factory Overhead. If actual overhead expenses exceed applied overhead, the overhead is said to be underapplied; if applied exceeds actual, it is overapplied. A relatively small balance in the under- or overapplied factory overhead account is usually charged or credited to Cost of Goods Sold.

VI. Accounting for Jobs Completed and Products Sold

When jobs are completed, cost sheets are moved from the in-process category to the finished work file. Completion of a job for stock results in a debit to Finished Goods and a credit to Work in Process. If the job is produced for a specific customer, Cost of Goods Sold is debited at the time the job is completed.

VII. Job Order Costing in Service Businesses

In service businesses, such as legal, architectural, and accounting services, several varieties of job order costing are used. The predetermined overhead rate is usually based on direct labor cost because direct labor is often the largest cost. It is also common to combine the labor cost rate with the predetermined overhead rate; thus, the amount charged to a job for each hour of labor time also represents overhead. The only remaining costs to be charged to the job are the directly traceable costs other than labor, such as travel, meals, and photocopying.

Part 1 ■ True/False

Instructions: *Indicate whether each of the following statements is **True** or **False**.*

True/False

1. In job order costing, the sheet on which direct materials, direct labor, and applied factory overhead are summarized for a job is called a job order cost sheet.... _____

2. A departmentalized job cost sheet will indicate the materials, labor, and overhead cost incurred in each department. _____

3. Job cost sheets are subsidiary records that are controlled by the factory overhead account. _____

4. If a job is produced for a specific customer, the cost of the completed job is debited directly to Cost of Goods Sold. _____

5. When indirect materials are issued, the requisitions are charged to the work in process account. _____

6. Time tickets are a basic source document in the computation of labor cost.... _____

7. Materials requisitions are documents prepared by production schedulers indicating the quantity of materials to be ordered. _____

8. When actual overhead expenses are greater than applied overhead, the overhead is said to be overapplied. _____

9. The applied factory overhead account is closed to the actual factory overhead account by debiting Factory Overhead Control and crediting Applied Factory Overhead. _____

10. Completion of a job for stock results in a debit to Finished Goods and a credit to Work in Process. _____

11. Service industries do not use job order costing because they provide a service rather than a product. _____

12. Only supplies that are used in the factory are charged to Factory Overhead Control. _____

13. In an automated factory with very little direct labor, all factory labor may be charged to Factory Overhead Control. _____

14. As automation increases in today's factories, more manufacturers are using direct labor hours as the overhead allocation base. _____

15. In service industries, it is common to combine labor cost with the overhead rate so that the amount charged to a job for each hour of direct labor represents both labor and overhead. _____

Part 2 ■ Matching

Instructions: *On the line at the left of each of the following items, place the letter from the columns below that identifies the term that best matches the statement. No letter should be used more than once.*

_____ 1. Item accounted for through the use of time tickets and clock cards and entered in the work in process account.

_____ 2. Document showing the time spent by one worker on a job order or other task.

_____ 3. Represents the difference between actual overhead and applied overhead.

_____ 4. The activity that "drives" most of the factory overhead cost.

_____ 5. The account in which labor costs are recorded before distribution.

_____ 6. Method of costing in which production costs are accumulated for each separate customer order.

_____ 7. Record on which the cost of each order produced for a given customer is recorded.

_____ 8. An accounting unit to which materials, labor, and factory overhead is assigned.

_____ 9. Purchase of direct materials is recorded here.

_____ 10. The individual usually responsible for issuing materials requisitions.

_____ 11. The individual who assembles the materials called for on the requisitions.

_____ 12. A subsidiary ledger for the recording of factory overhead items.

_____ 13. Item accounted for through the use of time tickets and clock cards and entered in the factory overhead control account.

_____ 14. Document prepared by production schedulers, specifying the job number and type and quantity of materials required.

_____ 15. Automates traditional labor-intensive production processes.

_____ 16. Determined based on the relationship of one factor to another.

_____ 17. The account in which estimated factory overhead is recorded.

_____ 18. The account in which actual factory overhead is recorded.

_____ 19. Factory overhead when actual expenses exceed applied expenses.

_____ 20. Factory overhead when applied expenses exceed actual expenses.

a. storekeeper
b. Factory Overhead Control
c. overhead allocation base
d. underapplied
e. factory overhead rate
f. job cost sheet
g. overapplied
h. cost variance
i. factory overhead analysis sheets
j. job order costing

k. labor time ticket
l. robotics
m. materials record card
n. materials requisition
o. direct labor
p. Applied Factory Overhead
q. job
r. indirect labor
s. Payroll
t. production scheduling clerk

Part 3 ■ Multiple Choice

Instructions: *On the line at the left of each of the following items, place the letter of the choice that most correctly completes each item.*

_____ 1. In job order costing, the basic document to accumulate the cost of each order is the:

    a. invoice   **d.** job cost sheet

    b. purchase order   **e.** none of the above

    c. materials requisition

_____ 2. In job order costing, details regarding the production costs on an individual customer's order are recorded on a:

    a. job cost sheet   **d.** factory overhead analysis sheet

    b. materials requisition form   **e.** none of the above

    c. labor time ticket

_____ 3. The tie-in between general accounts and cost accounts is often discussed in connection with accounting procedures. An example of a general account is:

    a. Work in Process   **d.** Accumulated Depreciation

    b. Finished Goods   **e.** none of the above

    c. Factory Overhead Control

_____ 4. Cost of Goods Sold is debited and Finished Goods is credited for a:

    a. purchase of goods on account

    b. transfer of completed production to the finished goods storeroom

    c. transfer of completed goods to the customer

    d. transfer of materials to the factory

    e. none of the above

_____ 5. Factory Overhead Control is debited and Materials is credited for:

    a. the issuance of direct materials into production

    b. the issuance of indirect materials into production

    c. the return of materials to the storeroom

    d. the application of materials overhead

    e. none of the above

_____ 6. Work in Process is debited and Payroll is credited for:

    a. recording the payroll   **d.** distributing withholding taxes

    b. distributing indirect labor costs   **e.** none of the above

    c. distributing direct labor costs

_____ 7. The activity chosen to be used in distributing overhead costs to jobs is known as the:

    a. predetermined overhead rate   **d.** base

    b. applied factory overhead   **e.** none of the above

    c. factory overhead control

_____ 8. Work in Process is debited and Applied Factory Overhead is credited to:

    a. close the estimated overhead account to actual overhead

    b. record the actual factory overhead for the period

    c. charge estimated overhead to all jobs worked on during the period

    d. record overapplied overhead for the period

    e. none of the above

_____ **9.** The best overhead allocation base to use in a highly automated manufacturing environment probably would be:
   a. materials cost
   b. machine hours
   c. direct labor hours
   d. direct labor dollars
   e. none of the above

_____ **10.** In service businesses the overhead allocation base most often used is:
   a. direct labor dollars
   b. direct labor hours
   c. machine hours
   d. materials costs
   e. none of the above

Part 4 ■ Problem

Instructions: *Complete the job cost sheet shown on page 38, using the following data. (Round all totals to the nearest dollar.)*

	Week Ending 3/12	Week Ending 3/19
Materials used, Cutting Dept.	$3,600 (Req. #6281)	$1,800 (Req. #6299)
Direct labor rate, Cutting Dept.	$10.80 per hour	$10.80 per hour
Labor hours used, Cutting Dept.	400	220
Materials used, Assembly Dept.	$240 (Req. #6288)	$360 (Req. #6308)
Direct labor rate, Assembly Dept.	$9.50	$9.50
Labor hours used, Assembly Dept.	200	300
Machine hours, Cutting Dept.	300	160
Applied factory overhead, Cutting Dept.	$7.50 per machine hour	$7.50 per machine hour
Applied factory overhead, Assembly Dept.	$6.00 per direct labor hour	$6.00 per direct labor hour

Marketing and administrative costs are charged to each order at a rate of 40% of the cost to manufacture. The sales price of the order is $40,000.

Obermyer Office Supply, Inc.
313 Oak Street, Cincinnati, OH 45227   Job Order No. **1215**

For:	Engleman Engineering
Product:	Executive Chairs
Specifications:	Attached
Quantity:	20

DATE ORDERED: 3/5/19--
DATE STARTED: 3/7/19--
DATE WANTED: 3/23/19--
DATE COMPLETED: 3/19/19--

Date	Department	Req. No.	Cost	Total

Date	Department	Hours	Hourly Rate	Cost	Total

Date	Department	Rate of Application	Hours	Cost	Total

Direct Materials . . . . $ _____	Sales Price		$ _____
Direct Labor . . . . _____	Factory Cost	$ _____	
Factory Overhead Applied . . . . _____	Marketing and Administrative Expenses	_____	
Total Factory Cost . . . . $ _____	Cost to Make and Sell		_____
	Profit		$ _____

Part 5 ■ Problem

Kravitz Corporation uses job order costing. At the beginning of March, two jobs were in process:

	Job 101	**Job 103**
Materials	$3,000	$ 800
Direct labor	6,000	2,250
Applied factory overhead	6,000	2,250

There was no inventory of finished goods on March 1. During the month, Jobs 105 through 110 were started. Materials requisitions for March totaled $25,000; direct labor cost, $30,000; and actual factory overhead, $28,500. Factory overhead is applied at a rate of 100% of direct labor cost. The only job still in process at the end of March is No. 110, with costs of $2,300 for materials and $1,500 for direct labor. Job 107, the only finished job on hand at the end of March, has a total cost of $9,000.

Instructions: *Using the T accounts below, record all of the information above, including the determination of the cost of goods sold, the closing of Applied Factory Overhead to Factory Overhead Control and, over- or underapplied factory overhead to Cost of Goods Sold.*

Work in Process

Finished Goods

Cost of Goods Sold

Factory Overhead Control

Applied Factory Overhead

Part 6 ■ Problem

Coldstream Products, Inc. provided the following data for May:

Materials and supplies:
Inventory, May 1 .... $10,000
Purchases on account 25,000
Factory labor:
Paid monthly on the last day of the month 33,000
Factory overhead costs:
Supplies (issued from materials)......................... 2,500
Indirect labor 5,500
Depreciation 1,000
Factory overhead costs
    (all from outside suppliers on account)................ 15,000

Work in process:

	Job 101	Job 102	Job 103	Total
Work in process, May 1	$4,000	--	--	$ 4,000
Job costs during May:				
Direct materials	9,000	$12,200	$8,000	29,000
Direct labor	7,500	12,000	8,000	27,500
Applied factory overhead (100% of direct labor cost).........	7,500	12,000	8,000	27,500

Job 101—started in April, finished during May, and sold to a customer for $40,000 cash.

Job 102—started in May, not yet finished.

Job 103—started in May, finished during May, and now in the finished goods warehouse awaiting customer's disposition.

Finished goods inventory, May 1 .... $0

Instructions: *Using the ruled forms on the following two pages, prepare general journal entries to record the following transactions for May:*

(1) Purchases of materials on account
(2) Liability for the monthly payroll
(3) Payment of the payroll
(4) Labor cost distribution
(5) Materials issued to production
(6) Depreciation for the month
(7) Acquisition of other overhead costs on credit
(8) Overhead applied to production
(9) Jobs completed and transferred to finished goods
(10) Sales revenue
(11) Cost of goods sold
(12) Applied factory overhead closed to the factory overhead control account
(13) The balance in the factory overhead control account closed to Cost of Goods Sold

JOURNAL

	DESCRIPTION	DEBIT	CREDIT	
1				1
2				2
3				3
4				4
5				5
6				6
7				7
8				8
9				9
10				10
11				11
12				12
13				13
14				14
15				15
16				16
17				17
18				18
19				19
20				20
21				21
22				22
23				23
24				24
25				25
26				26
27				27
28				28
29				29
30				30
31				31
32				32

JOURNAL

PAGE

	DESCRIPTION	DEBIT	CREDIT	
1				1
2				2
3				3
4				4
5				5
6				6
7				7
8				8
9				9
10				10
11				11
12				12
13				13
14				14
15				15
16				16
17				17
18				18
19				19
20				20
21				21
22				22
23				23
24				24
25				25
26				26
27				27
28				28
29				29
30				30
31				31
32				32

Process Costing

REVIEW SUMMARY

I. Purpose of the Chapter

The purpose of this chapter is to explain process cost accumulation and examine the environment in which it may be utilized. It then illustrates the calculation of equivalent units of production, the preparation of a cost of production report and journal entries to record process costs.

II. Process Cost Accumulation

Process costing is used when products are manufactured under conditions of continuous processing or under mass production methods. The cost of a completed unit is computed by dividing total cost incurred during a period by total units completed. Separate departmental work in process accounts are used to charge each department for the materials, labor, and factory overhead used to complete its share of a manufacturing process.

A. Costing by Departments and Production Flow

In process costing, manufacturing costs are generally charged to producing departments; however, if a department is organized into two or more cost centers, process costing may still be used as long as the units produced in each cost center are homogenous. Each item manufactured goes through the same set of operations in a **sequential product flow** format. In a **parallel product flow**, certain portions of the work are done simultaneously and then brought together for completion. When the initial product moves to different departments within the plant, depending upon the desired final product, this is called a **selective product flow** format.

B. Accounting for Materials Costs

The details involved in process costing for materials requisitions are usually fewer than those in job order costing because materials are charged to departments rather than jobs. The cost of materials used can be determined at the end of the period either by a periodic inventory (beginning inventory + purchases - ending inventory), or by requisitions that state the cost or quantity of materials put into process by various departments. The entry to charge direct materials to production consists of a debit to Work in Process Department X and a credit to Materials.

C. Accounting for Labor Costs

Daily time tickets or weekly time-clock cards are used to identify labor costs of departments in process costing. The entry to charge labor costs to production consists of debits to the various departmental work in process accounts and a credit to Payroll.

D. Accounting for Factory Overhead Costs

Factory overhead expenses should be accumulated in a factory overhead control account by means of an entry debiting Factory Overhead Control and crediting the various prepaid items, liabilities, etc. The use of a factory overhead control account requires a subsidiary ledger for both service and producing departments. The entry charging applied overhead to production consists of a debit to the various work in process accounts and a credit to Applied Factory Overhead. In highly automated manufacturing environments where direct labor is a relatively small proportion of total manufacturing costs, the trend is to combine the direct labor and factory overhead costs when computing the overhead rate that is used for charging costs to jobs.

III. The Cost of Production Report

A departmental cost of production report shows all costs chargeable to a department. Total cost is broken down by cost elements for each department head responsible for the costs incurred. The cost section of the report is divided into two parts: one showing total costs for which the department is accountable; the other showing the disposition of those costs.

A. Equivalent Units of Production

Computation of individual unit costs requires an analysis of the ending work in process inventory to determine its stage of completion. To assign costs equitably to in-process units and transferred units, units still in process must be restated in terms of completed units. To determine **equivalent units of production**, restated partially completed units are added to units actually completed during the period. Materials, labor, and overhead costs are then divided by the appropriate equivalent production figure to determine unit costs for each of these elements.

B. Average Costing Method

If the **average costing method** is used, the costs in beginning inventory are added to the costs of the new period. In the first department, the cost of materials already in process would be added to the materials cost for the period before dividing by the equivalent production figure. In a subsequent department, the portion of the work in process inventory representing the cost of work done in preceding departments is added to the cost of transfers received from the preceding department during the current period. A weighted average unit cost for work done in preceding departments is then computed. The other portion of the work in process inventory, representing costs added by the department under consideration, is entered as a departmental cost to be added to other departmental costs incurred during the period before dividing by the equivalent production figure.

C. FIFO Process Costing

In first-in, first-out costing, beginning work in process costs are kept separate from the additional new costs incurred in the next period, thus giving separate unit costs for beginning work in process units completed and for units started and finished in the new period. In the first department, the cost of completing units in process at the beginning of the period is computed first, followed by the computation of the cost of units started and finished within the period. Units in process at the beginning will usually have a completed unit cost that is different from the unit cost for work started and finished during the period. In departments subsequent to the first, the procedure is the same, except that the unit cost of units transferred into these departments is shown only as one figure, determined by dividing total units received into total costs received.

Part 1 ■ True/False

Instructions: *Indicate whether each of the following statements is **True** or **False**.*

True/False

1. In process costing, the cost of a completed unit is determined by dividing total costs incurred during the period by equivalent total units completed. . . . . _____

2. A single work in process account is used for materials, labor, and factory overhead, regardless of the number of producing departments. . . . . _____

3. In a parallel product flow, certain portions of the work are done simultaneously and then brought together in a final process. . . . . _____

4. When additional materials result in additional units, the preceding department's unit cost must be adjusted. . . . . _____

5. In highly automated manufacturing environments, direct labor is usually a lower percentage of manufacturing costs than it is in more traditional manufacturing settings. . . . . _____

6. If the average costing method is used, the cost of labor already in process would be added to the labor cost for the month before dividing by the equivalent production figure. . . . . _____

7. A weighted average unit cost is computed by adding two separate unit costs and dividing the sum by two. . . . . _____

8. When average costing is used, beginning units in process will usually have a completed unit cost that is different from the unit cost of work started and completed during the period. . . . . _____

9. In process costing, all costs chargeable to a department are summarized in a departmental cost of production report. . . . . _____

10. Equivalent production is determined by subtracting partially completed units in process from completed units. . . . . _____

11. A major difficulty associated with the use of process costing is obtaining an accurate estimate of the stage of completion of in-process inventories. . . . . _____

12. Some companies use both job order and process costing procedures. . . . . _____

13. An equivalent unit is a device for presenting the amount of costs accumulated and assigned to production during the month. . . . . _____

14. The work in process account is a subsidiary record that supports the cost of the production report. . . . . _____

15. When computing the cost of the ending work in process inventory of any department subsequent to the first, costs received from preceding departments must be omitted. _____

Part 2 ■ Matching

Instructions: *On the line at the left of each of the following items, place the letter from the columns below that identifies the term that best matches the statement. No letter should be used more than once.*

_____ **1.** Often referred to as continuous or mass production costing.

_____ **2.** Items when added to departments subsequent to the first may increase the number of units and cause a change in the unit cost.

_____ **3.** A product flow format in which the product moves to different departments, depending upon the desired final product.

_____ **4.** A product flow format in which each item manufactured goes through the same set of operations.

_____ **5.** A product flow format in which certain portions of the work are done simultaneously and then brought together in a final process for completion.

_____ **6.** Method of process costing, in which the cost of each equivalent unit contains a portion of the cost in beginning inventory and a portion of the cost added during the current period.

_____ **7.** Method of process costing in which equivalent units are computed for current period costs only.

_____ **8.** Often included in the computation of the overhead rate in highly automated manufacturing environments.

_____ **9.** A section of the cost of production report that indicates the disposition of the units started in process.

_____ **10.** Represents the number of units for which sufficient materials, labor, and overhead were issued to enable completion.

_____ **11.** A schedule showing quantities and costs chargeable to a department.

a.	process cost system	**g.**	equivalent production
b.	parallel product flow	**h.**	direct labor cost
c.	sequential product flow	**i.**	quantity schedule
d.	cost of production report	**j.**	materials
e.	average costing	**k.**	selective product flow
f.	fifo costing		

Part 3 ■ Multiple Choice

Instructions: *On the line at the left of each of the following items, place the letter of the choice that most correctly completes each item.*

_____ 1. The process flow format in which the product moves to different departments within the plant, depending upon the final product to be produced is:

    a. selective product flow   **d.** fifo product flow
    b. parallel product flow   **e.** none of the above
    c. sequential product flow

_____ 2. In highly automated factories, the distinction between direct and indirect labor is often:

    a. dependent upon what product is being manufactured
    b. heightened
    c. dependent upon whether job order or process costing is being used
    d. blurred
    e. none of the above

_____ 3. In a process costing system, procedures must be designed to:

    a. value inventory of work still in process
    b. determine a unit cost for each department
    c. accumulate materials, labor, and factory overhead costs by departments
    d. all of the above

_____ 4. A cost of production report for a department shows all of the following *except*:

    a. total and unit costs transferred from a preceding department
    b. the cost per job
    c. unit costs added by the department
    d. costs transferred to a subsequent department or to finished goods
    e. all of the above

_____ 5. Paducah Processing Co. uses the average costing method and reported a beginning inventory of 3,000 units that were 40% complete with respect to materials in one department. During the month, 18,000 units were started; 14,000 units were finished; and ending inventory amounted to 7,000 units that were 80% complete with respect to materials. Total materials cost during the period for work in process should be spread over:

    a. 15,400 units   **d.** 18,000 units
    b. 21,000 units   **e.** none of the above
    c. 19,600 units

_____ 6. A characteristic of process costing is that:

    a. work in process inventory is restated in terms of completed units
    b. costs are accumulated by order
    c. it is used by a company manufacturing custom machinery
    d. standard costs are not applicable
    e. none of the above   *(AICPA adapted)*

_____ 7. An error was made in computing the percentage of completion of the current year's ending work in process inventory. The error resulted in assigning a higher percentage of completion to each component of the inventory than actually was the case. The effect of this error on (a) computation of equivalent units in total, (b) computation of costs per equivalent unit, and (c) costs assigned to cost of goods completed for the period is:

	(a)	(b)	(c)
a.	understate	overstate	overstate
b.	understate	understate	overstate
c.	overstate	understate	understate
d.	overstate	overstate	understate

(AICPA adapted)

_____ 8. In process cost accumulation, transferred-in cost denotes:

a. labor that is transferred from another department within the same plant instead of hiring temporary workers from the outside

b. cost of the production of a previous internal process that is subsequently used in a succeeding internal process

c. supervisory salaries that are transferred from a service cost center to a production cost center

d. ending work in process inventory of a previous period that will be used in a succeeding process

e. none of the above

(AICPA adapted)

_____ 9. Larkin Company adds materials in the beginning of the process in the Shaping Department, which is the first of two stages of its production cycle. Information concerning the materials used in the Shaping Department in October is as follows:

	Units	**Materials Cost**
Work in process as of October 1	6,000	$ 3,000
Units started during October	50,000	25,560
Units completed and transferred to next department during October	44,000	

Using the average costing method, and assuming that there were no spoiled units, the materials cost of work in process at October 31 is:

a. $3,600
b. $5,520
c. $6,000
d. $3,060
e. none of the above

(AICPA adapted)

_____ 10. Kew Co. had 3,000 units in work in process at April 1 which were 60% complete as to conversion cost. During April, 10,000 units were completed. At April 30, 4,000 units remained in work in process; they were 40% complete as to conversion cost. Direct materials are added at the beginning of the process. How many units were started during April?

a. 9,900
b. 9,800
c. 10,000
d. 11,000
e. none of the above

(AICPA adapted)

Part 4 ■ Problem

Chiquita Company operates two producing departments whose quantity reports appear as follows:

	Department A	Department B
Beginning inventory........................	500	600
Department A—all materials, 75% conversion cost		
Department B—all materials, 50% conversion cost		
Started in process	3,000	2,500
	3,500	3,100
Transferred out	2,500	2,600
Ending inventory	1,000	500
Department A—all materials, 25% conversion cost		
Department B—all materials, 50% conversion cost		
	3,500	3,100

Instructions: *Using the form provided below, compute equivalent production figures for each department, using the average method.*

	Materials Units	Conversion Units
Department A:		
Transferred out		
Ending inventory		
Equivalent production		

	Units from Preceding Department	Conversion Units
Department B:		
Transferred out		
Ending inventory		
Equivalent production		

Part 5 ■ Problem

C. Cuesta, Production Manager of Hispanic Products Company, requested the ending work in process inventory figured on the average cost basis. The data are:

Units in beginning inventory, 10,000; 75% materials and 50% conversion costs.
Cost of beginning inventory: materials, $7,500 and conversion costs, $9,125.
Placed in process, 40,000 units. Cost: materials, $120,000 and conversion costs, $80,000.
Units completed and transferred, 35,000.
Units in process at the end, 15,000, 50% materials, 25% conversion costs.

Instructions: *Using the form provided below, determine the information requested by Cuesta. (Carry unit costs to three decimal places.)*

Materials . . . . $

Conversion . . . .   _____

Work in process inventory . . . . $_____

Computations:

Part 6 ■ Problem

Happy Valley Company manufactures a single product on a continuous plan in three departments. On June 1, the work in process in Department B was:

Cost from preceding department	$ 30,000
Labor—Department B	$ 2,000
Factory overhead—Department B	$ 1,000
Units in process..........................	5,000

Costs in Department B during June were:

Labor...................................	$ 25,000
Factory overhead	$ 12,500

During June, 45,000 units were received from Department A at a unit cost of $5; 40,000 units were completed in Department B, of which 38,000 were transferred to Department C and 2,000 units were on hand in Department B at the end of the month. The rest of the units were still in process, estimated to be one-half complete as to labor and factory overhead.

Instructions: *Complete the following cost of production report for Department B, using the average costing method for beginning work in process inventories. (Round all unit costs to two decimal places.)*

Happy Valley Company
Department B
Cost of Production Report
For the Month of June, 19--

Quantity Schedule	Materials	Labor	Overhead	Quantity
Beginning inventory				
Received from Department A				_____
				═════
Transferred to Department C				
Completed and on hand.......................				
Ending inventory				_____
				═════

Cost Charged to Department	Total Cost	Equivalent Units	Unit Cost
Beginning inventory:			
Cost from preceding department			
Labor...	$		
Factory overhead	_____		
Total cost in beginning inventory	$		
Cost added during period:			
Cost from preceding department...............	$		$
Labor..			
Factory overhead	_____		_____
Total cost added during period.............	$		
Total cost charged to the department	$		$

Cost Accounted for as Follows	Units	Percent Complete	Unit Cost	Total Cost
Transferred to Department C		%	$	$
Completed and on hand..............				
Work in process, ending inventory:				
Cost from preceding department.....				
Labor............................				
Factory overhead				_____
Total cost accounted for..............				$

Part 7 ■ Problem

(Based on material in the Appendix)

Cochrane Chemical Company operates three producing departments: Mixing, Refining, and Finishing. During May, the Refining Department transferred 40,000 units to the Finishing Department and had 5,000 units in process at the end of May. There were 10,000 units in process on May 1 in the Refining Department. The remaining units started in the Refining Department during May were received from the Mixing Department. The conversion costs incurred in the Refining Department during May were $89,900. The work in process inventory on May 1 was $10,000, consisting of $7,500 cost from the Mixing Department and $2,500 conversion cost. The costs transferred to the Refining Department from the Mixing Department amounted to $120,050. The Refining Department work in process inventory was one-half complete on May 1 and three-fourths complete on May 31.

Instructions: *Complete the following May cost of production report for the Refining Department, using the first-in, first-out method of accounting for beginning inventories.*

Cochrane Chemical Company
Refining Department
Cost of Production Report
For the Month of May, 19--

Quantity Schedule	Conversion Costs	Quantity
Beginning inventory	%	
Received from Mixing Department................		
Transferred to Finishing Department		
Ending inventory		

Cost Charged to Department	Total Cost	Equivalent Units	Unit Cost
Beginning inventory:			
Cost from preceding department	$		
Conversion			
Total cost in beginning inventory	$		
Cost added during current period:			
Cost from preceding department...............	$		$
Conversion			
Total cost added this period	$		
Total cost charged to the department	$		$

Cost Accounted for as Follows	Units	Percent Complete	Unit Cost	Total Cost
Transferred to finished goods inventory:				
From beginning inventory		%	$	$
Cost to complete this period:				
Conversion....................				
Started and completed this period ...				
Total cost transferred to finished goods				$
Work in process, ending inventory:				
Cost from preceding department.....		%	$	$
Conversion				
Total cost in ending inventory....				$
Total cost accounted for..............				$

CHAPTER 7

The Cost of Quality and Accounting for Production Losses

REVIEW SUMMARY

I.   Purpose of the Chapter

The purpose of the chapter is to explain the concept of quality costs and how these costs relate to production losses. The chapter identifies and differentiates between the three different kinds of quality costs; explains the concepts of total quality management and continuous improvement; computes the cost of scrap, spoilage, and rework in a job order cost system; and computes the cost of spoilage in a process cost system.

II.   Types of Quality Costs

Quality costs consist of (1) **prevention costs**, resulting from designing, implementing and maintaining the quality system; (2) **appraisal costs**, occurring from ensuring that materials and products meet quality standards; (3) **internal failure costs**, occurring when materials and products fail to meet quality standards; and (4) **external failure costs**, resulting from shipping inferior products to customers. The accounting system should aid in measuring these costs for control purposes.

III.   Total Quality Management (TQM)

Characteristics of a TQM approach to doing business include: (1) the company's emphasizing that the objective for business activity is to serve its customers, both internal employees and external consumers; (2) top management assuming an active role in quality improvement; (3) all employees being actively involved in quality improvement; (4) the company having a system of identifying quality problems, developing solutions, and setting quality improvement objectives; and (5) the company placing a high value on employees and providing continuous training as well as recognition for achievement.

IV.   Continuous Quality Improvement

The best approach to quality improvement is to concentrate on prevention—an approach that seeks out the causes of waste and inefficiency and develops systematic plans to eliminate them. The process should begin with product design and proceed through the production process. While prevention is important in building quality, performance appraisal is also important. *Statistical process control* may be used to monitor product quality improvement efforts and reduce product variability. Quality improvement efforts should also be extended to marketing activities such as packing, advertising, sales, and distribution.

V.   Accounting for Scrap in a Job Order Cost System

Scrap includes remains after processing materials, defective materials that cannot be used or returned, and broken parts resulting from the manufacturing process. The amount realized from sale of scrap may be: shown on the income statement under scrap sales or other income; credited to Cost of Goods Sold or to Factory Overhead Control; or may be treated as a reduction in the materials cost charged to a specific job, if it is directly traceable to a job.

VI.   Accounting for Spoiled Goods in a Job Order Cost System

Spoiled goods are units of the final product or component parts which are in some way defective and are either technically or economically not correctable. If spoilage is normal and results from an internal failure, its cost should be treated as factory overhead, included in the predetermined factory overhead rate, and prorated over all production of a period. If normal spoilage is caused by some action taken by the customer, such as exacting specifications, difficult processing, and so on, it should be charged to that specific job or order, and an allowance for normal spoilage should *not* be included in the predetermined factory overhead rate used to charge overhead to that specific job. Spoilage of a magnitude large enough to distort production costs should be reported separately as a loss on the income statement.

VII. Accounting for Rework in a Job Order Cost System

Rework is the process of correcting defective goods. If rework is caused by an internal failure, the additional cost to correct defective units should be included in predetermined factory overhead, based on previous experience, and all units produced during the period should be charged with a portion of the rework cost. Rework caused by the customer, such as special orders, may be charged directly to the specific job.

VIII. Accounting for Production Losses in a Process Cost System

Accounting for scrap and rework in a process cost system is essentially the same as in a job order cost system, except that the cost of rework should be charged to Factory Overhead Control rather than Work in Process because rework in a process cost system usually results from internal failure. The accounting treatment of spoiled goods in a process cost system often differs from its treatment in a job order system. The cost of units lost due to normal production shrinkage is spread over the remaining good units. The cost of units lost due to internal failures is charged either to Factory Overhead Control or directly to a current period expense and reported as a separate item in the cost of goods sold statement. **Normal production shrinkage** is uncontrollable spoilage that occurs in the production process under efficient operating conditions. Abnormal spoilage is due to internal failures such as inefficient operating conditions that could have been avoided with better control over production.

IX. Production Losses in Process Costing with a FIFO Cost Flow

In fifo costing, lost units must be identified as either beginning work in process units or new units started during the period. This identification is needed to determine which unit cost should be adjusted.

Part 1 ■ True/False

Instructions: *Indicate whether each of the following statements is **True** or **False**.*

True/False

1. The concept of "world class" that is used to designate the highest quality manufacturers also can be applied to the service sector of the economy. . . . .   _____

2. External failure costs occur during the manufacturing or production process. .   _____

3. Appraisal is the cost of designing high quality products and production systems, including the cost of implementing and maintaining such systems. . . . .   _____

4. Total quality management has become a pervasive philosophy and a way of doing business that applies to all areas of the company. . . . .   _____

5. The best way to approach the quality problem is to produce a large enough volume of products so that regardless of the number of rejects enough good units will survive to satisfy demand. . . . .   _____

6. Companies that are emphasizing quality are spending as much as 20% of revenue on quality costs. . . . .   _____

7. To reduce accounting for scrap to a minimum, often no entry is made until the scrap is actually sold. . . . .   _____

8. The cost of spoilage should always be charged to Factory Overhead. . . . .   _____

9. If rework is experienced in normal manufacturing operations, the additional cost to correct defective units should be considered in determining the factory overhead rate. . . . .   _____

10. In process costing, the effect of losing units in the first department is to increase the unit cost of the remaining good units. . . . .   _____

11. Accounting for scrap and rework in a process cost system is very different than in a job order system. . . . .   _____

12. The cost of normal production shrinkage is spread over the remaining good units.   _____

13. While the treatment of spoiled goods is conceptually the same in both job order and process cost systems, the accounting process differs. . . . .   _____

14. In average process costing, there is a need to identify whether lost units come from beginning work in process units or from units started during the period. . . . .   _____

15. In process costing, if spoilage is the result of an internal failure, the cost should be measured and charged to Factory Overhead Control. . . . .   _____

Part 2 ■ Matching

Instructions: *On the line at the left of each of the following items, place the letter from the columns below that identifies the term that best matches the statement. No letter should be used more than once.*

_____ 1. Includes the filings or trimmings remaining after processing materials, the defective materials that cannot be used or returned, and the broken parts resulting from employee or machine failures.

_____ 2. Costs that occur during the manufacturing or production process.

_____ 3. Units of the final product or of component parts that are not correctable due to technical or economic considerations.

_____ 4. Costs of designing high quality products and production systems, including the costs of implementing and maintaining such systems.

_____ 5. A pervasive philosophy and a way of doing business that applies to all functional areas of the company.

_____ 6. The process of correcting defective goods that resulted from either an action taken by the customer or from internal failures.

_____ 7. Requires the constant effort of everyone in the company and never ends nor gets easier.

_____ 8. Method of measuring and monitoring the variability in the output during a production process.

_____ 9. Costs that occur after the product has been sold, such as warranty repairs.

_____ 10. A static approach to finding the best solution given a set of fixed constraints.

_____ 11. The account that should be debited to record the cost of the rework when it is caused by internal failure.

_____ 12. Costs that are incurred to detect product failure, such as inspecting and testing materials.

_____ 13. Companies that are reorganizing their manufacturing system to improve efficiency and reduce costs, to emphasize product quality, and to successfully compete with the highest quality manufacturers.

_____ 14. Costs incurred when a product fails and may occur internally or externally.

_____ 15. The account that should be debited to record the cost of rework caused by the customer.

a. prevention costs	**i.** spoiled goods
b. appraisal costs	**j.** rework
c. failure costs	**k.** world-class manufacturers
d. internal failure costs	**l.** statistical process control
e. external failure costs	**m.** optimization
f. total quality management	**n.** Work in Process
g. continuous quality improvement	**o.** Factory Overhead Control
h. scrap	

Part 3 ■ Multiple Choice

Instructions: *On the line at the left of each of the following items, place the letter of the choice that most correctly completes each item.*

_____ 1. The quality costs that occur during the manufacturing or production process are:

    a. prevention costs   **d.** internal failure costs
    b. external failure costs   **e.** none of the above
    c. appraisal costs

_____ 2. The quality costs that are incurred to detect product failure are:

    a. prevention costs   **d.** internal failure costs
    b. external failure costs   **e.** none of the above
    c. appraisal costs

_____ 3. All of the following are characteristics of total quality management *except*:

    a. the company's objective for all business activity is to serve its customers
    b. top management provides an active leadership role in quality improvement
    c. all employees except those on probationary status are actively involved in quality improvement
    d. the company has a system of identifying quality problems, developing solutions, and setting improvement objectives

_____ 4. When spoilage occurs as a result of exacting specifications or customer changes, any loss is charged to:

    a. extraordinary losses   **c.** administrative expenses
    b. the specific job in which the   **d.** Factory Overhead Control
        spoilage occurred   **e.** none of the above

_____ 5. In contrast to spoilage caused by the customer, spoilage caused by an internal failure:

    a. is considered part of good production
    b. arises under efficient operating conditions
    c. is controllable in the short run
    d. results in lower profits
    e. none of the above

_____ 6. Units of the final product which are in some way defective and are not correctable due to technical or economic conditions are:

    a. spoiled goods   **d.** broken parts
    b. scrap   **e.** none of the above
    c. rework

_____ 7. When spoiled goods result from an internal failure, the unrecoverable spoilage cost should be debited to:

    a. Spoiled Goods Inventory   **d.** Factory Overhead Control
    b. Cost of Goods Sold   **e.** Applied Factory Overhead
    c. Work in Process

_____ 8. When rework costs are caused by the customer, the cost of the rework should be debited to:

    a. Work in Process   **d.** Factory Overhead Control
    b. Rework Inventory   **e.** Applied Factory Overhead
    c. Cost of Goods Sold

9. Dyno Products transferred 15,000 units to one department. An additional 5,000 units of materials were added in the department. At the end of the month, 12,000 units were transferred to the next department; while 6,000 units, 100% complete as to materials, remained in the work in process inventory. There was no beginning inventory, and lost units were the result of normal production shrinkage. The equivalent units of material would be:

    a. 21,000 units   **d.** 20,000 units

    b. 15,000 units   **e.** none of the above

    c. 12,000 units

10. Prime Products transferred 15,000 units to a department. An additional 5,000 units were added in this department. At the end of the month, 12,000 units were transferred to the next department, 6,000 units remained in Work in Process, 40% complete as to conversion costs and the remaining units were lost at the 75% stage of conversion. There was no beginning inventory and lost units were the result of internal failure. The equivalent units of material would be:

    a. 14,400   **d.** 15,900

    b. 18,000   **e.** none of the above

    c. 13,500

Part 4 ■ Problem

Furman Furniture Inc. accumulates fairly large quantities of wood shavings from the products it manufactures. At least once a month, the shavings are sold to a local pet supply company. This month's scrap sales on account totaled $4,300.

Instructions: *Using the general journal forms below, give the appropriate general journal entry to record the sale of the scrap for each of the following alternatives:*

1. The scrap sales are viewed as additional revenue.

JOURNAL

PAGE

	DESCRIPTION	DEBIT	CREDIT	
1				1
2				2
3				3
4				4
5				5
6				6
7				7
8				8
9				9
10				10

2. The scrap sales are viewed as a reduction of the cost of goods sold during the period.

JOURNAL

PAGE

	DESCRIPTION	DEBIT	CREDIT	
1				1
2				2
3				3
4				4
5				5
6				6

3. The scrap sales are viewed as a reduction of factory overhead.

JOURNAL

PAGE

	DESCRIPTION	DEBIT	CREDIT	
1				1
2				2
3				3
4				4
5				5
6				6

4. The scrap sales are traceable to individual jobs and are viewed as a reduction in the cost of materials used on the jobs.

JOURNAL

PAGE

	DESCRIPTION	DEBIT	CREDIT	
1				1
2				2
3				3
4				4
5				5
6				6

Part 5 ■ Problem

Perry Plastics Inc. manufactures custom plastics products. During the current period, an order for 500 custom tables began on Job 007. After completing the job, the tables are inspected and 20 units are defective. The customer has agreed to accept the order with only 480 units instead of the quantity originally ordered. The spoiled units can be sold as seconds for $10 each. Spoiled goods are kept in a separate inventory account from Finished Goods. Total costs charged to Job 007 follow:

Materials	$4,600
Labor (140 hours x $10 per hour)	1,400
Factory overhead ($22 per direct labor hour) . .	3,080
Total cost charged to Job 007	$9,080

Custom jobs are marked up 200 percent on cost.

Instructions:

1. Assuming that the defective units were the result of an internal failure (i.e., an employee error or a machine failure), prepare the appropriate general journal entries to record the transfer of the defective units to a separate inventory account and the completion and shipment of Job 007 to the customer.

	JOURNAL		PAGE
	DESCRIPTION	DEBIT	CREDIT
1			
2			
3			
4			
5			
6			
7			
8			
9			
10			
11			
12			
13			
14			
15			
16			
17			
18			

2. Assuming that the defective units were the result of a change in design specified by the customer after the units were completed, prepare the appropriate general journal entries to record the transfer of the defective units to the separate inventory account and the completion and shipment of Job 007 to the customer.

JOURNAL   PAGE

	DESCRIPTION	DEBIT	CREDIT	
1				1
2				2
3				3
4				4
5				5
6				6
7				7
8				8
9				9
10				10
11				11
12				12
13				13
14				14

Part 6 ■ Problem

Costa Company produced 1,000 units in a recent production run and discovered that 50 required reworking as follows.

Rework cost per unit:
Materials .... $ 5
Labor 10
Factory overhead .... <u>10</u>
    Total .... <u>$ 25</u>
Normal production cost per unit:
Materials .... $ 10
Labor 25
Factory overhead .... <u>25</u>
    Total .... <u>$ 60</u>

Instructions:

1. Using the journal form provided below, prepare journal entries to record the rework costs and to transfer the job cost to Finished Goods, assuming that rework costs were caused by an internal failure.

JOURNAL

	DESCRIPTION	DEBIT	CREDIT	
1				1
2				2
3				3
4				4
5				5
6				6
7				7
8				8
9				9
10				10

2. Using the journal form provided below, prepare the same journal entries as in Question 1, assuming that rework costs were caused by a change in customer specifications.

JOURNAL

	DESCRIPTION	DEBIT	CREDIT	
1				1
2				2
3				3
4				4
5				5
6				6
7				7
8				8
9				9
10				10

Part 7 ■ Problem

Laurel Company manufactures a single product in two departments, Cutting and Finishing. Units of product are started in the Cutting Department and then transferred to the Finishing Department where they are completed. Units are inspected at the end of the production process in the Finishing Department. Good units are transferred to Finished Goods Inventory and spoiled units are transferred to a separate inventory account. Spoiled units are inventoried at their salvage value of $25 each, and the unrecoverable cost of spoilage that was caused by an internal failure should be charged to the appropriate account.

At the end of June, 1,000 units were still in process in the Finishing Department, 75% complete as to materials and 40% complete as to conversion costs. During July, 7,500 units were transferred from the Cutting Department to the Finishing Department and 5,000 were transferred from the Finishing Department to Finished Goods Inventory. At the end of July, the Finishing Department still had 2,000 units in process, 50% complete as to materials and 25% complete as to conversion costs. Cost data related to July operations in the Finishing Department follow:

	Beginning Inventory	Added This Period
Costs charged to the department:		
Cost from preceding department...........	$8,850	$ 122,900
Materials	4,625	53,500
Labor...................................	3,150	33,600
Factory overhead	5,250	42,000

Instructions:

1. Complete the cost of production report on page 66 for the Finishing Department based on the data presented for July, assuming the company uses a process cost system with average costing to account for its production.

Laurel Corporation
Finishing Department
Cost of Production Report
For September, 19--

Quantity Schedule	Materials	Labor	Overhead	Quantity
Beginning inventory				
Received from Cutting Department				_____
Transferred to finished goods.				
Ending Inventory.	%	%	%	
Spoiled in process.	%	%	%	_____

Cost Charged to Department		Total Cost	Equivalent Units	Unit Cost
Beginning inventory:				
Cost from preceding department.		$		
Materials				
Labor				
Factory overhead		_____		
Total cost in beginning inventory		$_____		
Cost added during period:				
Cost from preceding department.		$		$
Materials				
Labor				
Factory overhead		_____		_____
Total cost added during period		$_____		
Total cost charged to the department		$_____		$_____

Cost Accounted for as Follows	Units	Percent Complete	Unit Cost		Total Cost
Transferred to finished goods.		%	$		$
Transferred to spoiled goods					
inventory at salvage value			$		
Charge to factory overhead for spoilage:					
Cost of completed spoiled units		%	$	$	
Less salvage value of spoiled units . .				_____	
Work in process, ending inventory:					
Cost from preceding department		%	$	$	
Materials					
Labor					
Factory overhead				_____	_____
Total cost accounted for					$_____

2. Prepare the appropriate general journal entry to record the transfer of cost out of the Finishing Department this period.

JOURNAL

PAGE

	DESCRIPTION	DEBIT	CREDIT	
1				1
2				2
3				3
4				4
5				5

Costing By-Products and Joint Products

REVIEW SUMMARY

I. Purpose of the Chapter

The purpose of this chapter is to distinguish by-products from joint products, to explain the various methods of assigning costs to by-products, and to describe the different methods of allocating joint production costs to joint products. Also, this chapter describes how management may use data on by-product and joint-product costing for decision making and profitability analysis.

II. Nature of By-Products

By-products are one or more products of relatively small total value that are produced simultaneously with a product of greater total value. By-products are classified into two groups according to their marketable condition at the split-off point: (a) those sold in their original form without need of further processing and (b) those that require further processing in order to be salable.

III. Nature of Joint Products

Joint products are produced simultaneously by a common process or series of processes, with each product possessing more than nominal value. A **joint cost** arises from the common processing or manufacturing of products. It is incurred prior to the point at which separately identifiable products emerge from the same process.

IV. Methods of Costing By-Products

The accepted methods for costing by-products are:

1. A joint product cost is not allocated to the by-product. Any revenue resulting from sales of the by-product is credited either to income or to cost of the main product.
2. Some portion of the joint production cost is allocated to the by-product.

The specific accounting methods used for (1) above are as follows:

(a) **Recognition of gross revenue.** Revenue from sales of the by-product is listed on the income statement either as other income, additional sales revenue, a deduction from the cost of goods sold of the main product, or a deduction from the total production cost of the main product.

(b) **Recognition of net revenue.** Revenue from sales of the by-product less its marketing and administrative expenses and additional processing costs is shown on the income statement as in (1) above.

(c) **Replacement cost method.** The cost assigned to the by-product is the purchase or replacement cost existing in the market.

The specific accounting methods used for (2) above are:

(a) **Market value (reversal cost) method.** The market value (reversal cost) method reduces the manufacturing cost of the main product by an estimate of the by-product's market value at the time of recovery. This estimate is determined by subtracting from the ultimate market value of the by-product the total of the by-product's estimated gross profit, its marketing and administrative expenses, and its estimated production costs after split-off.

V. Methods of Costing Joint Products

The allocation to joint products of the joint production cost incurred up to the split-off point can be made by one of the following methods:

1. The **market value method** prorates the joint cost of the items produced on the basis of their respective market values at the split-off point. For products that have no market value at the split-off point, a hypothetical market value must be computed by subtracting the after-split-off processing costs from the ultimate sales value of the product. If it is desired to make every joint product equally profitable, an overall gross profit percentage for all joint products is used to compute the gross profit for each product. The gross profit is then deducted from the ultimate sales value to find the total cost,

which in turn is reduced by each product's further processing cost, to determine the joint cost allocation to each product.

2. The **quantitative unit method** distributes the total joint cost on the basis of some unit of measurement, such as pounds, gallons, or tons.

3. The **average unit cost method** apportions total joint production cost to the various products on the basis of an average unit cost obtained by dividing total joint production cost by the total number of units produced.

4. The **weighted average method** multiplies finished production by weight factors to apportion the total joint cost to individual units. Weight factors include the size of the unit, difficulty to manufacture, time consumed in making the unit, and amount of materials used.

VI. Federal Income Tax Laws for Costing Joint-Products and By-Products

Federal income tax regulations state that the taxpayer may use "allocated cost as a basis for pricing inventories, provided such allocation bears a reasonable relation to the respective selling values of the different kinds, sizes, or grades of product."

VII. Joint Cost Analysis for Management Decisions

The method chosen to allocate joint product cost determines the degree of profitability of the various individual products. For profit planning, management should consider a product's contribution margin after separate or individual costs are deducted from sales.

VIII. Ethical Considerations

Ethical considerations require use of the joint cost allocation methods that most fairly present financial results. Several standards in the categories of integrity and objectivity of the *Standards of Ethical Conduct for Management Accountants* pertain to that topic.

Part 1 ■ True/False

Instructions: *Indicate whether each of the following statements is **True** or **False**.*

True/False

1. To be classified as a by-product, a product must have more than nominal value.   _____

2. The unit cost of a by-product or a joint product is difficult to determine because a true joint cost is indivisible. . . . .   _____

3. A by-product is a product of relatively small total value that is produced simultaneously with a product of greater value. . . . .   _____

4. An acceptable method of accounting for a by-product is to credit any revenue resulting from its sale to the cost of the main product. . . . .   _____

5. The replacement cost method of accounting for by-products is especially popular with firms that use the by-product within their own plant. . . . .   _____

6. In the market value method of accounting for by-products, the manufacturing cost of the main product is reduced by an estimate of the by-product's market value at the point of recovery. . . . .   _____

7. If joint products have no market value at the split-off point, the market value method of prorating joint costs cannot be used. . . . .   _____

8. An overall gross profit percentage for all joint products may be used for purposes of making each joint product equally profitable. . . . .   _____

9. The quantitative unit method distributes the total cost on the basis of some unit of measurement such as pounds or gallons. . . . .   _____

10. The weighted average method apportions total joint production cost to the various products on the basis of a predetermined standard or index of production. . . .   _____

11. Ethical considerations should be given to which joint cost allocation method most fairly represents actual financial results. . . . .   _____

12. Variables such as unit size, time needed to manufacture, and amount of materials consumed may be used as weight factors in allocating joint costs. . . . .   _____

13. Federal income tax regulations imply that the market value method is the preferred method for allocating by-product and joint product costs. . . . .   _____

14. Tax laws have solved the problem of costing joint products and by-products for the accountant and the manufacturer. . . . .   _____

15. The cost incurred up to the split-off point should be the key figure used by management in determining whether a particular joint product should continue to be marketed. . . . .   _____

Part 2 ■ Matching

Instructions: *On the line at the left of each of the following items, place the letter from the columns below that identifies the term that best matches the statement. No letter should be used more than once.*

_____ **1.** The cost that arises from the common processing or manufacturing of products produced from the same process.

_____ **2.** Produced simultaneously by a common process, with each product possessing more than nominal value.

_____ **3.** Products of relatively small total value produced simultaneously with a product of greater total value.

_____ **4.** Method in which sales of the by-product are listed on the income statement as other income, additional sales revenue, a deduction from the cost of goods sold of the main product, or a deduction from the total manufacturing cost of the main product.

_____ **5.** Method of accounting for by-products in which remelted scrap steel would be credited to the cost of finished steel at the market cost of equivalent grades purchased.

_____ **6.** Identifiable with the individual product and generally need no allocation.

_____ **7.** Method in which the allocation of joint production cost is based on the relative sales values of the individual products.

_____ **8.** To determine this, the after-split-off processing costs are deducted from the ultimate market value.

_____ **9.** Method of joint product costing that attempts to distribute the total joint cost on the basis of some unit of measurement such as pounds, gallons, or tons.

_____ **10.** Method in which the total joint production cost is apportioned to the various products on the basis of a predetermined standard or index of production.

_____ **11.** Irrelevant in deciding whether to sell a product at the split-off point or process it further.

_____ **12.** Method where finished production of every kind is multiplied by certain factors to apportion the total joint cost to individual units.

_____ **13.** A product of relatively large value produced simultaneously with products of relatively small total value.

_____ **14.** Point where joint products emerge as individual units.

_____ **15.** Method in which revenue from the sale of the by-product, less the costs of placing the by-product on the market and less any additional processing costs of the by-product, is shown on the income statement.

a.	quantitative unit method	**i.**	hypothetical market value
b.	separable product costs	**j.**	average unit cost method
c.	joint production cost	**k.**	joint cost
d.	by-products	**l.**	market value method
e.	weighted average method	**m.**	split-off point
f.	joint products	**n.**	recognition of gross revenue method
g.	main product	**o.**	recognition of net revenue method
h.	replacement cost method		

Part 3 ■ Multiple Choice

Instructions: *On the line at the left of each of the following items, place the letter of the choice that most correctly completes each item.*

_____ 1. Joint product costs generally are allocated using:

    a. market value at split-off   **d.** direct labor hours
    b. additional costs after split-off   **e.** contribution margin
    c. relative profitability

_____ 2. Costing difficulty because of indivisibility is encountered in dealing with:

	By-Products	**Joint Products**
a.	yes	yes
b.	yes	no
c.	no	yes
d.	no	no

(AICPA adapted)

_____ 3. One of the accepted methods of accounting for a by-product is to recognize the cost of the by-product as it is produced. Under this method, inventory costs for the by-product would be based on:

    a. an allocation of some portion of joint costs but not any subsequent processing costs
    b. neither an allocation of some portion of joint costs nor any subsequent processing costs
    c. subsequent processing costs less an allocation of some portion of joint costs
    d. an allocation of some portion of joint costs plus any subsequent processing costs
    e. none of the above   *(AICPA adapted)*

_____ 4. The components of production allocable as joint costs when a single manufacturing process produces several salable products are:

    a. materials, labor, and factory overhead
    b. materials and labor only
    c. labor and factory overhead only
    d. factory overhead and materials only
    e. factory overhead and commercial expenses   *(AICPA adapted)*

_____ 5. If two or more products share a common process before they are separated, the joint costs should be allocated in a manner that:

    a. assigns a proportionate amount of the total cost to each product by means of a quantitative basis
    b. maximizes total earnings
    c. minimizes variations in a unit of production cost
    d. does not introduce an element of estimation into the process of accumulating costs for each product
    e. none of the above   *(AICPA adapted)*

_____ 6. An accepted method by which to allocate joint cost is:

    a. market value   **d.** average unit cost
    b. weighted average method   **e.** all of the above
    c. relative weight, volume, or linear measure

(AICPA adapted)

_____ 7. Sandman Company manufactures Products C and R from a joint process. The total cost is $60,000. The market value is $75,000 for 8,000 units of Product C and $50,000 for 2,000 units of Product R. Assuming that the total joint cost is allocated using the average unit cost method, what was the joint cost allocated to Product C?

a. $48,000
b. $12,000
c. $24,000

d. $36,000
e. none of the above

(AICPA adapted)

_____ 8. Aquatics Company manufactures two products, Oar and Wade. Initially, they are processed from the same raw materials and then, after split-off, they are further processed separately before they can be sold. Additional information is as follows:

	Oar	Wade	Total
Final sales price	$9,000	$6,000	$15,000
Joint costs prior to split-off point	?	?	6,600
Costs after spilt-off point	3,000	3,000	6,000

Using the market value method, the assigned joint costs of Oar and Wade, respectively, are:

a. $3,300 and $3,300
b. $3,960 and $2,640
c. $4,400 and $2,200

d. $4,560 and $2,040
e. none of the above

(AICPA adapted)

_____ 9. St. Louis Corporation manufactures liquid chemicals A and B from a joint process. Joint cost is allocated on the basis of the market value at the split-off point. It costs $4,560 to process 500 gallons of A and 1,000 gallons of B to the split-off point. The market value at split-off is $10 per gallon for A and $14 for B. Product B requires an additional process beyond split-off at a cost of $2 per gallon if it is to be sold at the most profitable price. The resulting cost to produce 1,000 gallons of B is:

a. $3,360
b. $4,560
c. $5,360

d. $2,000
e. none of the above

(AICPA adapted)

_____ 10. The two standards in *the Standards of Ethical Conduct for Management Accountants* that pertain most specifically to consideration of joint cost allocation methods are:

a. competence and confidentiality
b. confidentiality and integrity
c. competence and integrity

d. integrity and objectivity
e. none of the above

Part 4 ■ Problem

The following data relate to the sale of a main product and by-product by the Dibble Company for September:

Main product:
    Sales (10,000 units @ $1.50) $15,000
    Beginning inventory (5,000 units @ $.75) 3,750
    Total production cost (9,000 units @ $.75) 6,750
    Marketing and administrative expenses 3,000
By-product:
    Revenue from sale of product 750

Instructions: *Prepare answers to the following:*

1. If by-product revenue is treated as other income, determine (a) the gross profit and (b) the income before income tax.

2. If by-product revenue is treated as additional sales revenue, determine (a) the gross profit and (b) the income before income tax.

3. If by-product revenue is treated as a deduction from the cost of goods sold, determine (a) the gross profit and (b) the income before income tax.

4. If by-product revenue is deducted from production cost, determine (a) the new average unit cost for the main product (round to three decimal places) and (b) the dollar amount of the ending inventory.

Part 5 ■ Problem

Greek Products Inc. manufactures one main product and two by-products. Data for July are:

	Main Product	By-Product Chi	By-Product Phi
Sales	$80,000	$12,000	$6,000
Manufacturing cost before separation	40,000	---	---
Manufacturing cost after separation	15,000	5,000	2,500
Marketing and administrative expense	8,000	2,000	750

Instructions: *Complete the income statement below. Assume no beginning or ending inventories and use the market value method for the by-products, allowing a 25% operating profit for Chi and a 20% operating profit for Phi.*

	Main Product	By-Product Chi	By-Product Phi	Total
Sales	$	$	$	$
Cost of goods sold:				
Manufacturing cost before separation:				
Cost assigned:				
Operating profit		$	$	
Marketing and administrative expense				
Manufacturing cost after separation				
Total		$	$	
Cost before separation	$	$	$	$
Manufacturing cost after separation				
Cost of goods sold	$	$	$	$
Gross profit	$	$	$	$
Marketing and administrative expense				
Operating profit	$	$	$	$

Part 6 ■ Problem

Waste Products Inc. manufactures three products that are processed through a joint refining process: Gunk, Sledge, and Grunge. Five gallons of input result in 1 unit of Gunk, 3 units of Sledge, and 5 units of Grunge. The total joint processing cost is $60.75 for 5 gallons of input. Outputs are complete at the end of the joint refining process. During January, 10,000 gallons were inputed to the process. There were no beginning inventories. Sales of the outputs were:

	Units Sold	Sales
Gunk	1,500	$ 15,000
Sledge	5,000	60,000
Grunge	8,000	56,000
Total		$131,000

Instructions: *On the form provided below, prepare the allocation of joint cost to Gunk, Sledge, and Grunge, using the market or sales value method. (Carry the joint cost allocation percentage to two decimal places.)*

Waste Products Inc.
Allocation of Joint Cost
For January, 19--

Chemical	Units Produced (1)	Units Sold	Units in Ending Inventory	Unit Sales Price at Split-Off (2)	Market Value of Production	Joint Cost Allocated (3)	Cost of Sales (4)	Ending Inventory
Gunk				$	$	$	$	$
Sledge								
Grunge								
					$	$	$	$

Computations:

(1)

(2)

(3)

(4)

Part 7 ■ Problem

Space Products Inc. produces Star and Trek from its centrifuge. For each gallon of Kirk placed in process, three-fourths of a gallon of Star and one-fourth of a gallon of Trek are produced. Star is sold at $10 per gallon, while Trek is sold at $15 per gallon. During April, the total cost of the centrifuge operation was $1,012,500, and 300,000 gallons of Kirk were processed. There were no inventories at either the beginning or end of April. No other processing was required for Star or Trek.

Instructions:

1. Complete the schedule below, showing the unit cost of sales and the unit gross profit for Star and Trek, using the quantitative unit method. (Round to the nearest tenth of a percent or tenth of a cent.)

Space Products Inc.
Quantitative Unit Method
For April, 19--

	Units Produced and Sold	Joint Cost Allocated	Unit Market Value	Unit Cost of Sales	Unit Gross Profit
Star		$	$	$	$
Trek.	_____	_____			
		$			

Computations:

2. Complete the schedule below, showing the unit cost and the unit gross profit for Star and Trek, using the relative sales value method.

Space Products Inc.
Market Value Method
For April, 19--

	Units Produced and Sold	Unit Market Value	Total Market Value	Joint Cost Allocation	Unit Cost of Sales	Unit Gross Profit
Star		$	$	$	$	$
Trek	_____		_____	_____		
	_____		$ _____	$ _____		

Computations:

Materials: Controlling, Costing, and Planning

REVIEW SUMMARY

I. Purpose of the Chapter

This chapter discusses materials procurement and use, and it identifies the components of the cost of acquiring materials. It also illustrates the calculation and use of the economic order quantity, the safety stock, and the order point, as well as describing the ABC plan for inventory control.

II. Purchase of Materials

The purchase of all materials is usually made by the purchasing department, although in small companies department heads sometimes have this authority. The purchasing department receives purchase requisitions; keeps informed as to sources of supply, prices, and shipping schedules; prepares and places purchase orders; and arranges for reports among the Purchasing, Receiving, and Accounting Departments. Supplies, services, and repairs should be purchased in a similar manner.

A. Purchasing Forms

The **purchase requisition** informs the purchasing agent of the quantity and type of materials needed. The **purchase order** is a written authorization to a vendor to supply specified quantities of described goods at agreed terms and at a designated time and place. Paperwork savings are enhanced by the use of **Electronic Data Interchange** (EDI), which is the exchange of documents and transactions by a computer in one company with the computer of another company. The **receiving report** certifies quantities received and may report results of inspection and testing for quality.

B. Invoice Approval

If the vendor's invoice is correct, the invoice clerk approves it, attaches it to the purchase order and the receiving report, and sends these papers to another clerk for the preparation of the voucher. The voucher data are entered in the purchases journal, the subsidiary records, and then the cash payments journal. The treasurer mails a check with the original voucher to the vendor, files a voucher copy, and returns one voucher to the Accounting Department.

C. Data Processing

Upon receipt of the invoice in an electronic data processing system, the data are directly input from the invoice to the computer and are edited, audited, and merged with the purchase order and receiving order data that are stored in the computer data bank. When in agreement, the cost data are entered into the accounts payable computer file with a date for later payment. It is equally important to post the invoice data in quantities and dollar values to the materials inventory file in the EDP system.

D. Cost of Acquiring Materials

Materials are commonly carried at the invoice price paid to the vendor, although all acquisition costs and price adjustments affect the materials cost. Acquisition costs are generally charged to Factory Overhead when it is not practical to follow a more accurate costing procedure. If it is decided that the materials cost should include incoming freight charges and other acquisition costs, an applied rate may be added to each invoice instead of charging these costs directly to Factory Overhead.

III. Storage and Use of Materials

The storekeeper is responsible for safeguarding the materials by placing them in bins or other storage areas and by seeing that they are taken from the storeroom only when properly requisitioned. The **materials requisition** is the authorization for the storeroom to issue materials to departments. Preparation of the materials requisition results in entries to the issued section of the materials record cards and in postings to the job order cost sheets, production reports, or the various expense analysis sheets for individual departments. The **materials record cards** record the receipt and the issuance of each class of materials and provide a perpetual inventory record. The **bill of materials**, a kind of master requisition, is a printed form that lists all the materials and parts necessary for a typical job or production run. Even with a perpetual inventory system, periodic physical counts are necessary to discover and eliminate discrepancies between the actual count and the balances on materials record cards. When the inventory count differs from the balance on the materials record card, the record card is adjusted to conform to the actual count.

IV.   Economic Order Quantity

The **economic order quantity** (EOQ) is the amount of inventory to be ordered at one time for purposes of minimizing annual inventory cost. The quantity to order at a given time must be determined by balancing two factors: (1) the cost of possessing (carrying) materials and (2) the cost of acquiring (ordering) materials. Costs of carrying inventory include interest expense, property tax and insurance, handling and storage, and deterioration and obsolescence of the items. Costs of not carrying enough inventory include extra purchasing, handling, and transportation costs; higher prices due to small order quantities; frequent stockouts resulting in disruption of production schedules; inflation-oriented increases in prices when inventory purchases are deferred; and lost sales and loss of customer goodwill.

A.   EOQ Formulas

The formula for the **economic order quantity** (EOQ) in units is:

$$\sqrt{\frac{2 \times \text{Annual required units} \times \text{Cost per order}}{\text{Cost per unit of material} \times \text{Carrying cost percentage}}}$$

The EOQ formula is equally appropriate in computing the optimum size of a production run in units:

$$\sqrt{\frac{2 \times \text{Annual required units} \times \text{Setup cost per run}}{\text{Variable manufacturing cost} \times \text{Carrying cost percentage}}}$$

V.   Determining the Time to Order

The question of when to order is controlled by the time needed for delivery, the rate of inventory usage, and the safety stock. A safety stock is often the least costly device for protecting against a **stockout**. The optimum safety stock is that quantity that results in minimal total annual cost of stockouts and safety stock carrying cost. The annual cost of stockouts depends upon the probability of their occurrence and the actual cost of each stockout. The **order point** is reached when inventory on hand and quantities due in are equal to the lead time usage quantity plus the safety stock quantity (I + QD = LTQ + SSQ).

VI.   Materials Control

Purchasing and production managers are primarily interested in unit control of inventory. Executive managers are concerned that dollars invested in inventory are utilized effectively as measured by an adequate return on capital employed. A basic objective of materials control is the ability to place an order at the appropriate time with the best source to require the proper quantity at the right place and quality.

A.   Materials Control Methods

A materials control method that examines periodically the status of quantities on hand of each class of items is the **order cycling method** or **cycle review method**. Under the **min-max method**, a maximum quantity for each item is established and a minimum level provides the margin of safety necessary to prevent stockouts during a reorder cycle. The **two-bin system** separates each stock item into two bins: the first bin contains enough stock to satisfy usage that occurs between receipt of an order and the placing of the next order; the second bin contains the normal amount used from order date to delivery date plus safety stock. The **ABC plan** is an analytical approach based on statistical averages. "A," or high-value items, are under the tightest control; whereas, "C" items are under simple physical controls, such as the two-bin system.

Part 1 ■ True/False

Instructions: *Indicate whether each of the following statements is **True** or **False**.*

True/False

1. With EDI, transactions are machine readable, and computers can transfer data between companies without extensive paperwork. . . . .   _____

2. The purchase order contains all necessary information regarding price, discount agreement, and delivery information. . . . .   _____

3. The receiving report is usually signed by the purchasing agent, and the original report and an acknowledgement copy are sent to the vendor. . . . .   _____

4. One copy of the receiving report is sent to the Accounting Department, where it is matched with the purchase order and the vendor's invoice and then paid. .   _____

5. Materials acquisition costs are generally charged to Factory Overhead when it is not practical to follow a more accurate costing procedure. . . . .   _____

6. The cost of carrying inventory and the cost of inadequate carrying are two conflicting kinds of costs. . . . .   _____

7. Costs of carrying inadequate inventory include frequent stockouts, additional clerical costs, and higher prices due to small order quantities. . . . .   _____

8. When calculating safety stock, the traditional rules of thumb, such as a two-week supply, furnish management with the soundest basis for determining the level of safety stock. . . . .   _____

9. In determining the economic order quantity, only the variable costs of procuring an order should be included. . . . .   _____

10. It is not unusual for order costs to amount to $20 or more per order and for carrying costs to amount to as much as 35% of the average inventory investment. . . . .   _____

11. The ideal order size is the point where the annual carrying charges exceed the ordering charges. . . . .   _____

12. If lead time or usage is less than expected during an order period, the new materials will arrive before the existing stock is consumed; thus, adding to the cost of carrying inventory. . . . .   _____

13. The optimum safety stock is that quantity that results in maximum total annual cost of stockouts and safety stock carrying cost. . . . .   _____

14. The order point is reached when inventory on hand and quantities due in equal the lead time usage quantity plus the safety stock quantity. . . . .   _____

15. Under the ABC plan of materials control, items are classified and ranked in descending order on the basis of the annual dollar value of each item. . . . .   _____

Part 2 ■ Matching

Instructions: *On the line at the left of each of the following items, place the letter from the columns below that identifies the term that best matches the statement. No letter should be used more than once.*

_____ 1. Provides the master plan from which details concerning materials requirements are eventually developed.

_____ 2. Exchange of documents and transactions by a computer in one company with the computer of another company.

_____ 3. Authorizes appropriate quantities to be delivered at specified dates.

_____ 4. Certifies quantities received and may report results of inspection and testing for quality.

_____ 5. Notifies the storeroom or warehouse to deliver specified types and quantities of materials to a given department.

_____ 6. Records the receipt and the issuance of each class of materials and provides a perpetual inventory record.

_____ 7. Another term for inventory cushion.

_____ 8. Method of materials control based on the premise that the quantities of most stock items are subject to definable limits.

_____ 9. A method illustrated by the physical observation that an order point has been reached.

_____ 10. Examines periodically the status of quantities on hand of each item or class.

_____ 11. Based on usage during the time necessary to requisition, order, and receive materials, plus an allowance for protection against stockout.

_____ 12. A computer simulation module that offers a modern method of dealing with each product's bill of materials, inventory status, and manufacturing process.

_____ 13. A printed or duplicated form that lists all the materials and parts necessary for a particular job or production run.

_____ 14. Represents the amount of inventory to be ordered at one time for purposes of minimizing annual inventory cost.

_____ 15. A materials costing method that charges issued materials at a predetermined price reflecting an expected future price.

_____ 16. Result in disruption of production schedules, overtime, and extra setup time.

_____ 17. An analytical approach based on statistical averages that concentrates on important stock items.

_____ 18. Time between the order and the delivery of materials.

_____ 19. Expressed as a percentage of the average inventory investment.

_____ 20. Informs the purchasing agent about the quantity and type of materials needed.

a.	purchase order	k.	Electronic Data Interchange (EDI)
b.	min-max method	l.	ABC plan
c.	stockouts	m.	purchase requisition
d.	inventory carrying cost	n.	standard cost
e.	materials requirement planning (MRP)	o.	production budget
f.	order points	p.	bill of materials
g.	materials record card	q.	order cycling
h.	economic order quantity	r.	lead time
i.	two-bin method	s.	safety stock
j.	receiving report	t.	materials requisition

Part 3 ■ Multiple Choice

Instructions: *On the line at the left of each of the following items, place the letter of the choice that most correctly completes each item.*

_____ 1. An auditor tests the quantity of materials charged to Work in Process by tracing these quantities to:

     a. cost ledgers   **d.** materials requisitions
     b. perpetual inventory records   **e.** none of the above
     c. receiving reports

_____ 2. The Weissbuch Company requires 40,000 units of Product Q for the year. It costs $60 to place an order and $10 annually to carry a unit in inventory. The economic order quantity in units is:

     a. 400   **d.** 693
     b. 490   **e.** none of the above
     c. 600   *(AICPA adapted)*

_____ 3. Magic Inc. manufactures wands. The cost of carrying one wand in inventory for one year is $.60. Magic manufactures 6,000 wands evenly throughout the year. Using the EOQ approach, the optimal production run would be 200 when the setup cost is:

     a. $2.00   **d.** $4.00
     b. $3.00   **e.** none of the above
     c. $3.50   *(AICPA adapted)*

_____ 4. A relevant factor in determining economic order quantity is:

     a. physical plant insurance costs   **d.** physical plant depreciation charges
     b. warehouse supervisory salaries   **e.** all of the above
     c. variable costs of processing a
         purchase order   *(AICPA adapted)*

_____ 5. A company buys a certain part for its manufacturing process. To determine the optimum size of a normal purchase order, the formula for the economic order quantity is used. In addition to the annual demand, other information necessary to complete the formula is:

     a. cost of placing an order and annual cost of carrying one unit in stock
     b. cost of the part and annual cost of carrying a unit in stock
     c. cost of placing an order
     d. cost of the part
     e. none of the above

_____ 6. If Frederick Company orders raw materials in quantities larger than the optimum quantity obtained using the basic EOQ model in order to obtain a quantity discount, the company will experience:

     a. ordering costs higher than if the optimum quantity were ordered
     b. ordering costs the same as if the optimum quantity were ordered
     c. carrying costs higher than ordering costs
     d. ordering costs higher than carrying costs
     e. none of the above   *(ICMA adapted)*

_____ **7.** A company's treasurer complains about an excessive investment in inventories. At the same time, the purchasing agent states that large inventory balances are necessary to take advantage of supplier discounts, and the production manager complains that production often is delayed by inventory shortages. The quantitative technique most relevant to this situation is:

a. economic order quantity models   **d.** probability analysis
b. linear programming   **e.** none of the above
c. payback analysis

(AICPA adapted)

_____ **8.** Ignoring safety stocks, a valid computation of the order point is:

a. the economic order quantity
b. the economic order quantity multiplied by the anticipated demand during lead time
c. the anticipated demand during lead time
d. the square root of the anticipated demand during the lead time
e. none of the above

(AICPA adapted)

_____ **9.** The purchase requisition:

a. contracts for quantities to be delivered
b. authorizes the storeroom or warehouse to deliver specified materials to a given department
c. informs the purchasing agent of the quantity and kind of materials needed
d. is a list of the materials requirements for each stop in the operations
e. none of the above

_____ **10.** If materials cost is to include purchasing department costs, the journal entry to record these costs should include a debit to materials and a credit to:

a. Applied Purchasing Department Costs   **c.** Applied Factory Overhead
    d. Cost of Goods Sold
b. Factory Overhead Control   **e.** none of the above

Part 4 ■ Problem

An invoice for Part 001, Part 002, and Part 003 is received from the Roman Chemical Company. Invoice totals are: Part 001, $22,500; Part 002, $16,000; and Part 003, $11,500. The freight charges on this shipment totalling 3,800 gallons is $950. Weights for the respective materials are 1,600, 1,400, and 800 gallons.

Instructions:

1. Allocate freight to materials based on cost.

2. Allocate freight to materials based on volume.

Part 5 ■ Problem

David Products Inc. uses 180,000 units of Material Yuk annually in its production. Order costs consist of $20 for placing a long-distance call to make the order, and $60 for delivering the order by truck to the company warehouse. Each Yuk costs $400, and the carrying cost is estimated at 20% of the inventory cost.

Instructions: *Compute the optimal order quantity in units for Yuk, and the total order cost and carrying cost for the year.*

Part 6 ■ Problem

Michael Manufacturing Inc. uses an item for which it places 100 orders per year. The cost of a stockout is $100, and the carrying cost is $2 per unit. The following probabilities of a stockout have been estimated for various levels of safety stock:

Probability	Safety Stock Level
50%	0 units
30	200
10	400
5	800

Instructions: *Determine the total carrying cost and stockout cost at each level of safety stock and indicate the optimum level of safety stock.*

Safety Stock Level	Expected Annual Stockouts	Total Stockout Cost	Total Carrying Cost	Total Stockout and Carrying Cost
0				
200				
400				
800				

Part 7 ■ Problem

The Tai-Chi Corporation has obtained the following costs and other data pertaining to one of its materials:

Working days per year......................	250 units
Normal use per day	100 units
Maximum use per day	150 units
Lead time.................................	10 days
Variable cost of placing one order	$25
Variable carrying cost per unit per year.........	$5

Instructions:

1. Determine the economic order quantity in units.

2. Determine the maximum safety stock needed.

3. Determine the order point.

4. Determine the maximum inventory, assuming normal lead time and usage.

CHAPTER 10

Just-in-Time and Backflushing

REVIEW SUMMARY

I. Purpose of the Chapter

This chapter describes just-in-time and illustrates accounting for the flow of production costs in a mature just-in-time system. It states the potential effect of JIT on production losses, describes JIT's effect on the purchasing function, and states the relationship between JIT and backflushing.

II. Just-in-Time

Just-in-time (JIT) is a philosophy centered on the reduction of costs through elimination of inventory. All materials and components should arrive at a work station only when they are needed, and products should be completed and available to customers only when the customers want them. In JIT, authorization for a part to be made at a work station is generated by the need for that part at the next work station in the production line. As parts are used in final assembly, the production of their replacements is authorized. To avoid inventory buildup, the entire production line is stopped if parts are missing at any stage or if defects are found. JIT seeks to reduce inventories because it views inventories as wasteful. Inventory represents resources not being used and is a form of slack or fat that covers up other forms of waste.

III. JIT and Velocity

There is an important and direct relationship between the size of Work in Process (WIP) and the speed of production. This relationship can be stated another way: If the rate of output is maintained while the number of units in process is cut in half, then the speed of the system has been doubled. The speed with which units or tasks are processed in a system is called the **velocity** and is inversely related to **throughput time**, the time that it takes to get through the system. The intent of JIT is to reduce total cycle time because the only time that value can be added to a product is when it is being processed; moving time, waiting time, and inspection time do not add value.

IV. JIT and Cost Savings

At individual work stations in a production line, the impact of WIP reduction is simple—fewer units will be waiting at, or moving to, each location. This can have an important impact on costs, resulting in both carrying cost savings and savings in cost of defects. Because of the connection between production losses and the size of WIP inventories, many successful JIT implementations have dramatically reduced such losses. Other potential advantages include the savings in setup costs that should be achieved to make the smaller average batch size economical, the savings due to improvements in customer satisfaction from quicker response to orders, and the possibility that the faster cycle time might permit all shipments to be made to order so that finished goods inventory is no longer needed. The potential costs include (1) handling a larger number of smaller batches of WIP, (2) the higher probability of shutdowns due to the smaller safety stock at each work station, and (3) the possibility that setup costs cannot be reduced enough to offset the larger number of setups performed.

V. JIT and Purchasing

The JIT approach to purchasing emphasizes reducing the number of suppliers and improving the quality of both the materials and the procurement function. The objective is to move materials directly from the supplier to the plant floor with little or no inspection and to eliminate storage except for brief periods directly on the plant floor. A single vendor for each material is the ideal. Well-developed JIT purchasing uses **blanket purchase orders**, which are agreements with vendors stating the total quantities expected to be needed over a period of three or six months. Received materials or their containers may have bar-coded labels that are read by hand-held or built-in scanners on the buyer's assembly line.

VI.   JIT and Factory Organization

One approach to JIT is to change from the traditional factory layout to **cells** or **work cells**. A cell is responsible for the entire production of one product or part or a family of very similar ones. Every worker in the cell is trained for multiple tasks so that labor is easily shifted to the point in the cell where it is needed. Scheduling, receiving, material handling, tool storage, setup, maintenance, repair, in-process inspection, and finished goods inspection are all performed by cell labor rather than by separate service departments. A high degree of worker empowerment is possible when a cell team has autonomy over every production step from receiving to final inspection and performs most of its own support functions as well.

VII.   JIT—A Balanced View

Many companies that are considered users of JIT purchasing handle only a small percentage of their materials requirements by JIT methods, because of:

1.   The time and effort required to convert many suppliers to a JIT shipping pattern.

2.   The difficulty of obtaining shipping at a cost low enough to justify many small deliveries.

3.   The likelihood of occasional shipping delays if suppliers are hundreds of miles away.

4.   The frustrating tendency for a low-cost, allegedly noncritical part to become critical when it does not arrive on time.

Among efforts to eliminate large WIP inventories, partial results again are the norm. A common reason for partial results is the continual shutdown of work stations because they are "starved" for work,

and there are no WIP safety stocks at those stations. Some so-called JIT factories contain only one or a few JIT cells, representing a small fraction of total output. Where product demand fluctuates greatly from hour to hour and day to day, JIT is less practical. JIT implementation can create conflicts with traditional performance measures that emphasize full utilization of productive capacity.

VIII.   Backflushing

Backflushing, also called **backflush costing** or **backflush accounting**, is an abbreviated approach to accounting for the flow of manufacturing costs. It is applicable to mature JIT systems in which velocity is so high that traditional accounting is impractical. A total cycle time of a few hours means an extremely small amount of work is in process at any time and an accurate assignment of costs to the very small WIP inventory is generally a trivial issue. For controlling a fast-moving WIP inventory, physical measures and visual observation are used.

IX.   The Essence of Backflush Costing

The purpose of backflush costing is to reduce the number of events that are measured and recorded in the accounting system. The work in process account is not adjusted throughout the accounting period to reflect all of the costs of units in process, but rather its balance is corrected by means of a single end-of-period adjusting entry and no subsidiary records are kept for work in process. Backflush costing determines the elements of the cost of completed work only after the work is completed. The cost of the completed work is then subtracted from the balance in the work in process account in a step called **postdeduction**.

Part 1 ■ True/False

Instructions: *Indicate whether each of the following statements is* **True** *or* **False**.

True/False

1. Just-in-time is a philosophy centered on the increase in revenues through adequate stocking of inventory quantities. . . . .   _____

2. High quality and balanced workloads are required in a JIT system to avoid costly shutdowns and customer ill will. . . . .   _____

3. JIT systems are applicable to manufacturing but not to service businesses. . . .   _____

4. The JIT ideal is to eliminate stocks of work in process (WIP) and produce parts only as needed. . . . .   _____

5. Businesses that have implemented JIT have found its objective of reducing inventory to zero to be relatively easy to achieve. . . . .   _____

6. The speed with which units on hand are processed in a system is called velocity and is positively correlated with throughput time. . . . .   _____

7. The intent of JIT is to reduce total cycle time, since the only time that value can be added to a product is when it is being processed. . . . .   _____

8. Potential costs of maintaining lower work in process (WIP) levels include handling a larger number of smaller batches, the higher probability of shutdowns due to smaller safety stock, and the larger number of setups. . . . .   _____

9. The JIT approach to purchasing emphasizes increasing the number of suppliers and improving the quality of both the materials and the procurement function. . . .   _____

10. In JIT purchasing, the goal is long-term vendor relationships, rather than short-run price breaks. . . . .   _____

11. JIT purchasing emphasizes the use of purchase requisitions, purchase orders, receiving reports, and materials requisitions. . . . .   _____

12. A JIT work cell is responsible for the entire production of a product or part.   _____

13. Most companies that are considered users of JIT purchasing handle almost all of their materials requirements by JIT methods. . . . .   _____

14. Backflush costing involves maintaining subsidiary records of the cost of WIP.   _____

15. Backflush costing determines some or all elements of the cost of output only after production is complete. . . . .   _____

Part 2 ■ Matching

Instructions: *On the line at the left of each of the following items, place the letter from the columns below that identifies the term that best matches the statement. No letter should be used more than once.*

_____   1. A philosophy centered on the reduction of costs through the elimination of inventory.

_____   2. A term for the JIT effort to reduce inventories of work in process and raw materials.

_____   3. The description for the average time that it takes for a unit to pass through the production system.

_____   4. The speed with which units or tasks are processed in a system.

_____   5. Emphasizes reducing the number of suppliers and improving the quality of both the materials and the procurement function.

_____   6. Agreements with vendors stating the total quantities expected to be produced over a period of three or six months.

_____   7. Responsible for the entire production of one product or part.

_____   8. Characterized by worker empowerment.

_____   9. Applicable to mature JIT systems in which velocity is so high that traditional accounting is impractical.

_____ 10. Step in which the cost of completed work is subtracted from the balance of the work in process account or an equivalent combined account.

a.	blanket purchase orders	**f.**	stockless production
b.	throughput time	**g.**	backflush costing
c.	TQM	**h.**	velocity
d.	postdeduction	**i.**	cell
e.	JIT purchasing	**j.**	just-in-time (JIT)

Part 3 ■ Multiple Choice

Instructions: *On the line at the left of each of the following items, place the letter of the choice that most correctly completes each item.*

_____   1. Just-in-time is a philosophy centered on:

    a. the increase in revenues through carrying adequate stock
    b. the reduction of costs through elimination of inventory
    c. the principles of job order costing
    d. the principles of process costing
    e. none of the above

_____   2. One of the dangers of JIT is that it:

    a. eliminates inventory storage costs
    b. eliminates inventory carrying costs
    c. eliminates the cushion against production errors
    d. has come to be closely identified with efforts aimed to eliminate waste
    e. none of the above

_____ **3.** JIT principles are applicable to all of the following, *except*:

   a. managing work in an office
   b. managing work in a service business
   c. managing a service department of a factory
   d. managing a job shop
   e. reducing inventory requirements in a factory

_____ **4.** All of the following are terms used to describe the JIT effort to reduce inventories of work in process and raw materials, *except*:

   a. zipless production
   b. stockless production
   c. lean production
   d. zero inventory production
   e. none of the above are appropriate terms

_____ **5.** The JIT production ideal is a batch size of:

   a. one hundred
   b. ten
   c. one
   d. zero
   e. none of the above

_____ **6.** The objective of reducing inventory to zero is possible if all of the following conditions are present, *except*:

   a. low or insignificant setup costs
   b. minimum lead times
   c. frequent engineering changes
   d. balanced and level workloads
   e. no interruptions due to stockouts

_____ **7.** The continuing reduction of inventories is achieved by all of the following steps *except*:

   a. inventories are reduced until a problem is discovered
   b. once the problem is defined the inventory level is increased to keep the system operating smoothly
   c. the problem is analyzed and practical ways are identified to reduce it
   d. once the problem is removed, the inventory level is reduced until another problem is discovered
   e. all of the above steps are required

_____ **8.** The speed with which units or tasks are processed in a system is called the:

   a. throughput time
   b. acceleration
   c. mass
   d. velocity
   e. none of the above

_____ **9.** The costing method that does not involve maintaining subsidiary records of the cost of WIP is:

   a. job order costing
   b. backflush costing
   c. process costing
   d. standard costing
   e. all of the above require subsidiary records for work in process

_____ **10.** In backflush costing, the step where the cost of completed work is subtracted from the balance of the work in process account is called:

   a. postdeduction
   b. inventory difference procedures
   c. manufacturing reduction
   d. throughput reduction
   e. none of the above

Part 4 ■ Problem

Ashcroft Assembly Company maintains a WIP inventory at each of 5 work stations, and the average size of the inventory is 100 units per station. The physical flow of units into and out of each WIP location is first-in, first-out. The total number of instances in which some work station goes out of its control limits is expected to be 300 during the coming year. In three-fourths of these instances, the out-of-control condition is expected to be discovered immediately by the operator at that station; in the other one-fourth of these instances, a defect will enter 10% of the units produced. These defective units enter WIP between stations, where they will be discovered by the next station's operator. Every out-of-control condition is corrected as soon as it is discovered. The average cost of a unit in WIP is $60, and the average loss from an out-of-control condition is $15 per defective unit produced. The annual cost of carrying WIP is 25% of the cost of the inventory.

Management plans to reduce the number of units held at every work station by 40%. The rate of final output will be unchanged, and no other changes will be made in the system.

Instructions:

1. Calculate the carrying cost savings.

2. Calculate the savings in cost of defects.

Part 5 ■ Problem

Modern Manufacturing has a cycle time of less than a day, uses a raw and in process (RIP) account, and expenses all conversion costs to Cost of Goods Sold. At the end of each month, all inventories are counted, their conversion cost components are estimated, and inventory account balances are adjusted accordingly. Raw material cost is backflushed from RIP to Finished Goods. The following information is for the month of March:

Beginning balance of RIP account, including $2,500 of conversion cost	$ 17,500
Beginning balance of finished goods account, including $7,500 of conversion cost	19,000
Raw materials received on credit	325,000
Ending RIP inventory per physical count, including $1,500 conversion cost estimate	14,000
Ending finished goods inventory per physical count, including $5,500 conversion cost estimate	13,000

Instructions: *Prepare all the journal entries that involve the RIP account and/or the finished goods account.*

JOURNAL   PAGE

	DESCRIPTION	DEBIT	CREDIT	
1				1
2				2
3				3
4				4
5				5
6				6
7				7
8				8
9				9
10				10
11				11
12				12
13				13
14				14
15				15

Computations:

Part 6 ■ Problem

Automaton Company had 50 units in process, 75% converted, at the beginning of a recent, typical month; the conversion cost component of this beginning inventory was $550. There were 40 units in process, 25% converted, at the end of the month. During the month, 5,000 units were completed and transferred to Finished Goods, and conversion costs of $200,000 were incurred.

Instructions:

1. Carrying calculations to three decimal places, find the conversion cost per unit for the month:

    (a) by the average cost method as used in process costing in Chapter 6.

    (b) by dividing the total conversion cost incurred during the month by the number of units completed during the month (do not calculate equivalent units).

    (c) by dividing the total conversion cost incurred during the month by the number of units started during the month.

2. Using the three unit costs from requirement (1), calculate three amounts for the total conversion cost of the ending inventory of work in process, to the nearest dollar.

3. What one attribute of Automaton Company's production system is the most important in explaining the results of requirements (1) and (2)?

CHAPTER 11

Labor: Controlling and Accounting for Costs

REVIEW SUMMARY

I. Purpose of the Chapter

The purpose of the chapter is to explain: (1) the nature of productivity and its relationship to labor costs; (2) the theory and application of incentive wage plans; and (3) the application of incentive wage plans. It also discusses the necessary organization for labor cost accounting and control and the accounting for nonwage benefits, payroll taxes, and other labor-related deductions.

II. Elements of Labor Cost

Labor cost represents an important cost factor. The basic pay for work performed is called the base rate or job rate. Fringe benefits also form a substantial element of labor cost and include such items as the employer's share of FICA tax, holiday pay, overtime premium pay, and pension costs. In recent years, employment costs—wages, salaries, and fringes—have risen more than output per labor hour, leading to higher prices to meet higher unit labor costs. To curtail the wage-price spiral requires labor cost increases that do not exceed the unit cost reduction resulting from increased productivity.

III. Productivity and Labor

Labor productivity is the measure of production performance using the expenditure of human effort as a yard stick. Setting a standard of labor performance is not easy. The pace at which an observed employee is working is referred to as a rating or performance rating. **Normal** or **standard time** is the time that it should take a person working at a normal pace to do a job, with allowances for rest periods. The **productivity-efficiency ratio** measures the output of an individual, relative to the performance standard.

IV. Increased Productivity Through Human Resources Management

Four fundamental assumptions of human resource management are: (1) workers are best qualified to improve their work; (2) decisions should be made at the lowest possible level in the organization; (3) worker participation increases job satisfaction; and (4) there is a vast pool of ideas in the workforce. Coupled with the need for better management through broader participation is the necessity for investment in better trained people.

V. Incentive Wage Plans

An **incentive wage plan** should reward workers in direct proportion to their increased output. To be successful, an incentive wage plan should (1) be applied to situations in which a worker can increase output, (2) provide for proportionately more pay for output above standard, and (3) set fair standards so that extra effort will result in bonus pay. The **straight piecework plan** pays wages above the base rate for production above the standard. Under the **100 percent bonus plan**, a standard time is allowed to complete a job or unit, and the worker is paid for the standard time at the hourly rate if the job or unit is completed in standard time or less. **Group bonus plans** depend upon the superior productive performance of an entire department or factory. In **organizational incentive plans** employee suggestions are the heart of these **gainsharing plans**, and the incentive equation is based on some ratio of labor costs to the value that is added to sales as a result of improved productivity.

VI. Learning Curves

Learning curve theory may be used in determining time standards. Learning curve theory stipulates that every time the cumulative quantity of units produced is doubled, the cumulative average time per unit is reduced by a given percentage. In highly automated manufacturing situations, the learning curve is not operative because the speed of the production process is machine controlled.

VII. Labor Cost Control

Labor cost control is based on pertinent and timely information submitted to management. It begins with an adequate production planning schedule supported by labor-hour requirements and accompanying labor costs, determined well in advance of production runs. The departments that should cooperate in this process include personnel, production planning, timekeeping, payroll, and cost.

VIII. Department Involvement in Labor Cost Control

The chief function of the personnel department is to provide an efficient labor force. The production planning department is responsible for scheduling work, releasing job orders to producing departments, and dispatching work in the factory. The timekeeping department gathers and collects total and specific time worked on a job, product, process, or in a department. A clock card shows the time a worker started and stopped work each day, with overtime or other premium hours clearly indicated. The time ticket provides information as to the type of work performed and the job on which it was performed. The payroll department determines the gross and net amount of earnings of each worker, computes the total payroll, and keeps earnings records for each employee. The cost department charges jobs, products, processes, or departments with the applicable costs as evidenced by the payroll distribution. With the advent of **bar coding**, companies are able to keep track of labor costs by operation as well as by employee.

The following notes are based upon the Appendix to the chapter.

IX. Nonwage Benefits

Major components of employee benefits include employer FICA and unemployment insurance contributions, vacation pay and paid holidays, employer contributions to pension funds and supplemental unemployment pay funds, and recreation, health services, life insurance, and medical care. Many employers offer cafeteria plans that enable employees to specify what benefits they want with a fixed dollar amount of coverage and to pay for the balance with pre-tax dollars.

X. Overtime Earnings

The Federal Wage and Hour Law established a minimum wage per hour with time and a half for hours worked in excess of 40 hours in one week. To comply with this law, the records for each employee must indicate the hours worked each day and each workweek, the basis on which wages are paid, the

total daily and weekly earnings at straight time, and the total wages paid during each pay period. When work is randomly scheduled, the overtime premium pay should be included in factory overhead rather than charged to the jobs that happened to be worked on in the overtime period.

XI. Accounting for Fringe Benefits

In theory, bonus payments, vacation pay, and other direct-labor-related costs are additional labor costs that should be charged to Work in Process. In practice, however, these costs are generally included in the predetermined factory overhead rate. **Guaranteed annual wage plans** guarantee a worker either a percentage of normal take-home pay during layoffs or that a worker's weekly paycheck will not fall below a minimum figure. In apprenticeship and training programs, the portion of the wages paid in excess of the standard paid for the productive output, plus the cost of instruction, is an indirect labor cost to be included in the factory overhead rate.

XII. Pension Plans

A **pension plan** provides retirement benefits for all employees in recognition of their work contributed to a company. Pension costs are chargeable currently to factory overhead or to commercial expense, although it may be many years before pension benefits are actually paid. The Pension Reform Act of 1974 (ERISA) was enacted in order to make certain that promised pensions are actually paid at retirement. The law prohibits a plan from excluding an employee due to advanced age and lack of years of service. Also, a plan's minimal annual contribution must include the normal cost for the year plus amortization of past service costs and certain other costs, including interest.

XIII. FICA Tax

Employers other than those in excluded classes of employment are required to pay FICA tax on wages paid and certain fringe benefits, equal to the amount paid by the employees. The employer is further required to collect the FICA tax from employees by deducting the current percentage from the wages paid each payday up to the current annual limit or base to which the tax applies. Federal income tax withheld and employee and employer FICA taxes must be deposited with either an authorized commercial bank depository or a Federal Reserve Bank on a periodic basis and a quarterly report must be filed.

XIV. FUTA Tax

Under the Federal Unemployment Tax Act, an employer in covered employment must pay an unemployment insurance tax to the federal government. While the federal act requires no employee contribution, some states levy an unemployment insurance tax on the employee. The federal portion of the unemployment tax is generally payable quarterly, and the related tax return is due annually on January 31. The various state unemployment compensation laws also require reports from employers to determine their liability to make contributions, the amount of taxes to be paid, and the amount of benefit to which each employee is entitled if unemployment occurs.

XV. Worker's Compensation and Income Taxes Withheld

Workers' compensation insurance laws provide insurance benefits for workers or their survivors for losses caused by accidents or occupational diseases suffered in the course of employment. While the benefits, premium costs, and other details vary from state to state, the total insurance cost is borne by the employer. Income taxes are withheld from each wage payment in accordance with the amount of the employee's earnings and withholding allowances claimed on the W-4 form.

XVI. Recordkeeping

For each payroll, the total amount earned by workers is debited to Payroll with credits to Accrued Payroll and to the withholding accounts. The cost of labor purchased is summarized and recorded as debits to Work in Process, Factory Overhead Control, Marketing Expenses Control, and Administrative Expenses Control, and as a credit to Payroll. Employer payroll taxes and other labor-related costs are recorded and, at appropriate times, payments are made to discharge payroll-related liabilities.

Part 1 ■ True/False

Instructions: *Indicate whether each of the following statements is **True** or **False**.*

                                                     True/False

1. Labor cost control begins with an adequate production planning schedule. . . . .   _____

2. Many U.S. manufacturers employ advanced manufacturing technologies to enhance productivity and competitiveness, but relatively few take the required steps to reconfigure their human resource needs to reap the full benefits of technological innovation. . . . .   _____

3. Fringe costs are generally accounted for as direct labor costs. . . . .   _____

4. Bar coded employee identification badges are replacing clock cards and time tickets as a means of collecting payroll data and measuring the activity of workers and machines. . . . .   _____

5. Effective control of labor costs is best achieved by comparisons between actual performance and predetermined standards. . . . .   _____

6. In recent years in the U.S., output per labor hour has risen less than employment costs. . . . .   _____

7. The chief function of a payroll department is to provide an efficient labor force.   _____

8. Replacement hiring usually requires authorization by executive management. . .   _____

9. The cost accounting records should include a record of the time each worker spends on each job or process or in each department. . . . .   _____

10. In comparing the accounting for labor with the accounting for materials, the job ticket is comparable to the materials requisition, whereas the clock card is comparable to the materials invoice. . . . .   _____

11. A fundamental assumption of human resource management is that people who perform the work are best qualified to improve it. . . . .   _____

12. By utilizing a special payroll bank account, only one check, drawn on the general bank account, appears in the cash payments journal each payroll period. . . . .   _____

13. An incentive wage plan should reward workers in direct proportion to their increased high-quality output. . . . .   _____

14. A production planning department is responsible for the scheduling of work, the release of job orders to the producing departments, and the dispatching of work in the factory. . . . .   _____

15. Learning-curve theory is more applicable to simple, repetitive tasks than to complex tasks. . . . .   _____

Part 2 ■ Matching

Instructions: *On the line at the left of each of the following items, place the letter from the columns below that identifies the term that best matches the statement. No letter should be used more than once.*

_____ **1.** Developed a productivity measure that considers the use of capital, raw materials, energy, and labor related to a plant's output.

_____ **2.** Under this, the company sets a predetermined formula; if improvement above a certain amount occurs, all employees including management participate in the bonus.

_____ **3.** Factor based on the pace at which an observed employee is working.

_____ **4.** The time it should take a person working at a normal pace to do the job, with allowances for rest periods, possible delays, etc.

_____ **5.** Inherent in these is an employee-centered management style that places great emphasis on the involvement and participation of all employees.

_____ **6.** Unquestionable evidence of the employee's presence in the plant.

_____ **7.** Symbols that can be processed electronically to identify numbers, letters, or special characters.

_____ **8.** Items such as employer portion of FICA tax, pension costs, and vacation pay.

_____ **9.** Should be established for each operation in a plant or office and grouped by class of operation.

_____ **10.** Amount of goods and services that a worker produces.

_____ **11.** Shows the specific use that has been made of the labor purchased and is comparable to the materials requisition.

_____ **12.** A phase of production where no further learning takes place.

_____ **13.** Its chief function is to provide an efficient labor force.

_____ **14.** Starts with a labor requisition sent to the personnel department by a department head or supervisor.

_____ **15.** Requires authorization by executive management, resulting from its approval of the labor requirements of a production schedule.

_____ **16.** Responsible for the scheduling of work, the release of job orders to the departments, and the dispatching of work in the factory.

_____ **17.** Measures the output of an individual relative to the performance standard.

_____ **18.** Under this, a standard time is allowed to complete a unit, and the worker is paid for the standard time at the hourly rate if the unit is completed in standard time or less.

_____ **19.** Under this, the production standard is computed in minutes per piece and is then translated into money per piece.

_____ **20.** Stipulates that every time the cumulative quantity of units produced is doubled, the cumulative average time per unit is reduced by a given percentage.

a. standard time
b. time ticket
c. bar codes
d. steady-state condition
e. replacement hiring
f. base rate
g. productivity-efficiency ratio
h. expansion hiring
i. labor productivity
j. fringe costs
k. performance rating
l. straight piecework plan
m. learning-curve theory
n. 100 percent bonus plan
o. American Standards for Productivity Measurement
p. production planning department
q. clock card
r. personnel department
s. organizational incentive plans
t. Scanlon plan

Part 3 ■ Multiple Choice

Instructions: *On the line at the left of each of the following items, place the letter of the choice that most correctly completes each item.*

_____   1. Effective internal control over the payroll function includes:

  a. reconciling total time recorded on clock cards to job reports by employees responsible for those specific jobs
  b. supervising payroll department employees by personnel department management
  c. maintaining employee personnel records by payroll department employees
  d. comparing total time spent on jobs with total time indicated on clock cards
  e. all of the above

_____   2. An 80% learning curve was in effect for a certain industry. The first time the task was performed required a time of 100 minutes. When the task was performed for the fourth time, the cumulative average time per task unit equaled:

  a. 100 minutes   **d.** 144 minutes
  b. 80 minutes   **e.** none of the above
  c. 64 minutes

_____   3. In (2) above, the total estimated minutes that would have been required to perform the task four times would be:

  a. 400   **d.** 256
  b. 144   **e.** none of the above
  c. 320

_____   4. The document that provides evidence of an employee's total time in the plant is the:

  a. time ticket   **d.** requisition
  b. daily performance report   **e.** none of the above
  c. clock card

_____   5. The incentive program that bases a department's bonus on meeting an objective that has been stated in terms of time per output unit is the:

  a. group straight piecework plan   **d.** 100 percent group bonus plan
  b. Emerson efficiency system   **e.** none of the above
  c. group learning-curve plan

_____   6. In the process of setting labor standards, the rate or speed at which a person is working is the:

  a. performance rating   **d.** physical output per labor hour
  b. standard time   **e.** none of the above
  c. base rate

_____   7. An example of a fringe cost is:

  a. the direct labor wage rate   **d.** overtime premium pay
  b. withheld taxes   **e.** none of the above
  c. union dues paid by the employee

_____   8. All of the following assumptions characterize better human resource management, *except*:

  a. people who do the work are best qualified to improve it
  b. advanced manufacturing technology inherently results in better human resource management
  c. decision making should be pushed down to the lowest level possible
  d. worker participation increases commitment to company objectives
  e. there is a vast pool of ideas in the workplace waiting to be tapped

_____ **9.** If prices are to be kept from rising, it is necessary that:

    a. increased productivity must be reflected in lower prices rather than higher wages

    b. unit cost increases must be greater than wage increases

    c. direct labor cost increases must be in the form of fringe benefits

    d. productivity increases must be met by corresponding wage increases

    e. none of the above

_____ **10.** The company division that is responsible for recording the direct labor costs on the appropriate job cost sheets and indirect costs on the departmental cost analysis sheets is the:

    a. payroll department   **d.** production planning department

    b. timekeeping department   **e.** none of the above

    c. cost department

Part 4 ■ Problem

Instructions: *Complete the following table, assuming that standard production is 20 units per hour and the 100 percent bonus plan is in use. (When the efficiency ratio is less than 100, no bonus is earned.) Round all computations to two decimal places.*

Worker	Hours Worked	Output Units	Standard Units	Efficiency Ratio	Base Rate	Base x Efficiency Ratio	Total Earned	Labor Cost per Unit	Overhead per Hour	Overhead per Unit	Conversion Cost per Unit
Allen	40	840			$15.00				$20.00		
Birge	40	800			15.00				20.00		
Cole	40	880			15.00				20.00		
Duffy	36	750			10.00				20.00		
Easton	40	720			7.50				20.00		

Part 5 ■ Problem

D. Lucero, an employee of the Cuernavaca Co., submitted the following data for work activities last week:

Day	Units Produced Each Day
Monday	30
Tuesday	32
Wednesday	46
Thursday	28
Friday	34

During the week, Lucero worked 8 hours each day. The company guarantees a flat hourly wage of $12 of its straight piecework plan. Standard production is 4 units per hour. Wages are computed on a daily basis.

Instructions: *Complete the schedule below. (Round labor cost per unit to two decimal places.)*

Day	Units Produced	Daily Earnings	Labor Cost per Unit Produced Each Day
Monday		$	$
Tuesday			
Wednesday			
Thursday			
Friday			

Part 6 ■ Problem

Tonto Company uses labor standards in manufacturing its products. Based upon past experience, the company considers the effect of an 80% cumulative average time learning curve when developing standards for direct labor costs.

The company is planning the production of an item that requires the assembly of purchased components. Production is planned in lots of 10 units each. A steady-state production phase with no further increases in labor productivity is expected after the eighth lot. The first production lot of units requires 150 hours of direct labor time at a standard rate of $17.50 per hour.

Instructions:

1. Complete the schedule below demonstrating the 80% cumulative average time learning curve that the company expects to experience in producing the units. (Round to two decimal places.)

Cumulative Lots x	Cumulative Average Time per Lot =	Cumulative Time (Total Hours)
1		
2		
4		
8		

2. Compute the standard amount allowed for direct labor cost to produce the first 8 lots.

3. Compute the standard amount allowed for direct labor cost to produce an order for 7 lots, assuming that 1 lot had already been produced.

Part 7 ■ Problem

(The following problems are based on material in the Appendix.)

An employee of the Finishing Department is paid $14 per hour for a regular work week of 40 hours. During the week ended July 15, the employee worked 50 hours and earned time and a half for overtime hours.

Instructions:

1. Prepare the entry to distribute the labor cost if the job worked on during overtime was a rush order, the contract price of which included the overtime premium.

JOURNAL   PAGE

	DESCRIPTION	DEBIT	CREDIT	
1				1
2				2
3				3
4				4

2. Prepare the entry to distribute the labor cost if the job worked on during overtime was the result of random scheduling.

JOURNAL   PAGE

	DESCRIPTION	DEBIT	CREDIT	
1				1
2				2
3				3
4				4
5				5
6				6
7				7

Part 8 ■ Problem

A production worker earns \$3,300 per month and the company pays the worker a year-end bonus equal to one month's wages. The worker is also entitled to a one-month paid vacation per year. Bonus and vacation benefits are treated as indirect costs and accrued during the 11 months that the employee is at work.

Instructions: *Prepare the journal entry to record and distribute the labor cost of the production worker for a month. Assume that there are no deductions from gross wages.*

JOURNAL   PAGE

	DESCRIPTION	SUBSIDIARY RECORD	DEBIT	CREDIT	
1					1
2					2
3					3
4					4
5					5
6					6
7					7
8					8
9					9
10					10
11					11
12					12
13					13
14					14
15					15
16					16
17					17
18					18
19					19
20					20
21					21
22					22
23					23
24					24
25					25
26					26

*F*actory Overhead: *Planned, Actual, and Applied*

REVIEW SUMMARY

I.   Purpose of the Chapter

This chapter discusses the methods and bases available for applying overhead, describes the classification and accumulation of actual overhead costs, and shows the computation and disposition of over- or underapplied overhead.

II.   Nature of Factory Overhead

Factory overhead consists of indirect materials, indirect labor, and all other factory expenses that cannot conveniently be identified with or charged directly to specific jobs or products. Since automation has increased in modern manufacturing processes, factory overhead as a percentage of total product cost has increased. As production volume changes, the combined effect of different overhead patterns (i.e., fixed, variable, or semivariable) causes unit manufacturing cost to fluctuate considerably, unless some method is provided to stabilize the overhead charged to units produced.

III.   Use of a Predetermined Overhead Rate

A **predetermined factory overhead rate** is used to equitably allocate overhead because of the impossibility of tracing overhead costs to specific jobs or products. Its use is the only feasible method of computing product overhead costs promptly enough to serve management needs, identify inefficiencies, and smooth out uncontrollable month-to-month fluctuations in unit costs.

IV.   Factors Considered in Selecting Overhead Rates

Types of overhead rates differ not only from one company to another, but also from one department, cost center, or cost pool to another within the same company. At least five factors influence the selection of overhead rates. The three factors discussed in this chapter are: (1) the base to be used, (2) activity level selection, and (3) inclusion or exclusion of fixed overhead.

A.   Selection of Overhead Rate Base

In applying factory overhead, the base selected should be closely related to functions represented by the overhead cost being applied. All other things being equal, the simplest base should be used in order to minimize clerical costs. The following bases are used for applying factory overhead:

1.   The **physical output** base in which the factory overhead charge per unit is determined by dividing the estimated factory overhead for the period by the estimated units of production for the same period. This base is satisfactory when a company manufactures one product or closely related products whose difference is merely one of weight or volume.

2.   The **direct materials cost** base, in which the percentage of estimated materials cost is multiplied by the materials cost for the job or product to obtain the factory overhead to be charged to the order. This base has limited usage because in most instances there is no logical relationship between the direct materials cost of a product and the factory overhead used in its production.

3.   The **direct labor cost** base, in which the percentage of the estimated factory overhead to estimated direct labor cost is multiplied by the direct labor cost for the job or product to obtain the factory overhead charge. Its use is particularly favored when there is a direct relationship between direct labor cost and factory overhead and the rates of pay per hour for similar work are comparable.

4.   The **direct labor hour** base, in which the factory overhead rate is determined by dividing the estimated factory overhead by the estimated direct labor hours. This rate is then multiplied by the number of direct labor hours worked on a job or product to determine the overhead charge. As long as labor operations are the chief factor in production processes, the direct labor hour base is an equitable base for applying overhead.

5.   The **machine hour** base, in which the factory overhead rate is determined by dividing the estimated factory overhead by the estimated

machine hours. This rate is then multiplied by the number of machine hours used in completing a job or product to determine the overhead charge. This base is considered an accurate method of applying overhead if it is composed predominantly of facility-related costs, such as depreciation, maintenance, and utilities.

6. The **transactions-base approach**, in which each activity, such as setups or inspections, is viewed as a transaction, with costs assigned to products based on the number and complexity of the transactions. *Transactions* such as setups, inspections, and materials movements often are responsible for a large percentage of overhead costs, and the key to managing overhead is controlling the transactions that drive overhead. The transactions-base approach gives particular attention to the fact that certain overhead costs are not volume-driven.

B. Activity Level Selection

The **theoretical capacity** of a department is its ability to produce at full speed without interruption, and this capacity is achieved only if the department is producing at 100% of its rated capacity. **Practical capacity** is theoretical capacity less allowances for such things as unavoidable interruptions, unsatisfactory materials, labor shortages, and model changes. The **normal capacity concept** advocates an overhead rate in which expenses and production are based on average utilization of the physical plant over a period long enough to level out production highs and lows. The **expected actual capacity concept** advocates a rate in which overhead and production are based on the expected actual output for the next production period. The argument for using normal capacity is that a job or product should not cost more to produce in any one accounting period just because production was lower and fixed expenses were spread over fewer units. **Idle capacity** results from the idleness of production workers and facilities due to a temporary lack of sales; whereas, **excess capacity** results either from greater productive capacity than the company could ever hope to use or from an imbalance of equipment or machinery.

C. Including or Excluding Fixed Overhead

Under **full** or **absorption costing**, both fixed and variable expenses are included in overhead rates. Under **direct costing**, only variable expenses are included in overhead rates, and fixed expenses are charged against income in the period in which they are incurred.

V. Calculation of a Factory Overhead Rate

Variable expenses change in total with production volume and remain constant on a per-unit basis. *Fixed expenses* remain the same in total, but the expense per unit is different for each production level. The factory overhead rate can be broken down into its fixed and variable components as follows:

Fixed factory overhead rate =
$$\frac{\text{Estimated fixed factory overhead}}{\text{Estimated direct labor hours (or other base)}}$$

Variable factory overhead rate =
$$\frac{\text{Estimated variable factory overhead}}{\text{Estimated direct labor hours (or other base)}}$$

VI. Actual Factory Overhead

The principal source documents used for recording overhead are purchase vouchers, materials requisitions, labor time tickets, and general journal vouchers. Actual factory overhead expenses are summarized in a factory overhead control account in the general ledger. Individual factory overhead accounts are kept in a subsidiary ledger. Debits to the factory overhead control account are for actual expenses incurred during the period, while credits are for applied expenses.

VII. Over- or Underapplied Factory Overhead

A debit balance in the factory overhead control account indicates that overhead has been underapplied (i.e., actual overhead charges for the period exceeded factory overhead applied). A credit balance in the factory overhead control account indicates that overhead has been overapplied (i.e., factory overhead applied to production exceeded actual factory overhead expense for the period). If the balance is significant, it may instead be allocated to inventories and cost of goods sold. The procedure most often used for disposing of over- or underapplied factory overhead, provided the amount involved is not significant, is to close it to Cost of Goods Sold or Income Summary (thus treating it as a period cost rather than a product cost).

VIII. Changing Overhead Rates

Changes in production methods, prices, efficiencies, and sales expectancy make review of overhead rates necessary at least annually. The extent to which a company revises its rates depends on the frequency of these changes and on management's need and desire for current costs. Since a rate is an estimate, small differences between actual and applied overhead should be expected.

Part 1 ■ True/False

Instructions: *Indicate whether each of the following statements is **True** or **False**.*

True/False

1. Factory overhead includes all factory costs *except* costs of direct materials and direct labor. . . . . _____

2. Fixed costs are constant per unit, whereas variable costs per unit vary inversely with production volume. . . . . _____

3. Predetermined overhead rates are uniquely associated with job order costing, while actual overhead should be used with process costing. . . . . _____

4. The overhead rate should be changed if, at the end of the period, any difference exists between the actual factory overhead and the factory overhead applied. . _____

5. Since automation has increased in modern manufacturing processes, factory overhead as a percentage of total cost has increased. . . . . _____

6. During a predicted and severe recession (and accompanying reduction in production and sales), use of expected actual capacity for costing would result in higher product unit costs than would use of normal capacity. . . . . _____

7. The primary objective in selecting an overhead base is to minimize clerical cost and effort. . . . . _____

8. If the machine hours base is used, the fixed overhead rate should be calculated by dividing estimated fixed overhead by actual machine hours. . . . . _____

9. Labor time tickets are used to record only direct labor charges. . . . . _____

10. Actual factory overhead is recorded as a debit on the books, while applied overhead is shown as a credit. . . . . _____

11. When direct labor dollars are used for the overhead base, the amount of overhead applied is calculated by multiplying the overhead rate by the number of direct labor dollars actually expended. . . . . _____

12. It is logical to use a direct labor cost base rather than a direct labor hour base when the rates of pay for similar work are comparable. . . . . _____

13. Under the direct costing method, only fixed overhead is included in overhead rates. _____

14. The Internal Revenue Service requires that inventories include an allocated portion of significant annual overhead variances. . . . . _____

15. The amount by which applied overhead is less than actual overhead is known as overapplied overhead. . . . . _____

Part 2 ■ Matching

Instructions: *On the line at the left of each of the following items, place the letter from the columns below that identifies the term that best matches the statement. No letter should be used more than once.*

_____ **1.** Expected production volume for the coming year.

_____ **2.** Method of measuring activity that assumes that a large part of overhead costs arise from machinery.

_____ **3.** Method of product costing that results in high unit costs during recessions and low costs in prosperity.

_____ **4.** Estimated factory overhead divided by estimated materials cost times 100.

_____ **5.** The simplest overhead costing base in multiproduct plants.

_____ **6.** Total overhead rate times direct labor hours worked or other base.

_____ **7.** An appropriate overhead base for single-product plants.

_____ **8.** Indirect materials, indirect labor, and all other factory expenses that cannot conveniently be identified with or charged directly to specific jobs or products.

_____ **9.** An equitable method for applying overhead, as long as labor operations are the chief factor in production processes.

_____ **10.** The account to which actual factory overhead costs are charged.

_____ **11.** Actual overhead less applied overhead.

_____ **12.** Total overhead rate less the fixed overhead rate.

_____ **13.** A costing method that associates all production costs with product units.

_____ **14.** Results from the lack of utilization of production workers and facilities due to a temporary lack of sales.

_____ **15.** Account debited when Applied Factory Overhead is credited for actual production times the overhead rate.

_____ **16.** Costing method that associates only variable production costs with product units.

_____ **17.** Results either from greater productive capacity than the company could ever hope to use or from an imbalance in equipment or machinery.

_____ **18.** Achieved only if the department is producing at 100% of its rated capacity.

_____ **19.** Approach to overhead costing that gives particular consideration to the fact that certain overhead costs may not be driven by volume of output.

_____ **20.** Includes allowances for such things as unavoidable interruptions, unsatisfactory materials, labor shortages, and model changes.

a.	direct costing	**k.**	idle capacity
b.	actual unit cost	**l.**	machine hours base
c.	applied overhead	**m.**	direct materials cost base
d.	practical capacity	**n.**	factory overhead
e.	direct labor cost	**o.**	theoretical capacity
f.	expected annual capacity	**p.**	over/underapplied overhead
g.	direct labor hour base	**q.**	excess capacity
h.	Factory Overhead Control	**r.**	units of production
i.	transactions base	**s.**	variable overhead rate
j.	absorption costing	**t.**	Work in Process

Part 3 ■ Multiple Choice

Instructions: *On the line at the left of the following items, place the letter of the choice that most correctly completes each item.*

_____ 1. Overapplied factory overhead will always result when a predetermined factory overhead rate is employed and:

 a. production is greater than practical capacity
 b. actual overhead costs are more than expected
 c. practical capacity is less than normal capacity
 d. overhead incurred is less than applied overhead
 e. none of the above   *(AICPA adapted)*

_____ 2. The difference for the period between actual factory overhead and applied factory overhead will usually be minimized when the predetermined overhead rate is based on:

 a. normal capacity   **d.** practical capacity
 b. expected actual capacity   **e.** none of the above
 c. theoretical capacity

_____ 3. If a predetermined factory overhead rate is not used and the volume of production is decreased from the level planned, the cost per unit would be expected to:

 a. remain unchanged for fixed cost and increase for variable cost
 b. decrease for fixed cost and remain unchanged for variable cost
 c. increase for fixed cost and remain unchanged for variable cost
 d. decrease for fixed cost and decrease for variable cost
 e. none of the above   *(AICPA adapted)*

_____ 4. All of the following are other terms used for factory overhead, *except*:

 a. factory burden   **d.** manufacturing overhead
 b. manufacturing expense   **e.** all of the above
 c. direct manufacturing cost

_____ 5. Factory overhead should be allocated on the basis of:

 a. an activity basis that relates   **c.** direct labor cost
    to cost incurrence   **d.** machine hours
 b. direct labor hours   **e.** none of the above

_____ 6. Overapplied factory overhead costs are:

 a. fixed factory costs not allocated to units produced
 b. factory overhead costs not allocated to units produced
 c. excess variable factory overhead costs
 d. costs that cannot be controlled
 e. fixed factory costs that are overallocated to units produced

_____ 7. A company found that the differences in product costs resulting from the application of predetermined factory overhead rates rather than actual factory overhead rates were immaterial, even though actual production was substantially less than planned production. The most likely explanation is that:

 a. factory overhead was composed chiefly of variable costs
 b. several products were produced simultaneously
 c. fixed factory overhead was a significant cost
 d. costs of factory overhead items were substantially larger than anticipated
 e. none of the above   *(AICPA adapted)*

_____ 8. When a manufacturing company has a labor-intensive manufacturing plant producing many different products with employees of varying wage rates, the most appropriate base for applying factory overhead to work in process is:

    a. direct labor hours   **d.** cost of materials used

    b. direct labor dollars   **e.** none of the above

    c. machine hours   *(AICPA adapted)*

_____ 9. According to the Internal Revenue Service regulations, significant underapplied factory overhead should be disposed of by:

    a. decreasing cost of goods sold

    b. increasing cost of goods sold

    c. decreasing cost of goods sold, work in process inventory, and finished goods inventory

    d. increasing cost of goods sold, work in process inventory, and finished goods inventory

    e. none of the above

_____ 10. Examples of factory overhead include all of the following, *except*:

    a. wages of punch press operators

    b. wages of materials handlers

    c. salary of factory manager

    d. wages of production schedulers

    e. all of the above

Part 4 ■ Problem

Bono Company's budget data for March are shown below:

Estimated factory overhead............................	$500,000
Production scheduled	25,000 units
Direct labor hours scheduled........................	50,000 hours
Estimated direct labor cost..........................	$400,000
Machine hours scheduled............................	10,000 hours

Instructions:

1. Compute the overhead rate using the various bases given and complete the table below.

Activity Base	Total Overhead Rate
Physical output	_____
Direct labor hours.....................................	_____
Direct labor cost	_____
Machine hours...	_____

2. Assuming that the total overhead estimate is composed of a variable estimate of $200,000 and a fixed estimate of $300,000, complete the table below. (The machine hour base is used.)

Variable overhead rate	_____
Fixed overhead rate	_____
Total overhead rate....................................	_____

3. Prepare a journal entry that would be required to charge the predetermined overhead of $500,000 to production.

JOURNAL   PAGE

	DESCRIPTION	DEBIT	CREDIT	
1				1
2				2
3				3

4. Complete the following journal entry.

JOURNAL   PAGE

	DESCRIPTION	DEBIT	CREDIT	
1	?	550,000		1
2	Stores (factory supplies)		120,000	2
3	Accumulated Depreciation—Machinery		150,000	3
4	Prepaid Insurance—Factory Building		60,000	4
5	Accrued Payroll (indirect labor)		161,000	5
6	Accounts Payable (repairs)		59,000	6
7				7

5. Assume that Bono Company uses direct labor hours for the overhead base, that 52,000 direct labor hours were worked in March, and that actual overhead was $550,000.

(a) Prepare the entry in the T accounts below to charge predetermined overhead to production and to record the actual factory overhead. (Assume that a separate applied factory overhead account is not used.)

Work in Process	Factory Overhead Control

(b) Was the factory overhead over- or underapplied during March? _____

By how much? _____

(c) Complete the table below, using the data given in Questions 1, 2, and 5 above for direct labor hours.

	Overhead Rate	March Overhead Applied
Variable cost	$ _____	$ _____
Fixed cost	_____	_____
Total overhead..................................	_____	_____

Part 5 ■ Problem

Instructions: *The format for an overhead budget is shown below. Calculate the amount that should be budgeted for each indicated level of activity by completing the schedule. (Round to two decimal places.)*

Factory Expense Category	Budget Rate	Level of Activity (Machine Hours)			
		45,000	50,000	55,000	60,000
Variable costs (per machine hour):					
Indirect labor	$2.00	$ _____	$ _____	$ _____	$ _____
Indirect materials	.80				
Repairs...................	.60				
Total variable cost.......	$3.40	$ _____	$ _____	$ _____	$ _____
Fixed costs (total):					
Depreciation—factory and machinery..............	$200,000	$ _____	$ _____	$ _____	$ _____
Insurance—factory and machinery..............	50,000				
Total fixed cost	$250,000	$ _____	$ _____	$ _____	$ _____
Total overhead budget		$ _____	$ _____	$ _____	$ _____
Factory overhead rate per hour .		$ _____	$ _____	$ _____	$ _____
Fixed overhead rate per hour ..		$ _____	$ _____	$ _____	$ _____
Variable overhead rate per hour		$ _____	$ _____	$ _____	$ _____

Computations:

Part 6 ■ Problem

The following information is available concerning the inventory and cost of goods sold accounts of Blossom Company at the end of the most recent year:

	Work in Process	Finished Goods	Cost of Goods Sold
Direct material	$ 2,000	$ 5,500	$13,000
Direct labor	3,500	9,000	24,000
Applied overhead.	4,500	10,500	28,000
Year-end balance	$ 10,000	$ 25,000	$65,000

Applied overhead has already been closed to Factory Overhead Control.

Instructions: *Give the journal entry to close Factory Overhead Control, assuming:*

1. Underapplied overhead of $11,000 is to be allocated to inventories and Cost of Goods Sold in proportion to the balances in those accounts.

JOURNAL
PAGE

	DESCRIPTION	DEBIT	CREDIT	
1				1
2				2
3				3
4				4
5				5

2. Underapplied overhead of $11,000 is to be allocated to inventories and Cost of Goods Sold in proportion to the amounts of applied overhead contained in those accounts. (Round percentages to two decimal places and dollars to the nearest whole dollar.)

JOURNAL   PAGE

	DESCRIPTION	DEBIT	CREDIT	
1				1
2				2
3				3
4				4
5				5

Computations:

CHAPTER 13

Factory Overhead: Departmentalization

REVIEW SUMMARY

I. Purpose of the Chapter

This chapter describes the concept of departmentalization, distinguishes between service and producing departments and between direct and indirect departmental costs; further, it describes departmentalization in nonmanufacturing and nonprofit organizations. Last, the chapter illustrates the computation and use of departmental overhead rates and the accumulation of actual departmental overhead costs.

II. Departmentalization

Departmentalization of factory overhead means dividing the plant into segments, called departments, to which costs are charged. A job or product going through a department is charged with factory overhead for work done in that department, using the department's predetermined overhead rate. Responsible control of overhead costs is possible because departmentalization makes the incurrence of costs the responsibility of a specific supervisor or manager.

A. Producing and Service Departments

Producing departments engage in the actual manufacture of the product, whereas **service departments** render a service that contributes indirectly to the manufacture of the product. Examples of producing departments include Assembly, Machining, and Refining; while service departments include Production Control, Maintenance, and Personnel. The most common approach in establishing producing departments for the purpose of costing and controlling costs is to divide the factory along lines of functional activities, with each activity or group of activities constituting a department. Determination of the kinds and number of service departments to be established should consider the number of employees needed for each service function, the cost of providing the service, the importance of the service, and the assignment of supervisory responsibility.

III. Direct and Indirect Departmental Costs

Direct departmental costs are generally readily identified with the originating department and can be charged directly to that department. These costs include supervision, indirect labor, overtime, labor fringe benefits, indirect materials and factory supplies, repairs and maintenance, and equipment depreciation. **Indirect departmental costs** do not originate with any specific department but are incurred for all departments; they must, therefore, be prorated to the user departments. Indirect departmental costs include factory costs such as building depreciation, property tax, and insurance. To charge each department with its fair share of an indirect departmental cost, a base using some factor common to all departments (such as square footage in prorating building depreciation) must be found.

IV. Departmental Overhead Rates

The use of **departmental overhead rates** requires separate consideration of each producing department's overhead, which often results in the use of different bases for applying overhead for different departments. Sometimes different overhead bases and rates are used for cost pools within a single producing department. For example, there may be a pool of machine-related overhead costs and labor-related overhead costs all within the same work center. To establish departmental factory overhead rates, one must:

1. Estimate or budget the total direct factory overhead of producing and service departments at the selected activity levels.

2. Prepare a factory survey for the purpose of distributing indirect factory overhead and service department costs.

3. Estimate or budget total indirect factory overhead at the selected activity levels and allocate these costs among the departments.

4. Distribute service department costs to benefiting departments.

5. Calculate departmental factory overhead rates.

V.   Distributing Service Department Costs

The costs of service departments must ultimately be transferred to producing departments to establish predetermined factory overhead rates. Service department costs may be transferred only to producing departments, using the **direct method**, if there is no material difference in the final costs of a producing department when the costs of a service department are not prorated first to other service departments. Otherwise, service department costs should be transferred on the bases of producing and other service departments' use of the respective services, using the **step method**, with the costs of the service department serving the greatest number of other service departments or providing the largest dollar value of services to other service departments transferred first. Once costs for a service department are distributed, that department is usually considered closed and no further distributions are made to it. If greater precision is desired in overhead distribution so that service departments receive cost prorations from each other before distribution to producing departments, the **simultaneous method** using simultaneous equations for overhead distribution may be used.

VI.   Actual Overhead—Departmentalized

Departmentalization of factory overhead requires that each cost be charged to a department as well as to a specific expense account via **departmental cost analysis sheets**. When all overhead has been assembled in the producing departments at the end of the fiscal period, it is possible to compare actual with applied overhead and to determine the over- or underapplied factory overhead for each department.

VII.   Multiple Overhead Rates

Many job order settings involve a diverse product line with products that can be produced in several sizes, grades, and configurations. As a result, reliable product cost data cannot be obtained using any single predetermined overhead rate. One approach is to divide overhead costs into two or more overhead cost pools and to calculate an overhead rate for each pool. In determining the cost of a job, the result would be a multipart overhead cost calculation within a single department.

VIII.   Nonmanufacturing Businesses

Nonmanufacturing businesses and not-for-profit organizations should also departmentalize for cost planning and control. Examples of entities that have done so include retail stores, financial institutions, insurance companies, and educational institutions.

Part 1 ■ True/False

Instructions: *Indicate whether each of the following statements is True or False.*

True/False

1. Producing departments render a service that contributes indirectly to the manufacturing of a product.. _____

2. Examples of service departments include Production Control, Maintenance, and Shipping. .... _____

3. A departmentalized factory is usually divided along lines of functional activities. _____

4. When relatively few employees are involved, service functions are generally combined for the sake of economy.. _____

5. Indirect departmental expenses do not originate within specific departments but are incurred for all departments. .... _____

6. The overtime premium portion of overtime paid to direct labor employees should usually be charged to direct labor. .... _____

7. Indirect departmental expenses include factory costs such as power, light, and rent. _____

8. Factory costs such as building depreciation, property tax, and insurance would most appropriately be allocated by using the floor area as a distribution base. ..... _____

9. It is unusual to use different distribution bases for applying overhead to different departments... _____

10. Repairs and maintenance are usually classified as direct departmental expenses because they frequently originate in a maintenance department before being charged to the department receiving service. .... _____

11. The costs of service departments must ultimately be transferred to producing departments to establish predetermined factory overhead rates.............. _____

12. Selecting appropriate bases for the distribution of indirect departmental expenses has, for the most part, been reduced to an exact science................. _____

13. Usually, service department costs are transferred in the order of the amount of service rendered and received, with the costs of the department serving the greatest number of other departments and receiving service from the smallest number of other departments transferred first. .... _____

14. Using the step method, once costs for a service department are distributed, that department is usually considered closed and no further distributions are made to it. .... _____

15. Sometimes multiple overhead rates are used for cost pools within the same department.. _____

Part 2 ■ Matching

Instructions: *On the line at the left of each of the following items, place the letter from the columns below that identifies the term that best matches the statement. No letter should be used more than once.*

_____ 1. The act of dividing the plant into segments to which costs are charged.

_____ 2. Engages in the actual manufacture of the product by changing the shape, form, or nature of the material worked upon.

_____ 3. Contributes indirectly to the manufacturing of the product.

_____ 4. The specific service is not identified if service costs applicable to producing and service functions accumulate in this.

_____ 5. Costs that include fringe benefits, small tools, and supplies.

_____ 6. The straight-time portion of overtime paid to assemblers would be charged to this expense.

_____ 7. States that, in allocating direct and indirect costs, a department should be homogeneous; and specifies that this criterion is met if each significant activity of which costs are included has the same or a similar beneficial or causal relationship as the other activities for which costs are included in the department.

_____ 8. The cost of a service if each department obtained it separately rather than centrally at a lower aggregate price.

_____ 9. Costs that include repairs and maintenance, setups, lubricants, and energy.

_____ 10. Prepared for the purpose of facilitating the distribution of indirect factory overhead and service department costs.

_____ 11. An approach to overhead distribution that results in the most precise proration of service department costs.

_____ 12. To use this procedure for allocating service department costs, a decision must be made as to the order in which service departments are closed because no further distributions are made to a department once its costs have been distributed.

_____ 13. Method of distributing service department costs that can be justified if there is no material difference in the final costs of a producing department when the costs of a service department are not first prorated to other service departments.

_____ 14. Place where charges to a department for its share of factory overhead are recorded.

_____ 15. Example of a nonmanufacturing business that has practiced departmentalization for many years.

_____ 16. An overhead grouping used in nonmanufacturing businesses that is equivalent to the general factory grouping in a manufacturing business.

_____ 17. Used most often in job order settings involving some combination of labor-related overhead, machine-related overhead, and materials related overhead.

a. factory survey
b. simultaneous method
c. retail store
d. direct labor
e. multiple overhead rates
f. step method
g. CAS 418
h. occupancy
i. stand-alone cost

j. departmentalization
k. service department
l. general factory cost pool
m. direct method
n. labor-related overhead costs
o. departmental cost analysis sheet
p. producing department
q. machine-related overhead costs

Part 3 ■ Multiple Choice

Instructions: *On the line at the left of each of the following items, place the letter of the choice that most correctly completes each item.*

_____ 1. A segment of an organization is referred to as a producing department if it has:
  a. responsibility for developing markets for and selling of the organization's output
  b. responsibility for combining the raw materials, direct labor, and other production factors into a final output
  c. authority to make decisions affecting the major determinants of profit, including the power to choose its markets and sources of supply
  d. authority to provide specialized support to other units within the organization
  e. none of the above   *(ICMA adapted)*

_____ 2. A department that would be classified as a producing department is:
  a. Materials Handling   d. Storage
  b. Fabricating   e. none of the above
  c. Inspection

_____ 3. A department that would be classified as a service department is:
  a. Plating   d. Purchasing
  b. Knitting   e. none of the above
  c. Cutting

_____ 4. Alpha Company operates with two producing departments (P1 and P2) and two service departments (S1 and S2). Factory overhead before allocation of service department costs, together with the usage of services from the service departments, follows:

Department	Overhead Before Allocation of Service Department Costs	Services Provided S1	S2
P1	$400,000	40%	30%
P2	300,000	30	50
S1	52,640	--	20
S2	105,280	30	--
	$857,920	100%	100%

Assuming that the step allocation method is used, what is the total factory overhead (including service department costs) charged to Department P1?
  a. $400,000   d. $461,062
  b. $461,664   e. none of the above
  c. $473,696

_____ 5. The most reasonable base for allocating supervision is:
  a. number of employees   d. building depreciation
  b. materials used   e. none of the above
  c. square footage

_____ 6. The method for allocating service department costs that results in the least precision is the:
  a. step method   d. direct method
  b. simultaneous equation method e. none of the above
  c. algebraic method

_____ 7. Deadwood Corp. has three producing departments, A, B, and C, with 35, 25, and 40 employees respectively in each department. Factory payroll costs other than direct labor are accumulated in a payroll department account and are assigned to producing departments on the basis of number of employees. The total payroll in each department is: A, $300,000; B, $275,000; C, $325,000; and payroll, $100,000. Other costs accumulated in the payroll department amounted to $190,000. The amount of payroll department costs chargeable to Department B is:

    a. $72,500   **d.** $47,500
    b. $25,000   **e.** none of the above
    c. $80,556

_____ 8. Factors to be considered in deciding what kinds of departments are required for establishing accurate departmental overhead rates with which to control costs include all of the following *except*:

    a. similarity of operations, processes, and machinery in each department
    b. location of operations, processes, and machinery
    c. the number of employees within each department
    d. number of departments and cost centers
    e. none of the above

_____ 9. All of the following are generally direct departmental overhead costs *except*:

    a. depreciation, insurance, and property taxes on the factory building
    b. supervision, indirect labor, and overtime
    c. labor fringe benefits
    d. equipment depreciation
    e. none of the above

_____ 10. All of the following departmental expenses logically might use square footage as the distribution base *except*:

    a. factory rent   **d.** fixed portion of electricity
    b. building repairs   **e.** none of the above
    c. variable portion of electricity

Part 4 ■ Problem

The factory overhead work sheet shown below for Godzilla Products Company had the indicated columnar totals after the actual direct charges and the indirect departmental expense allocations had been made. The company has three service departments, X, Y, and Z, and two producing departments, A, and B.

Instructions: *Complete the work sheet if the service department costs are allocated in the following order:*

Department X costs: 40% to Y; 30% to Z; 20% to A; 10% to B.
Department Y costs: 40% to Z; 35% to A; 25% to B.
Department Z costs: 70% to A; 30% to B.

1. Using the step method of allocation:

	Service Departments			Producing Departments		Total
	X	Y	Z	A	B	
Total	$ 40,000	$ 30,000	$ 25,000	$100,000	$150,000	$ 345,000
Dept. X distribution	$					
Dept. Y distribution		$				
Dept. Z distribution			$			
Total				$	$	$

2. Using the direct method of allocation:

	Service Departments			Producing Departments		Total
	X	Y	Z	A	B	
Total	$ 40,000	$ 30,000	$ 25,000	$100,000	$150,000	$ 345,000
Dept. X distribution	$					
Dept. Y distribution		$				
Dept. Z distribution			$			
Total				$	$	$

Part 5 ■ Problem

Kokomo Candy Co. consists of three producing departments and four service departments. For the purpose of creating factory overhead rates, the accountant prepared the cost distribution sheet, shown below, containing operational data that were gathered. For the distribution of expenses of the service departments, the following procedures had been decided upon:

(a) Utilities: 70% on metered hours—power; 30% on floor square footage
(b) Maintenance: Maintenance hours excluding Utilities' hours
(c) Materials Handling: 45% to Preparation; 35% to Mixing; and 20% to Packaging; pounds handled—300,000 in Preparation; 500,000 in Mixing
(d) Factory Office: Preparation, 40%; Mixing, 40%; Packaging, 20%

Instructions: *Complete the cost distribution sheet on the next page using the step method of cost allocation. Factory overhead rates should be based on pounds handled in Preparation and Mixing and on direct labor cost of $20,000 in Packaging. (Round off all amounts except overhead rates to the nearest dollar. Overhead rates should be rounded to four decimal places.)*

	Total	Producing Departments			Service Departments			
		Preparation	Mixing	Packaging	Utilities	Maintenance	Materials Handling	Factory Office
Operational Data:								
Floor space—sq. ft.	53,000	18,000	13,000	12,000	3,000	2,000	1,000	4,000
Maintenance hours	7,000	3,000	1,500	600	1,000	—	600	300
Metered hours	5,000	1,500	1,800	700	—	500	300	200
Expenses:								
Indirect labor	$ 26,000	$ 4,500	$ 4,000	$ 3,500	$ 6,000	$ 3,500	$ 2,500	$ 2,000
Payroll taxes	2,500	450	400	350	500	350	250	200
Indirect materials	6,000	900	1,100	3,000	500	200	50	250
Depreciation	1,000	150	200	100	200	150	75	125
Total	$ 35,500	$ 6,000	$ 5,700	$ 6,950	$ 7,200	$ 4,200	$ 2,875	$ 2,575
Distribution of								
service departments costs:								
Utilities:								
70% metered hours								
30% sq. footage					$			
Maintenance						$		
Materials handling							$	
Factory office		$	$	$				$
Bases:								
Pounds handled								
Direct labor cost								
Rates	$							

Part 6 ■ Problem

Keith Mills, Inc. has two service departments that not only serve the two producing departments but also one another. The relationships between the four departments can be expressed as follows:

Percentage of Services Consumed by Departments

Service Departments	Milling Dept.	Planing Dept.	Utilities Dept.	Maintenance Dept.	Service Costs To Be Distributed
Utilities	50%	40%	--	10%	$25,000
Maintenance	40%	35%	25%	--	$40,000

Instructions:

1. Determine the amount of service costs applicable to each service department, using the simultaneous method. (Round answers to the nearest whole dollar.)

2. Compute the total factory overhead in each producing department if primary overhead amounts to $90,000 in the Milling Department and $60,000 in the Planing Department. (Round to the nearest dollar.)

	Total	Milling	Planing	Utilities	Maintenance
Primary overhead	$	$	$	$	$
Distribution of:					
Utilities					
Maintenance					
	$	$	$	$	$

CHAPTER 14

Activity Accounting: Activity-Based Costing and Activity-Based Management

REVIEW SUMMARY

I. Purpose of the Chapter

The purpose of this chapter is to define activity-based costing and activity-based management, identify the circumstances in which activity-based costing gives more credible results than product costing, and identify the different levels of costs and activity drivers in activity-based costing. The chapter also calculates product costs using activity-based costing. Further, the chapter identifies the strategic performance of activity-based costing in pricing and product-line decisions and identifies ways in which activity-based management can achieve improvements in an organization.

II. Activity-Based Costing

Activity-based costing (ABC) is a costing system in which multiple overhead cost pools are allocated using bases that include one or more non-volume-related factors. Compared to traditional accounting, ABC represents a more thorough application of cost tracing. ABC recognizes that many other costs in addition to direct materials and direct labor are traceable—not to units of output but to the activities required to produce output.

III. Levels of Costs and Drivers

In ABC, the bases used to allocate overhead costs are called **drivers**. A **resource driver** is a base used to allocate the cost of a resource to the different activities using that resource. An **activity driver** is a base used to allocate the cost of an activity to products, customers, or other final cost objects. ABC recognizes activities, activity costs, and activity drivers at different **levels of aggregation** within a production environment.

A. Unit Level

Unit-level costs are the costs that inevitably increase whenever a unit is produced, such as electricity cost if electric machinery is used in producing each unit. **Unit-level drivers** are measures of activi-ties that vary with the number of units produced and sold, such as direct labor hours, direct labor cost, and machine hours.

B. Batch Level

Batch-level costs are costs caused by the number of batches produced and sold, such as setup costs and most material handling costs. **Batch-level drivers** are measures of activities that vary with the number of batches produced and sold, such as setups, work orders, and material requisitions.

C. Product Level

Product-level costs are costs incurred to support the number of different products produced, such as the costs of new products' design, development, prototyping, and product engineering. **Product-level drivers** are measures of activities that vary with the number of different products produced and sold, such as design changes, design hours, and the number of different kinds of parts needed.

D. Plant Level

Plant-level costs are the costs of sustaining capacity at a production site, such as rent, depreciation, property taxes, and insurance on the factory building. Floor space occupied is referred to often as the **plant-level driver** for assigning plant-level costs.

IV. Comparison of ABC and Traditional Costing

Traditional costing systems are characterized by their exclusive use of unit-level measures as bases for allocating overhead to output, whereas ABC systems use all four of the above measures. The number of overhead cost pools and allocation bases tends to be higher in ABC systems. Another difference is that all the costs within an activity cost pool are very much alike in their logical relationship to the activity driver, while the same cannot be said in many traditional systems. Another distinction between ABC and traditional systems is that all ABC systems are two-stage costing systems, while traditional systems may be one- or two-stage systems.

V.   ABC and Product Cost Distortion

One circumstance necessary for product cost distortion is a complex cost structure, which means significant amounts of non-volume-related costs. If non-volume-related costs were insignificant, the traditional system's distortions would be insignificant because they would be percentages of insignificant amounts. The other circumstance necessary for product cost distortion is a diverse product line, which means different products consume different mixes of volume-related and non-volume-related costs.

VI.   Strategic Advantage of ABC

The subtle choice of a system for calculating product costs can have important strategic implications. Using the wrong product costing system can lead to disaster. The strategic advantage of ABC lies in its potential to save a company from mistakenly discontinuing a product due to inappropriate cost allocation.

VII.   Strengths and Weaknesses of ABC

ABC produces more credible product cost information but is nonetheless a system of allocation. Particularly for plant-level costs, ABC has little or no advantage over traditional costing. ABC requires managers to make a radical change in their way of thinking about costs, in that ABC, which is designed to be a long-term decision-making tool, treats all costs as variable.

ABC does not show the costs that will be avoided by discontinuing a product or by producing fewer batches of it. ABC attempts to show each products' long-run consumption of resources; it does not predict how spending will be affected by certain decisions. Finally ABC requires data-gathering efforts beyond those needed to satisfy external reporting requirements.

VIII.   Activity-Based Management

Activity-based management (ABM) is the use of information obtained from ABC to make improvements in the firm. Over the long term, ABC information can help management position the firm to take better advantage of its strengths. When ABC's revelations about the processes used to produce goods and services become available to management, they usually reveal opportunities for improvement. The contribution of ABC to TQM is that it measures the cost of setups and every other significant activity, making it clear where improvement efforts should be devoted first.

IX.   Behavioral Changes

The design of products is a third area where activity cost information can be used. Activity cost information can show the cost of each significant activity, including ordering, receiving, and inspecting purchased components. An ABC system can provide information that will elicit the desired behavior because it permits designers to make cost-based decisions accurately. The best a traditional system can do is accurately capture the costs of unit-level activities, but it then distorts them by allocating batch- and product-level costs using unit-level allocation bases.

Part 1 ■ True/False

Instructions: *Indicate whether each of the following statements is* **True** *or* **False.**

True/False

1. Compared to traditional accounting, ABC represents a more thorough application of cost tracing. . . . .   _____

2. In ABC, the four levels of aggregation within a production environment are the unit, batch, product, and plant. . . . .   _____

3. An example of a batch-level cost would be inspection labor if each unit requires inspection. . . . .   _____

4. Examples of plant-level costs include rent, depreciation, and insurance on the factory building. . . . .   _____

5. ABC systems are characterized by their exclusive use of unit-level measures as bases for allocating overhead to output. . . . .   _____

6. The number of overhead cost pools and allocation bases tend to be higher in ABC systems than in traditional costing systems. . . . .   _____

7. A distinction between ABC and traditional costing systems is that all ABC systems are two-stage costing systems, while traditional systems may be one- or two-stage systems. . . . .   _____

8. Compared to ABC, a traditional cost system reports a lower unit cost for the high-volume products and a higher unit cost for the low-volume products. . . . .   _____

9. If non-volume-related costs are insignificant, a traditional cost system's product cost distortions would be insignificant. . . . .   _____

10. If different products consume different mixes of volume-related and non-volume-related costs, product cost distortion will not be a problem. . . . .   _____

11. The strategic advantage of ABC lies in its potential to save a company from mistakenly discontinuing a product due to inappropriate cost allocation. . . . . . .   _____

12. ABC has a tremendous advantage over traditional costing, particularly for plant-level costs. . . . .   _____

13. ABC's treatment of all costs as if they were variable is appropriate because it is designed to be a long-run, strategic decision-making tool. . . . .   _____

14. Revised product costs may prompt management to reexamine the strategic importance of high-volume products that are found to be costly to produce. . . . .   _____

15. Activities may be managed to achieve improvements in a process by activity reduction, activity elimination, activity selection, and activity sharing. . . . .   _____

Part 2 ■ Matching

Instructions: *On the line at the left of each of the following items, place the letter from the columns below that identifies the term that best matches the statement. No letter should be used more than once.*

_____ 1. A costing system in which multiple overhead cost pools are allocated using bases that include one or more non-volume-related factors.

_____ 2. Bases used to allocate overhead costs.

_____ 3. A base used to allocate the cost of a resource to the different activities using that resource.

_____ 4. A base used to allocate the cost of an activity to products, customers, or other final cost objects.

_____ 5. Costs that inevitably increase whenever a unit is produced.

_____ 6. Examples include direct labor hours, direct labor cost, and machine hours.

_____ 7. Examples include setup costs and most materials handling costs.

_____ 8. Measures of activities that vary with the number of batches produced and sold.

_____ 9. Examples include the cost of new products' design, development, and production engineering.

_____ 10. Measures of activities that vary with the number of different products produced and sold.

_____ 11. Costs of sustaining capacity at a production site.

_____ 12. Frequent example is floor space occupied.

_____ 13. Synonym for traditional costing systems.

_____ 14. Use of information obtained from ABC to make improvements in the firm.

_____ 15. Examples include complying with laws and regulations and moving and storing materials.

a. activity driver
b. batch-level costs
c. product-level drivers
d. unit-based systems
e. non-value-added activities
f. drivers
g. plant-level driver
h. unit-level costs

i. product-level costs
j. activity-based management (ABM)
k. plant-level costs
l. activity-based costing (ABC)
m. batch-level drivers
n. unit-level drivers
o. resource driver

Part 3 ■ Multiple Choice

Instructions: *On the line at the left of each of the following items, place the letter of the choice that most correctly completes each item.*

_____ 1. Examples of activities at the unit-level of costs include:

   a. soldering, painting, and assembling
   b. scheduling, setting up, and moving
   c. designing, developing, and warehousing
   d. heating, lighting, and cooling
   e. all of the above

_____ 2. Examples of batch-level costs are:

   a. portions of electricity and indirect materials
   b. salaries of schedulers and setup personnel
   c. salaries of designers and programmers
   d. depreciation and insurance on buildings
   e. none of the above

_____ 3. Examples of product-level activity drivers include:

   a. units of output and direct labor hours
   b. number of batches and material moves
   c. number of products and design changes
   d. square footage occupied
   e. all of the above

_____ 4. Examples of plant-level activities include:

   a. cutting, soldering, and painting   d. heating and providing security
   b. scheduling and setting up   e. none of the above
   c. designing and developing

_____ 5. Traditional costing systems are characterized by their use of which of the following measures as bases for allocating overhead to output:

   a. unit-level drivers   d. plant-level drivers
   b. batch-level drivers   e. none of the above
   c. product-level drivers

_____ 6. ABC systems are characterized by their use of which of the following measures as bases for allocating overhead to output:

   a. unit-level drivers   d. plant-level drivers
   b. batch-level drivers   e. all of the above
   c. product-level drivers

_____ 7. All of the following are distinctions that usually exist between traditional and ABC costing systems, *except* that:

   a. the number of overhead cost pools tends to be higher in ABC systems
   b. the number of allocation bases tends to be fewer in ABC systems
   c. costs within an ABC cost pool tend to be more homogeneous than the costs within a traditional system's cost pool
   d. all ABC systems are two-stage costing systems, while traditional systems may be one- or two-stage systems
   e. all of the above are distinctions

_____ **8.** All of the following are limitations of ABC costing, *except* that:

    a. ABC does not show the costs that will be avoided by discontinuing a product

    b. ABC has little or no advantage over traditional costing in allocating plant-level costs

    c. ABC treats all costs as if they were variable

    d. it is necessary to replace the traditional accounting system with ABC to get ABC benefits

    e. all of the above are limitations of ABC

_____ **9.** All of the following are ways in which activities may be managed to achieve improvements in a process, *except*:

    a. activity reduction   **d.** activity sharing

    b. activity elimination   **e.** all of the above are ways in which activities may

    c. activity selection   be managed

_____ **10.** All of the following are examples of non-value-added activities, *except*:

    a. materials conversion   **d.** materials handling

    b. materials storage   **e.** all of the above are non-value-added activities

    c. materials movement

Part 4 ■ Problem

Instructions: *Each of the following is a potential activity driver. Identify the most likely level of each activity driver by placing a check mark in the appropriate column.*

Item	Unit-Level Driver	Batch-Level Driver	Product-Level Driver	Plant-Level Driver
1. Number of setups				
2. Number of design changes				
3. Units of output				
4. Square footage occupied				
5. Number of part numbers				
6. Loads of materials moved				
7. Machine hours				
8. Marketing promotions				
9. Number of production orders				
10. Direct material cost				

Part 5 ■ Problem

Gernhardt Company manufactures a variety of high-volume and low-volume products, including Product #747, in its New Rochelle plant. The following information pertains to the most recent year:

	Total for Product #747	Total for New Rochelle
Unit-level overhead		$100,000
Batch-level overhead		150,000
Product-level overhead		250,000
Plant-level overhead		200,000
Total overhead		$700,000
Units produced	200	10,000
Direct labor hours	400	40,000
Setups	12	240
Design hours	140	2,000

Instructions:

1. If the New Rochelle plant accumulates all overhead in a single cost pool and allocates it on the basis of direct labor hours, how much overhead will be allocated to a unit of Product #747?

2. If the New Rochelle plant uses ABC with setups as the driver for all batch-level overhead, design hours as the driver for all product-level overhead, and direct labor hours as the driver for all unit- and plant-level overhead, how much overhead cost will be allocated to a unit of Product #747?

Part 6 ■ Problem

The Herold Company produces two products, Standard and Custom, and uses a cost system which accumulates all overhead in a single cost pool and allocates it based on direct labor cost. Herold's management has decided to implement ABC, having just finished a study that revealed significant amounts of overhead cost are related to setup activity and design activity. The number of setups and the number of design hours were selected as the activity drivers for the two new cost pools, and direct labor cost will continue as the base for allocating the remaining overhead. Information concerning Herold Company's most recent year of operations is as follows:

	Standard	Custom	Total
Units produced	39,000	1,000	40,000
Direct material cost:			
Per unit	$ 10	$ 80	
Total	$ 390,000	$ 80,000	$ 470,000
Direct labor cost	$1,900,000	$100,000	$2,000,000
Setups	15	10	25
Design hours	2,000	1,500	3,500
Overhead:			
Setup-related			$ 250,000
Design-related			700,00
Other			1,050,000
Total overhead			$2,000,000

Instructions:

1. Calculate the total and per-unit costs reported for the two products by the existing costing system, using the format below.

Herold Company
Product Costs from Existing Cost System

Overhead Rate:

	Standard	Custom	Total
Direct material	$	$	$
Direct labor			
Overhead:			
Total cost	$	$	$
Units produced			
Cost per unit	$	$	

2. Calculate the total and per-unit costs reported for the two products by the ABC system, using the format below.

Herold Company
Product Costs from Existing Cost System

Overhead Rates:

	Standard	Custom	Total
Direct material.....................................	$	$	$
Direct labor			
Overhead:			
Total cost......................................	$	$	$
Units produced			
Cost per unit..................................	$	$	

Budgeting: Profits, Sales, Costs, and Expenses

REVIEW SUMMARY

I. Purpose of the Chapter

This chapter distinguishes between long-range and short-range planning, discusses the advantages of profit planning and enumerates the fundamental principles of budget development and implementation. It also indicates employee motivational hazards in the budgeting process, discusses budgeting system requirements to avoid such hazards, and illustrates a complete operating budget.

II. Profit Planning

Profit planning is a well-thought-out operational plan with its financial implications expressed in the form of long- and short-range income statements, balance sheets, and cash budgets. Using the *a priori* **method** of setting profit objectives, management specifies a given rate of return that it seeks to realize in the long run by means of planning toward that end. Under the *a posteriori* **method**, the determination of profit objectives is subordinated to the planning, and the objectives emerge as the product of the planning itself. Using a target rate of profit derived from experience, expectations, or comparisons, management establishes a relative profit standard considered satisfactory for the company under the **pragmatic method**.

III. Long- and Short-Range Profit Planning

Market trends and economic factors, inflation, growth of population, personal consumption expenditures, and indexes of industrial production form the background for long-range planning. Quantitative and dollar sales estimates for a three- to five-year forecast may be developed from this information. Long-range plans with their future expectancy of profits and growth must be incorporated into a shorter-range budget for both planning and control of the contemplated course of action. Although one year is the usual planning period, the short-range budget may cover periods of three, six, or twelve months, depending on the nature of the business.

IV. Principles of Budgeting

A company's organization chart and its chart of accounts form the basic framework on which to build a coordinated and efficient system of managerial planning and budgetary control. The budget process is usually directed by a budget committee that decides on general policies, reviews and suggests revisions in individual budget estimates, approves budgets, analyzes budget reports, and recommends action designed to improve efficiency. Budget development should include adherence to the following principles: (1) provide adequate guidance so that all management levels are working on the same assumptions, targeted objectives, and agenda; (2) encourage participation in the budgeting process at each level within the organization; (3) structure the climate of budget preparation to eliminate anxiety and defensiveness; (4) structure the preparation of the budget so that there is a reasonably high probability of successful attainment of objectives; and (5) evaluate numerous sets of assumptions in developing the budget through the use of computers and probability theory. Principles of budget implementation include establishing reward contingencies that will lead to achieving the organizational objectives, focusing on rewarding achievement rather than punishing failure, and providing rapid feedback on the performance of each work team or individual.

V. Budgeting and Human Behavior

Cost accounting and budgeting play an important role in influencing individual and group behavior at these stages of the management process: (1) setting goals, (2) informing employees of the contributions expected of them, (3) motivating desired performance, (4) evaluating performance, and (5) suggesting corrective action. A manager's attitude toward the budget will depend greatly upon the relationship within the management group. Suggestions for motivating a company's personnel include (1) a compensation and promotion system that ties results to rewards, (2) a performance appraisal system that employees understand, (3) an open and honest communications system, (4) a counseling and career-planning system that considers employee skills and capacities, and (5) a system that emphasizes attainable standards.

VI.   The Sales Budget

One of the most important and most difficult-to-predict elements in a budgetary control system is a realistic sales forecast based on analysis of past sales and the present market. The preparation of sales estimates is usually the responsibility of the marketing manager, assisted by individual salespeople and market research personnel. In most large organizations, the forecasting procedure usually starts with known factors such as (1) the company's sales of past years broken down by product groups and profit margins, (2) industry or trade sales volumes and profits, and (3) unusual factors influencing sales in the past. In addition, a sound basis for determining future sales may be established by applying probability analysis techniques to the consideration of general business conditions, the industry's prospects, the company's potential share of the total industry market, and the plans of the competitors.

VII.   Sales Budgeting Techniques

A sales budget not only should be placed on a monthly basis for each product but also should be classified by territories or districts and by types of customers. A detailed sales budget can be a strong means for analyzing possible new trade outlets and for identifying and investigating reasons for a drop in sales. Prior to the final acceptance of a sales budget, the factory's capacity to produce the estimated quantities must be determined. If factory capacity is available, production should be planned at a level that will keep workers and equipment operating all year. A sales forecast follow-up should occur at intervals for purposes of determining the (1) accuracy of past estimates, (2) location of major estimation errors, (3) best method by which to update estimates, and (4) steps needed for improving the making and monitoring of future estimates.

VIII. Manufacturing Budgets

The **production budget** is stated in physical units and deals with the scheduling of operations, the determination of volume, and the establishment of maximum and minimum quantities of materials and finished goods inventories. With the forecast sales translated into physical units in the production budget, the estimated manufacturing costs essential to the sales and production program can be com-

puted. The **direct materials budget** indicates the quantity and cost of materials required to produce the predetermined units of finished goods and is usually the first cost budget to be prepared. The **direct labor budget**, based upon specifications drawn up by production engineers, guides the personnel department in determining the number and types of workers needed. The **factory overhead budget** is usually prepared on a departmental basis, with expenses grouped according to natural classification. It is usually prepared as a report that enables executive management and individual department supervisors to make monthly comparisons of budgeted and actual expenses. Not only must inventory quantities be determined for materials, work in process, and finished goods, but the inventories must be costed in order to make available the necessary information leading to preparation of a budgeted cost of goods manufactured and sold statement.

IX.   Budgeting Commercial Expenses

The company's chart of accounts is the basis for budgetary control of commercial expenses, which include both marketing and administrative expenses. To control commercial expenses effectively, it is necessary to group them by functional activities or operating units. The **marketing expenses budget** is prepared by the supervisors of functions connected with marketing activities, which include the costs of obtaining and filling an order. The **administrative expenses budget** includes costs such as professional fees and certain taxes that are peculiar to the administrative function, as well as costs such as purchasing and personnel that are shared with the production and marketing activities.

X.   The Budgeted Income Statement and Balance Sheet

A **budgeted income statement** contains summaries of the sales, manufacturing, and expense budgets. It projects net income, and it offers management the opportunity to judge the accuracy of the budget work and to investigate causes of variances. Percentages of sales figures are often included to aid in determining whether income statement components are in line with expectations.

A balance sheet for the beginning of the budget period, incorporating all changes in assets, liabilities, and capital in the budgets submitted by the various departments, is the starting point for the preparation of a budgeted balance sheet for the end of the budget period. The **budgeted balance sheet** discloses unfavorable ratios and serves as a check on the accuracy of all other budgets.

Part 1 ■ True/False

Instructions: *Indicate whether each of the following statements is* **True** *or* **False**.

                                                                                     True/False

1. In most firms, budgeting is one of the most popular management activities...   _____

2. Under the *a priori* method of setting profit objectives, management uses a target rate of profit derived from experience, expectations, or comparisons.........   _____

3. Accountants cannot ignore the behavioral sciences because the "information for decision making" function of accounting is essentially a behavioral function. .   _____

4. The rate of return on capital employed is an important statistic in long-range profit planning..........   _____

5. A complete motivational system for factory workers is unnecessary as long as you have an incentive pay system tied to productivity. ....   _____

6. Continuous budgeting adds a month or quarter in the future as each current month or quarter is ended. ....   _____

7. One of the advantages of profit planning is that sales forecasting can be reduced to an exact science. ....   _____

8. A budgetary system has performed inadequately whenever it motivates an individual to take an action that is not in the best interests of the organization........   _____

9. A company's organization chart and its chart of accounts form the basic framework on which to build a coordinated and efficient system of budgetary control...   _____

10. Studies have usually shown that there is a high correlation between employees' acceptance of a budget and their general attitude towards the company's management.........   _____

11. The task of preparing the sales budget usually involves judging and evaluating both external and internal influences. ....   _____

12. The sales variable is often the budget component that is the easiest to predict with reasonable precision..........   _____

13. An advantage of a budgeted balance sheet is that it discloses unfavorable ratios that management may wish to change..........   _____

14. The production budget is prepared from the direct materials budget........   _____

15. A company's marketing activities can be divided into two broad categories: (a) obtaining an order and (b) filling an order........   _____

Part 2 ■ Matching

Instructions: *On the line at the left of each of the following items, place the letter from the columns below that identifies the term that best matches the statement. No letter should be used more than once.*

_____ **1.** Represents the expected profit level or target to which management strives.

_____ **2.** Method of setting profit objectives where the profit objectives take precedence over the planning process.

_____ **3.** Method under which the determination of profit objectives is subordinated to the planning, with objectives emerging as the product of the planning itself.

_____ **4.** Method of setting profit objectives under which management, using a target rate of profit derived from experience, expectations, or comparisons, establishes a relative profit standard considered satisfactory for the company.

_____ **5.** Provides the basic framework on which to build a coordinated and efficient system of managerial planning and budgetary control.

_____ **6.** Directs the budgeting process and is usually composed of the sales manager, the production manager, the chief engineer, the treasurer, and the controller.

_____ **7.** Level of revenue or cost that the organization predicts will occur.

_____ **8.** Plans not stated in precise terms nor expected to be completely coordinated future plans.

_____ **9.** Costs of obtaining an order and costs of filling an order.

_____ **10.** General trend of industrial activity, governmental policies, purchasing power of the population, and changing buying habits.

_____ **11.** Sales trends, factory capacities, seasonal products, and establishment of quotas for salespersons.

_____ **12.** Incorporates all changes in assets, liabilities, and capital in the budgets submitted by the various departments.

_____ **13.** Use of this results in sound basis for determining future sales when applied to general business conditions, the industry's prospects, and the plans of competitive companies.

_____ **14.** Should be placed on a monthly basis for each product, as well as being classified by territories or districts and by types of customers.

_____ **15.** Deals with the scheduling of operations, the determination of volume, and the establishment of maximum and minimum quantities of materials and finished goods inventories.

_____ **16.** Summarization of the estimated cost of materials, labor, and factory overhead, often based on standard costs.

_____ **17.** Indicates the quantity and cost of materials required to produce the predetermined units of finished goods and is usually the first cost budget to be prepared.

_____ **18.** Based on specifications drawn up by product engineers, guides the personnel department in determining the number and type of workers needed.

_____ **19.** Include both marketing and administrative expenses.

_____ **20.** Used to update plans throughout the budget period, and in some cases, to extend planning horizons beyond the current budget period.

a.	*a posteriori* method	**k.**	pragmatic method
b.	budget committee	**l.**	commercial expenses
c.	budgeted cost of goods manufactured and sold statement	**m.**	*a priori* method
		n.	direct materials budget
d.	internal influences	**o.**	organization chart
e.	probability analysis techniques	**p.**	budgeted balance sheet
f.	direct labor budget	**q.**	external influences
g.	continuous budgeting	**r.**	forecast
h.	sales budget	**s.**	profit plan
i.	marketing expenses	**t.**	long-range plans
j.	production budget		

Part 3 ■ Multiple Choice

Instructions: *On the line at the left of each of the following items, place the letter of the choice that most correctly completes each item.*

_____ 1. A continuous budget:

    a. drops the current month or quarter and adds a future month or quarter as the current month or quarter is completed

    b. presents the plan for only one activity level and does not adjust to activity-level changes

    c. presents the plan for a range of activity so that the plan can be adjusted for activity-level changes

    d. classifies budget requests by activity and estimates the benefits arising from each activity

    e. none of the above   *(ICMA adapted)*

_____ 2. Probability (risk) analysis:

    a. ignores probability weights under 50%

    b. is only for situations in which there are three or fewer possible outcomes

    c. does not enhance the usefulness of sensitivity analysis data

    d. helps provide a sound basis for estimating future sales

    e. none of the above   *(AICPA adapted)*

_____ 3. When management sets profit objectives by specifying a given rate of return, which it then seeks to realize in the long run, the procedure is called the:

    a. *a priori* method   **d.** *a posteriori* method

    b. *ad hoc* method   **e.** none of the above

    c. pragmatic method

_____ 4. The development of an atmosphere of profit-mindedness, the encouragement of attitudes of cost-mindedness, and maximum resource utilization are advantages of:

    a. production analysis studies   **d.** profit planning

    b. product costing   **e.** none of the above

    c. sales objectives

_____ 5. Of the following items, the one used to form the background for long-range plans is:

    a. economic factors and market trends   **d.** precise future product costs

    b. current inventory levels   **e.** none of the above

    c. direct labor costs

_____ 6. A principal function of the budget committee is to:

    a. determine inventory values   **d.** prepare individual budget estimates

    b. prepare the budget report   **e.** all of the above

    c. suggest revisions to budget estimates

_____ 7. To point out possible unfavorable financial ratios at the end of a forecast period, management should prepare a:

    a. sales budget   **d.** budgeted balance sheet

    b. forecasted cash flow statement   **e.** none of the above

    c. treasurer's budget

_____ 8. A limitation of profit planning is that:

    a. installation of a budgetary system takes time

    b. the budget could focus management's attention on the wrong goals

    c. profit planning does not eliminate the role of administration

    d. all of the above

    e. none of the above

_____ **9.** The budget component that is usually the most difficult to predict with reasonable precision is:

    a. sales   **d.** commercial expenses

    b. production   **e.** none of the above

    c. factory overhead

_____ **10.** If estimated sales and beginning inventory in units are 60,000 and 18,000 respectively, and the amount of required production is 54,000 units, the ending inventory in units would be:

    a. 6,000   **d.** 3,000

    b. 0   **e.** none of the above

    c. 12,000

Part 4 ■ Problem

Hamaeuchi Products prepares a budget forecast of its needs for the coming year. Last year's data are presented for the three models of videocassette recorders (VCRs) sold by the company. In addition, salespersons' estimates for the coming year are as follows:

	Last Year		This Year	
VCR Model No.	Unit Price	Unit Sales	Units—Ending Inventory	Salespersons' Unit Estimates
007	$500	500	40	1,000
2525	450	700	20	1,600
1984	400	1,200	110	2,600

Management notes that the salespersons are very optimistic and that their predictions of sales levels must be halved to be realistic. In addition, the company wants an ending inventory equal to 10% of sales.

Instructions:

1. Complete the schedule below, predicting unit sales for each VCR and the production required to provide for sales and inventory needs.

VCR Model No.	Predicted Unit Sales	Less: Beginning Inventory	Plus: Ending Inventory	Production Required
007	_____	_____	_____	_____
2525	_____	_____	_____	_____
1984	_____	_____	_____	_____

2. Determine the dollar revenues to be obtained for each VCR.

VCR Model No.	Unit Sales	Unit Price	Total Sales
007	_____	_____	_____
2525	_____	_____	_____
1984	_____	_____	_____
Total Sales			$ _____

3. Determine the working capital required if each VCR produced costs 60% of the selling price and if the company requires working capital equal to 20% of total production costs.

VCR Model No.	Units Produced	Production Cost
007	_____	_____
2525	_____	_____
1984	_____	_____
Total production cost		$ _____

Working capital required:

Part 5 ■ Problem

The Nanni Noodle Company prepared the following figures as a basis for its 19B budget:

Product	Expected Sales	Estimated Per-Unit Sales Price	Required Materials per Unit	
			Flour	Cheese
Ravioli.........	40,000 units	$5	4 lbs.	2 lbs.
Tortellini	20,000	8	5 lbs.	--
Cavatelli	50,000	3	--	3 lbs.

Estimated inventories at the beginning and desired quantities at the end of 19B are:

Material	Beginning	Ending	Purchase Price per Pound
Flour	5,000 lbs.	6,000 lbs.	$ .50
Cheese	6,000	7,500	1.00

Product	Beginning	Ending	Direct Labor Hours per 1,000 Units
Ravioli.........	2,500 units	3,000 units	200 units
Tortellini	2,000	1,000	400
Cavatelli	5,000	4,000	50

The direct labor cost is budgeted at $20 per hour and variable factory overhead at $10 per hour of direct labor. Fixed factory overhead, estimated to be $100,000, is a joint cost and is not allocated to specific products in developing the master budget for internal management use.

Instructions:

1. Prepare the production budget.

	Ravioli	Tortellini	Cavatelli
Units required to meet sales budget . .			
Add desired ending inventories			
Total units required.			
Less estimated beginning inventories . .			
Planned production			

2. Determine the budgeted quantities and dollar amounts of purchase requirements for each material.

	Flour	Cheese
Ravioli		
Tortellini.		
Cavatelli		
Add desired ending inventories		
Less estimated beginning inventories . .		
Budgeted quantities of materials purchased.		
Budgeted price per pound	$	$
Budgeted dollar amounts of materials purchased.	$	$

3. Prepare the manufacturing budgets by product and in total.

	Ravioli	**Tortellini**	**Cavatelli**	**Total**
Materials:				
Flour:	$ _____			$ _____
		$ _____		_____
Cheese:	_____			_____
			$ _____	_____
	$ _____	$ _____	$ _____	$ _____
Direct labor:				
	$ _____			$ _____
		$ _____		_____
	_____	_____	$ _____	_____
	$ _____	$ _____	$ _____	$ _____
Factory overhead– Variable:				
	$ _____			$ _____
		$ _____		_____
			$ _____	_____
	$ _____	$ _____	$ _____	$ _____
Total variable manufacturing cost	$ _____	$ _____	$ _____	$ _____
Fixed manufac- turing cost . .				_____
Total manufac- turing cost . .				$ _____

Part 6 ■ Problem

The following financial information relates to the operations of L. H. Herold Company for the year ending December 31, 19C:

Materials:
Beginning inventory................................ $ 87,500
Purchases 568,663
Ending inventory 107,125
Direct labor 2,161,680
Factory overhead..................................... 226,503

Finished goods:
Beginning inventory................................ 84,745
Ending inventory 60,895

Sales... 3,650,000
Commercial expenses:
Marketing expenses 300,000
Administrative expenses........................... 200,000
Income tax rate...................................... 35%

Instructions:

1. Prepare a budgeted cost of goods manufactured and sold statement.

L. H. Herold Company
Budgeted Cost of Goods Manufactured and Sold Statement
For the Year Ending December 31, 19C

Materials:

Beginning inventory............................. $

Add purchases .... _____

Total materials available for use................ $

Less ending inventory .... _____

Cost of materials used.......................... $

Direct labor ....

Factory overhead.................................. _____

Total manufacturing cost .... $

Add beginning inventory of finished goods .... _____

Cost of goods available for sale .... $

Less ending inventory of finished goods .... _____

Cost of goods sold .... $

2. Prepare a budgeted income statement.

L. H. Herold Company
Budgeted Income Statement
For the Year Ending December 31, 19C

	Amount
Sales	$ _____
Cost of goods sold	_____
Gross profit	$ _____
Commercial expenses:	
Marketing expenses .... _____	
Administrative expenses .... _____	_____
Income from operations	$
Less provision for income tax	_____
Net income........................	$ _____

(Round dollar amounts to the nearest whole dollar.)

Part 7 ■ Problem

The 19D forecast for Gabriel Corporation appears below in the form of a prospective trial balance as of December 31, 19D (000s omitted):

Cash	2,400	
Accounts Receivable	120,000	
Finished Goods Inventory (1/1/19D, 50,000 units)	60,000	
Plant and Equipment......................	480,000	
Accumulated Depreciation.............................		82,000
Accounts Payable....................................		65,000
Accrued Payables....................................		40,000
Notes Payable (due in 1 year)........................		75,000
Common Stock......................................		95,000
Retained Earnings		197,900
Sales		900,000
Other Income.......................................		15,000
Manufacturing costs:		
Materials	225,000	
Direct Labor	270,000	
Variable Factory Overhead.....................	140,000	
Depreciation	15,000	
Other Fixed Factory Overhead	9,000	
Marketing:		
Salaries	21,000	
Commissions	25,000	
Promotion and Advertising......................	55,000	
General and Administrative:		
Salaries	25,000	
Travel	4,000	
Office Costs...................................	11,000	
Income Tax	?	
Dividends	7,500	
	$1,469,900	$1,469,900

Adjustments for the change in inventory and for income tax have not been made. The scheduled production for 19D is 500,000 units, while the sales volume will reach 475,000 units. A full cost, first-in, first-out inventory system is used. There were no beginning nor ending inventories of raw materials or work in process. The company is subject to a 30% income tax rate.

Instructions:

1. Prepare a prospective statement of income and retained earnings for the year 19D, including the computation of the cost of the ending inventory. (Use the forms provided below and on page 145. Round unit costs to four decimal places and dollar totals to the nearest dollar.)

Gabriel Corporation
Prospective Statement of Income and Retained Earnings
For the Year Ending December 31, 19D
(000s omitted)

Revenue:

    Sales .... $

    Other income .... _____ $

Costs of goods manufactured and sold:

    Materials .... $

    Direct labor ....

    Variable factory overhead ....

    Fixed factory overhead .... _____

    $

    Beginning inventory .... _____

    $

    Ending inventory .... _____* $

Marketing:

    Salaries .... $

    Commissions ....

    Promotion and advertising .... _____

General and administrative:

    Salaries .... $

    Travel ....

    Office costs .... _____ _____ _____

Income before tax .... $

Income tax .... _____

Net income .... $

Beginning retained earnings .... _____

    Subtotal .... $

    Less dividends .... _____

Ending retained earnings .... $

*Inventory

Units:

    Beginning inventory . . . .

    Added to inventory . . . .   _____

    Ending inventory . . . .   _____

Cost:

    19D Manufacturing costs . . . . $ _____

    Units manufactured . . . .   _____

    Cost per unit . . . . $ _____

    Ending units . . . .   _____

    Cost of ending inventory . . . . $ _____

2. Prepare a prospective balance sheet for 19D.

Gabriel Corporation
Prospective Balance Sheet
December 31, 19D
(000s omitted)

<u>Assets</u>

Current assets:

    Cash . . . . $

    Accounts receivable . . . .

    Inventory . . . .   _____ $

Plant and equipment . . . . $

    Less accumulated depreciation . . . .   _____   _____

    Total assets . . . . $ _____

<u>Liabilities and Shareholders' Equity</u>

Current liabilities:

    Accounts payable . . . . $

    Accrued payables . . . .

    Income tax payable . . . .

    Notes payable . . . .   _____ $

Shareholders' equity:

    Common stock . . . . $

    Retained earnings . . . .   _____   _____

    Total liabilities and shareholders' equity . . . . $ _____

Budgeting: Capital Expenditures, Research and Development Expenditures, and Cash; PERT/Cost

REVIEW SUMMARY

I. Purpose of the Chapter

The purpose of this chapter is to describe specific budgets, such as the capital expenditures and research and development budgets, which play a significant role in long-term and short-term planning. In addition to cash budgeting, budgeting for nonmanufacturing businesses and not-for-profit organizations, zero-base budgeting, PERT and PERT/cost and probabilistic budgeting are all described and illustrated.

II. Capital Expenditures Budget

Capital expenditures are long-term commitments of resources to realize future benefits. Managerial control of capital expenditures requires facts regarding engineering estimates, expected sales volumes, production costs, and marketing costs. Management is interested in making certain that a project will contribute to the earnings position of the company.

III. Research and Development Budget

The research and development (R&D) budget involves identifying program components and estimating their costs. It is considered the best tool for (1) balancing the R&D program, (2) coordinating the program with the company's other projects, and (3) checking certain phases of nonfinancial planning. The overall R&D program should be supported by a specific budget request that indicates the jobs or steps within each project, the necessary labor hours, the service department time required, and required direct departmental funds. Generally, R&D costs should be expensed in the period incurred, due to the uncertainty of the length of future benefits to the company.

IV. Cash Budget

A **cash budget** involves detailed estimates of anticipated cash receipts and disbursements for the budget period. A cash budget does the following:

1. Indicates cash requirements for current operations.
2. Focuses on cash usage priorities, currently unavoidable and required versus postponable or permanently avoidable.
3. Indicates the effect on cash position of such factors as seasonal requirements and speed in collecting receivables.
4. Indicates the availability of cash for taking discounts.
5. Indicates the cash requirements for plant expansion.
6. Assists in planning the financial requirements of bond retirements, income taxes, and pension funds.
7. Shows the availability of excess funds for investment.
8. Shows the need for additional funds from sources such as bank loans.
9. Serves as a basis for evaluating the actual cash management performance of individuals.

A long-range cash management projection may cover periods ranging from three to five years and is useful in planning business growth, investments in projects, and introduction of new products. A yearly cash budget should usually be prepared by months, with changes made at the end of each month to incorporate deviations from the previous forecast and to add a month to replace the month just past. A short-range cash budget depicts the daily availability of cash for current operations and indicates needs for short-term financing.

A. Preparation of a Cash Budget

In cash budget preparation, all anticipated cash receipts are carefully estimated, primarily based on the sales budget and the company's experience in collecting accounts receivables. Similarly, cash requirements for items such as payroll, materials purchases, loan repayments, and equipment must be determined. After all the cash receipts and cash disbursements have been estimated for each month of the budget year, the year-end cash balance for inclusion in the budgeted balance sheet can be determined.

B. Electronic Cash Management

Electronic cash management involves cash concentration by means of nationwide electronic transfers that accelerate the collection of deposits from local banks into a central account on a same-day basis. For whatever number of bank accounts a firm may have, electronic balance reporting affords a valuable aid to cash management. **Electronic funds transfer systems** are designed to reduce the number of paper documents and to increase the use of electronic data in carrying out banking cash transfer functions, thus reducing bank transaction costs and expediting cash transfers.

V. Nonmanufacturing Businesses

The merchandise budget of a retail store shows predetermined sales and profits, generally on a six-month basis following the two merchandising seasons. It also includes purchases, expenses, capital expenditures, cash, and annual statements. Other nonmanufacturing businesses, such as banks and insurance companies, should also create long-range profit plans coordinating long-term goals and objectives.

VI. Not-for-Profit Organizations

While business organizations are concerned with profits, the not-for-profit sector is concerned with programs. A comprehensive budget format, by program, is required to indicate the purpose of expenditures and to provide adequate detail for control. An example of an effort to base a budget on a managerial approach is **planning, programming, budgeting system (PPBS)**, which is an analytical tool designed to aid in the analysis of the alternatives in allocating resources to accomplish goals and objectives. In the same way that governmental units have become budget conscious; not-for-profit organizations, such as hospitals, churches,

and school districts are adopting strong measures of budgetary control.

VII. Zero-Base Budgeting

Zero-base budgeting is a budget-planning procedure for the reevaluation of an organization's program and expenditures. It requires each manager to justify the entire budget request in detail, and it places the burden of proof on the manager to justify why authorization to spend money should be granted. Zero-base budgeting proponents assert that building the budget from zero causes managers to look at different ways of performing the same activity and to consider different levels of effort in performing it.

VIII. Financial Forecasts

Recent years have seen increasing recognition of the importance of financial forecasts for external users because investors and potential investors seek to enhance the process of predicting the future. The AICPA recommends that financial forecasts should (1) be presented in the same format as historical financial statements; (2) include a description of what management intends to present; (3) include a statement that the assumptions are based on information existing at the time the prospective information was prepared; (4) include a caveat that the prospective results may not be achieved; and (5) include a summary of significant assumptions.

IX. PERT/Cost Systems

Many companies have been using PERT or CPM in planning, scheduling, and costing such diverse projects as constructing buildings, installing equipment, and research and development. PERT is a probabilistic diagram of the interrelationships of a complex series of activities. The major use of PERT is in the determination of the longest time duration for the completion of an entire project. The **PERT/Cost system** is an expansion of PERT. It assigns cost to time and activities, thereby providing a financial planning and control tool.

Part 1 ■ True/False

Instructions: *Indicate whether each of the following statements is **True** or **False**.*

True/False

1. Capital expenditures are long-term commitments of resources to realize future benefits. . . . . _____

2. The greatest advantage of computerized budgeting over conventional budgeting is that it negates the need for planning time. . . . . _____

3. Research and development projects compete with other projects for available financial resources. . . . . _____

4. Research and development costs generally should be capitalized and written off over the periods of anticipated benefit. . . . . _____

5. Even if a company does not prepare extensive budgets for sales and production, it should set up a budget of cash receipts and disbursements as an aid to cash management. . . . . _____

6. Presently, Security and Exchange Commission regulations encourage but do not require inclusion of prospective financial data in annual reports. . . . . _____

7. Electronic funds transfer systems are designed to reduce the number of paper documents and to increase the use of electronic data in carrying out banking transactions. . . . . _____

8. A probabilistic budget is developed based on one set of assumptions as to the most likely performance in the forthcoming period. . . . . _____

9. An SEC-regulated company and its auditors always are exposed to legal liability should the prospective financial forecasts fail to materialize. . . . . _____

10. Nonmanufacturing businesses generally do a better job of planning and budgeting than do manufacturing businesses. . . . . _____

11. The difficulty of planning and budgeting in governments and nonprofit organizations is measuring the benefits or outputs of programs. . . . . _____

12. In zero-base budgeting, what a manager is already spending is acceptable as a starting point for budget negotiations. . . . . _____

13. The major task of PERT is to determine the longest time duration needed for the completion of an entire project. . . . . _____

14. If available slack time is not exceeded, noncritical activities can be delayed without delaying a project's completion date. . . . . _____

15. The PERT/cost system assigns cost to time and activities, thereby providing total financial planning and control by functional responsibility. . . . . _____

Part 2 ■ Matching

Instructions: *On the line at the left of each of the following items, place the letter from the columns below that identifies the term that best matches the statement. No letter should be used more than once.*

_____ 1. Long-term commitments of resources to realize future benefits.

_____ 2. Provision must be made in the current budget for these.

_____ 3. Will not be implemented in the current budget period and need only be stated in general terms.

_____ 4. The amount of time that can be added to an activity without increasing the total time required on the critical path.

_____ 5. The translation of research findings or other knowledge into a plan for a new product or for a significant improvement to an existing product.

_____ 6. Type of account where research and development costs are charged because of the uncertainty of the extent or length of future benefit to the company.

_____ 7. Type of account that public utilities charge research and development to because of the rate-regulated aspects of the industry.

_____ 8. Involves detailed estimates of anticipated cash receipts and disbursements for the budget period.

_____ 9. Should be included in external financial statements when they will enhance the reliability of users' predictions.

_____ 10. Designed to reduce the number of paper documents and to increase the use of electronic data in carrying out banking transactions.

_____ 11. Involves cash concentration by means of nationwide electronic transfers that accelerate the collection of deposits from local banks into a central account on a same-day basis.

_____ 12. Use of cash during the time that it takes a check to be cleared back to a central account.

_____ 13. In zero-base budgeting, identifies an activity in a definite manner for evaluation and comparison with other activities.

_____ 14. If shortened in a PERT network, the total time to complete a task results.

_____ 15. Using statistical estimation to spread a forecast of the total monthly minor cash flow components over the days of the month in order to reflect the known intramonth cash flow.

_____ 16. A tool to assist management in the analysis of alternatives as the basis for rational decision making.

_____ 17. A budget planning procedure for the reevaluation of an organization's program and expenditures.

_____ 18. A probabilistic diagram of the interrelationships of a complex series of activities.

_____ 19. The construction of a cash forecast from information-system-based data, such as disbursement data from invoices and purchase authorizations.

_____ 20. An integrated management information system designed to furnish management with timely information for planning and controlling schedules and costs of projects.

a. slack time
b. cash budget
c. float
d. long-range projects
e. PERT
f. PERT/cost
g. scheduling
h. distribution
i. capital expenditures
j. PPBS

k. expense
l. development
m. critical path
n. financial forecasts
o. zero-base budgeting
p. asset
q. short-range projects
r. electronic funds transfer systems
s. electronic cash management
t. decision package

Part 3 ■ Multiple Choice

Instructions: *On the line at the left of each of the following items, place the letter of the choice that most correctly completes the item.*

_____ **1.** A budget system referred to as PPBS:

    a. drops the current month or quarter and adds a future month or quarter as the current month or quarter is completed

    b. consolidates the plans of separate departments into an overall plan

    c. classifies budget requests by activity and estimates the benefits arising from each activity

    d. presents the plan for a range of activity so that the plan can be adjusted for changes in activity levels

    e. all of the above   *(ICMA adapted)*

_____ **2.** The critical path is the:

    a. amount of time an activity may be delayed without delaying the total project beyond its target time

    b. earliest starting time that an activity for a project can begin

    c. shortest time path from the first event to the last event for a project

    d. longest time path from the first event to the last event for a project

    e. none of the above   *(ICMA adapted)*

_____ **3.** In preparing a cash budget, usually the starting point for projecting cash requirements is with:

    a. fixed assets   **d.** inventories

    b. sales   **e.** none of the above

    c. accounts receivables   *(CIA adapted)*

_____ **4.** Zero-base budgeting:

    a. involves the review of changes made to an organization's original budget

    b. does not provide a projection of annual expenditures

    c. is a method peculiar to budgeting by program

    d. involves the review of each cost component from a cost/benefit perspective

    e. emphasizes the relationship of effort to projected annual revenues   *(CIA adapted)*

_____ **5.** A company is controlling a complex project by determining the activities that must take place and the relationship between these activities. Attention then is focused upon those activities that have the greatest influence on the project's estimated completion date. The quantitative technique most relevant to this situation is:

    a. cost-volume-profit analysis   **d.** queuing analysis

    b. parametric programming   **e.** none of the above

    c. Program Evaluation and Review Technique (PERT)   *(AICPA adapted)*

_____ **6.** Cinnamon Company has budgeted its activity for April. Selected data are as follows:

Net income $120,000
Increases in gross amount of trade accounts receivable during month   35,000
Decrease in accounts payable during month   25,000
Depreciation expense   65,000
Provision for income tax   80,000
Provision for doubtful accounts receivable   45,000

On the basis of the above data, Cinnamon had budgeted a cash increase for the month in the amount of:

    a. $90,000   **d.** $300,000

    b. $195,000   **e.** none of the above

    c. $250,000   *(AICPA adapted)*

_____ 7. Vikings Inc. is preparing its cash budget for November. The following information is available concerning its inventories:

Estimated inventories at beginning of November......................	$180,000
Estimated cost of goods sold for November..........................	900,000
Estimated inventories at end of November..........................	160,000
Estimated payments in November for purchases prior to November	210,000
Estimated percentage of payments in November for purchases in November..	80%

The estimated cash disbursements for inventories in November are:

a. $720,000   **d.** $1,042,000
b. $930,000   **e.** none of the above
c. $914,000   _(AICPA adapted)_

_____ 8. Farfield Inc. is considering a three-phase research project. The time estimates for completion of Phase 1 of the project are:

	Months
Optimistic...	4
Most likely...	8
Pessimistic...	18

Using the Program Evaluation and Review Technique (PERT), the expected time for completion of Phase 1 should be:

a. 8 months   **d.** 18 months
b. 10 months   **e.** none of the above
c. 9 months   _(AICPA adapted)_

_____ 9. Clinton Corporation had the following transactions in 19A, its first year of operations:

Sales (90% collected in 19A)	$1,500,000
Receivables write-offs	60,000
Disbursements for costs and expenses	1,200,000
Disbursements for income taxes	90,000
Payments for plant assets.....................................	400,000
Depreciation on plant assets	80,000
Proceeds from issuance of common stock	500,000
Proceeds from short-term borrowings	100,000
Payments on short-term borrowings	50,000

The cash balance at December 31, 19A is:

a. $150,000   **d.** $280,000
b. $170,000   **e.** none of the above
c. $260,000   _(AICPA adapted)_

_____ 10. Success in implementing zero-base budgeting requires:

a. linkage of zero-base budgeting to the planning process
b. sustained support and commitment from top management
c. innovation among the managers who make up the budget decision packages
d. sale of the concept to the people who must perform the work
e. all of the above   _(AICPA adapted)_

Part 4 ■ Problem

Cleaver Candy Co. prepared cash estimates for the next four months. The following estimates were developed for certain items:

Item	March	April	May	June
Cash sales	$20,000	$12,000	$16,000	$22,000
Credit sales	10,000	4,000	12,000	18,000
Payroll	4,000	3,000	5,000	6,000
Purchases	6,000	5,200	5,600	8,000
Other expenses	5,000	4,800	5,200	5,600

In February, credit sales totaled $18,000, and purchases totaled $10,000. January credit sales were $24,000. Accounts receivables collections amount to 60% in the month after the sale and 35% in the second month after the sale; 5% of the receivables are never collected. Payroll and other expenses are paid in the month incurred, as are 50% of the purchases. The remainder of the purchases are paid in the following month. The cash balance was $5,000 on March 1. A $35,000 tax payment is due on June 15.

Instructions: *Prepare a cash budget for the four-month period (March through June), using the form provided below.*

Cleaver Candy Co.
Cash Budget
For March-June, 19X

Receipts From:	March	April	May	June
Cash sales	$	$	$	$
January credit sales				
February credit sales				
March credit sales				
April credit sales				
May credit sales				
Total receipts	$	$	$	$
Disbursements for:				
Payroll	$	$	$	$
Other expenses				
February purchases				
March purchases				
April purchases				
May purchases				
June purchases				
Tax payment				
Total disbursements	$	$	$	$
Net increase (decrease) in cash:				
Receipts less disbursements	$	$	$	$
Cash balances:				
Beginning				
Ending	$	$	$	$

Part 5 ■ Problem

A budget prepared the following time estimates for a contemplated project with 72 days as the target date:

Event	Activity	t_o	t_m	t_p
B	A-B	4	6	8
C	A-C	16	18	20
D	A-D	6	9	12
E	B-E	6	10	14
F	C-F	5	9	19
F	D-F	3	5	7
H	E-H	10	16	22
E	F-E	3	7	11
G	F-G	4	6	14
H	G-H	7	11	15

Instructions:

1. Prepare a calculation for t_e (expected time) for each activity.

Activity	t_e
A-B	
A-C	
A-D	
B-E	
C-F	
D-F	
E-H	
F-E	
F-G	
G-H	

2. Design the PERT network for the data in 1.

3. Determine the total t_e for each path and identify the critical path for the project.

Path	t_e
1	
2	
3	
4	
5	

Part 6 ■ Problem

Hickok Company is preparing a cash budget for July. The following estimates were made:

a. Expected cash balance, July 1, $10,000.

b. Income tax rate is 30%, based on accounting income for the month, payable in the following month.

c. Hickok's customers pay 25% of their purchases during the month of purchase and the balance during the following month. Bad debts are expected to be 5%.

d. Merchandise is purchased on account for resale, with 50% of purchases paid for during the month of purchase and the balance paid during the following month.

e. Marketing and administrative expenses are all paid in the current month.

f. Dividends of $25,000 are expected to be declared and paid during July.

g. Hickok's desire is to have a minimum month-end cash balance of $10,000.

h. Other budgets include the following estimates:

	June	July
Sales (all on account)	$50,000	$55,000
Purchases	20,000	23,000
Depreciation expense	7,500	7,500
Cost of goods sold	25,000	27,000
Other marketing and administrative expenses	13,000	14,500

Instructions:

1. Prepare a cash budget for July, using the form provided on page 155.

Hickok Company
Cash Budget
For July

Cash balance, July 1 .... $

Cash receipts:

    June sales .... $

    July sales...................................   _____   _____

Cash available .... $

Cash disbursements:

    June purchases .... $

    July purchases...............................

    Other marketing and administrative expenses .....

    Income tax ....

    Dividends ....   _____   _____

Cash balance, July 31 .... $

Calculation of June income tax:

    Sales .... $

    Cost of goods sold..........................   _____

    Gross profit................................ $

Commercial expenses:

    Depreciation .... $

    Other marketing and administrative ....   _____   _____

Taxable income .... $

Income tax .... $

2. What financial action needs to be taken as a result of this cash budget?

Responsibility Accounting and Reporting

REVIEW SUMMARY

I.   Purpose of the Chapter

This chapter defines responsibility accounting and reporting, explains the organizational requirements necessary for its implementation, and explains the characteristics of a useful responsibility report. It also illustrates the preparation of a flexible budget, the computation of spending and idle capacity variances, and the preparation of a variance report. Lastly, it criticizes the usefulness of information provided by responsibility reports to managers and the practice of using responsibility reports to measure managerial performance.

II.   Responsibility Accounting Principles

Business activity drives cost; therefore, costs can be controlled only if the individuals in the company who control business activities are held accountable for the efficient conduct of those activities. A responsibility accounting and reporting system is designed to promote and enhance accountability. To be effective:

1. Each individual must have a clear understanding of his or her responsibilities, and there must be no overlapping lines of responsibility.

2. Individuals with responsibility must have sufficient authority to take the actions necessary to meet those responsibilities.

3. The accounting system must be able to segregate controllable costs from those that are not controllable and provide timely reports to responsible managers.

III.   Responsibility for Overhead Costs

The distribution of service hours provided to a recipient department should be based on what is termed a **predetermined billing rate**, **sold-hour rate**, **charging rate**, or **transfer rate**. This rate is determined as follows:

1. Estimate or budget the costs directly traceable to the service department.

2. Allocate a share of plantwide costs to the service department.

3. Allocate a share of the budgeted costs of other service departments to the service department.

4. Determine the billing rate by dividing total estimated service department cost by the number of service department hours.

IV.   Responsibility Reports

Responsibility reports are accountability reports intended to inform managers of their performance in responsible areas and to motivate managers to generate the direct action needed to improve performance. Responsibility reports should (1) be addressed primarily to the individuals responsible for controlling the items covered in the report; (2) be consistent in form and content each time they are issued; (3) be prompt and timely; (4) be issued regularly; (5) be easy to understand; (6) convey sufficient but not excessive detail; (7) include comparative figures of predetermined standards and actual results; (8) analyze underlying data and reasons for poor performance; and (9) be stated in physical units as well as in dollars.

V.   Flexible Budgeting

The fact that costs and expenses are affected by fluctuations in volume limits the use of the fixed budget and leads to the use of a flexible budget. The preparation of a flexible budget results from the development of formulas indicating the fixed amount or variable rate for each department and for each account within a department. The application of the formulas to the level of activity actually experienced produces the allowable expenditures for the volume of activity attained. These budget figures are compared with actual costs in order to measure the performance of each department.

VI.   Variance Analysis

The **spending variance** is the difference between actual factory overhead and the budget allowance estimated for the capacity utilized. It is attributable to the differences in the actual and budgeted prices and quantities of the items that comprise overhead. The **idle capacity variance** is the difference between the budget allowance estimated for the capacity utilized and the applied factory overhead. It is a measure of capacity utilization (i.e., the amount of over- or underapplied budgeted fixed factory overhead).

VII. Responsibility Accounting—Dysfunctional Behavior by Managers

The traditional view of responsibility accounting and reporting assigns responsibility for inefficiencies to individuals, and a variance from the budget (or standard) is the measure of inefficiency. Since individuals are evaluated rather than the operating systems, the individuals tend to do whatever it takes to minimize or eliminate variances. This can have the following dysfunctional results:

1. Managers tend to take actions that are self-serving rather than beneficial to the company as a whole.

2. Managers concentrate on meeting the budget rather than the best level of performance that can be achieved.

3. Managers tend to focus their attention on short-run targets and ignore the long-term needs of the business.

4. Managers who are unable to subvert the system sufficiently to get acceptable evaluations but who are otherwise competent and efficient become frustrated, do not get promoted, and often leave the company.

Probably the most effective step in solving the problem of dysfunctional behavior is to discontinue the practice of using variance reports as a basis for evaluating individual managers. By shifting the focus of variance reporting to evaluating activities and business systems, individuals are not placed in the position of defending their actions.

VIII. Responsibility Accounting—Usefulness of Data to Managers

The traditional view of responsibility accounting and reporting is that the costs incurred in conducting a business activity should be reported to the manager who controls the business activity. Problems with this view include:

1. Most responsibility accounting and reporting systems improperly base allowable budgets on volume-based measures of activity, which have little to do with cost incurrence.

2. Control data available in a responsibility reporting system are too aggregated to be useful.

3. Control data available to managers are financial and not easily interpreted by all operating-level managers.

4. Control data available to managers are not timely enough to be useful.

To a great extent, these problems stem from poorly designed responsibility accounting systems and from attempts to use responsibility reporting as the primary or exclusive cost control mechanism.

Part 1 ■ True/False

Instructions: *Indicate whether each of the following statements is **True** or **False**.*

	True/False

1. A well-designed information system should provide a control mechanism encompassing responsibility accounting. . . . . _____

2. Responsibility accounting is based on the concept that the individual in charge of each responsibility classification should be accountable for the expenses of his or her activity. . . . . _____

3. Generally, costs charged directly to a department, with the exception of fixed costs, are controllable by the department's manager. . . . . _____

4. The distribution of service hours to the user department is based on what is called a billing rate. . . . . _____

5. A billing rate is determined by dividing the total actual departmental cost by the number of hours the service is expected to be used. . . . . _____

6. The charge for the services of a maintenance department is usually based on a fixed rate per transaction plus a standard variable charge. . . . . _____

7. The flexible budget is a useful planning device because it provides cost behavior information that can be used to evaluate the effects of different volumes of activity and profit. . . . . _____

8. Maintenance engineers control the quantity of people and materials required to serve the various departments, while factory supervisors control the amount of maintenance work. . . . . _____

9. Manufacturing expenses are prepared on a flexible budget basis; whereas, marketing and administrative expenses are prepared on a fixed budget basis. . . . . _____

10. An unfavorable spending variance suggests that variable overhead costs were not adequately controlled. . . . . _____

11. Supervisors are responsible for costs incurred by their subordinates. . . . . _____

12. The idle capacity variance is calculated by comparing actual overhead costs with what should have been spent for the actual activity of the period. . . . . _____

13. Under the traditional view of responsibility accounting, operating systems are evaluated rather than individuals. . . . . _____

14. Most responsibility accounting systems improperly base allowable budgets on volume-based measures of activity which have little to do with cost incurrence. . . . . _____

15. Responsibility accounting is the reporting phase of responsibility reporting. . . . _____

Part 2 ■ Matching

Instructions: *On the line at the left of each of the following items, place the letter from the columns below that identifies the term that best matches the statement. No letter should be used more than once.*

_____ **1.** Especially effective in offering opportunities to convey information, raise questions, and voice opinions.

_____ **2.** The difference between actual costs and budgeted costs.

_____ **3.** An organizational unit having a single head accountable for activities of the unit.

_____ **4.** Based on a classification of managerial departments at every level in the organization for the purpose of establishing a budget for each.

_____ **5.** The starting point for a responsibility accounting system.

_____ **6.** Especially effective in conveying qualitative information and analyzing and interpreting quantitative data.

_____ **7.** Basis of distribution of service hours to the recipient center.

_____ **8.** Provides a measure of what costs should be under any given set of conditions.

_____ **9.** The difference between actual cost and the budget allowance.

_____ **10.** If actual volume differs from that planned, a comparison of actual results with this type of budget may be misleading.

_____ **11.** Control the amount of maintenance work performed.

_____ **12.** Control the quantity of people and materials required to serve the maintenance needs of various departments.

_____ **13.** The difference between the budget allowance for actual activity and the amount of cost charged to the products manufactured.

_____ **14.** Issued to inform managers of their performance in responsible areas and to motivate them to generate the direct action needed to improve their performance.

_____ **15.** Relevant in deciding which costs should be assigned to a responsibility center.

a.	organization chart	**i.**	idle capacity variance
b.	spending variance	**j.**	responsibility accounting
c.	responsibility reports	**k.**	static budget
d.	degree of controllability	**l.**	oral presentations
e.	flexible budget	**m.**	factory supervisors
f.	billing rate	**n.**	maintenance supervisors
g.	written reports	**o.**	variance
h.	responsibility		

Part 3 ■ Multiple Choice

Instructions: *On the line at the left of each of the following items, place the letter of the choice that most correctly completes each item.*

_____ 1. Generally the item that should *not* appear on a monthly cost control report of a department manager is:

    a. departmental direct labor cost   **d.** cost of materials used in the department

    b. departmental supplies cost   **e.** none of the above

    c. salary of department manager   *(AICPA adapted)*

_____ 2. Periodic internal performance reports based on a responsibility accounting system should *not*:

    a. distinguish between controllable and uncontrollable costs

    b. be related to the organization chart

    c. include allocated fixed overhead in determining performance variation

    d. include variances between actual and controllable costs

    e. all of the above   *(AICPA adapted)*

_____ 3. A flexible budget is:

    a. not appropriate when costs and expenses are affected by fluctuations in volume

    b. appropriate for any relevant level of activity

    c. appropriate for control of factory overhead but not for control of direct materials and direct labor

    d. appropriate for control of direct materials and direct labor but not for control of factory overhead

    e. none of the above   *(AICPA adapted)*

_____ 4. Of most relevance in deciding how or which costs should be assigned to a responsibility center is the degree of:

    a. avoidability   **d.** variability

    b. causality   **e.** none of the above

    c. controllability   *(AICPA adapted)*

_____ 5. A spending variance for factory overhead is the difference between actual factory overhead cost and factory overhead cost that should have been incurred for the actual hours worked and results from:

    a. price differences for factory overhead costs

    b. quantity differences for factory overhead costs

    c. price and quantity differences for factory overhead costs

    d. differences caused in production volume variation

    e. none of the above

_____ 6. The most desirable measure for evaluating the performance of the departmental manager is departmental:

    a. revenue less controllable expenses   **d.** revenue less departmental expenses

    b. net income   **e.** none of the above

    c. contribution to indirect expenses   *(AICPA adapted)*

_____ 7. The term that identifies an accounting system in which the operations of the business are broken down into cost centers and the control function of the supervisor or the manager is emphasized is:

    a. responsibility accounting   **d.** budgetary accounting

    b. operations-research accounting   **e.** none of the above

    c. control accounting   *(AICPA adapted)*

_____ **8.** If a company uses a predetermined rate for applying factory overhead, the idle capacity variance is the:

    a. over- or underapplied fixed cost element of budgeted overhead

    b. over- or underapplied variable cost element of overhead

    c. difference in budgeted costs and actual cost of fixed overhead items

    d. difference in budgeted costs and actual cost of variable overhead items

    e. none of the above

_____ **9.** In general, costs incurred under a long-term lease for production equipment, when the lease calls for a level annual payment, are controllable by the:

    a. line supervisor   **d.** company treasurer

    b. production vice president   **e.** none of the above

    c. users of the equipment

_____ **10.** The EDP Department provides service to producing departments at the exact level predicted for the current period. Variances in cost for this department are charged to:

    a. producing departments on the basis of usage

    b. producing departments on the basis of capacity provided

    c. miscellaneous overhead

    d. the EDP Department as a spending variance

    e. none of the above

Part 4 ■ Problem

International Falls Products Inc. has two producing departments (Fabricating and Assembly) and one service department (Utilities). Allocation of fixed service costs is based on standby capacity available to each department. Variable service department costs are charged on the basis of actual consumption. These costs are distributed to departments at a predetermined rate based on variable costs at capacity. Data related to capacity and to the current month of July are as follows:

	Fabricating	Assembly	Utilities
Power consumption (July)	85,000 kwh	45,000 kwh	
Capacity available	100,000 kwh	50,000 kwh	
Fixed cost (July)			$25,000
Budgeted variable cost at capacity			48,000
Variable cost (July)			40,000

Instructions:

1. Compute the rate per kilowatt-hour (kwh) used to distribute variable costs.

2. Distribute the fixed and variable Utilities Department costs for the month to the Fabricating and Assembly Departments. (Round to the nearest dollar.)

	Fabricating	Assembly
Fixed cost distribution:	$	
		$
Variable cost distribution:		
Total cost distributed	$	$

3. Determine the over- or underdistributed variable cost for July.

Total variable cost..................................		$
Costs distributed:		
Fabricating	$	
Assembly.......................................		
Over- or underdistributed cost.....................		$

Part 5 ■ Problem

Ajax Adhesives Inc. has two service departments that provide the following data:

Service Center	Monthly Budget	Service Hours Available	Actual Monthly Expense
General maintenance...............	$100,000	10,000	$94,000
Machine repairs	40,000	2,000	45,000

The two service departments serve three producing departments that show the following budgeted and actual cost and service hours data:

	Estimated Services Required		Actual Services Used	
Department	General Maintenance	Machine Repairs	General Maintenance	Machine Repairs
Machining........	5,000	1,200	4,600	1,300
Assembling	3,000	600	2,500	650
Finishing........	2,000	200	1,600	250

Instructions:

1. Determine the billing-hour rates for the two service departments.

General Maintenance:

Machine Repairs:

2. Compute the amounts charged to the producing departments for services rendered.

| | Department | | | |
	Machining	Assembling	Finishing	Total
General Maintenance	$	$	$	$
Machine Repairs				
Total	$	$	$	$

3. Determine the spending variance for the two service departments, assuming that 75% of the budgeted expense is fixed in General Maintenance and 60% in Machine Repairs.

	Monthly Budget	Fixed Cost Percentage	Fixed Cost	Variable Cost	Variable Rate per Hour
General Maintenance	$	%	$	$	$
Machine Repairs	$	%	$	$	$

	General Maintenance	Machine Repairs
Actual overhead	$	$
Budget allowance:		
Fixed overhead	$	$
Variable overhead:		
Spending variance	$	$

4. Determine the idle capacity variance for the two service departments.

	General Maintenance	Machine Repairs
Budget allowance	$	$
Costs charged out		
Idle capacity variance	$	$

Part 6 ■ Problem

Tijuana Taco Inc. employs 30 production workers at normal capacity who work 8 hours per day, 20 days per month; normal capacity is 5,000 units per month. The direct labor wage rate is $12 per hour; direct materials are budgeted at $4 per unit produced. Fixed factory overhead is $2,500; supplies average $.50 per direct labor hour; indirect labor is 1/4 of direct labor cost, and other manufacturing charges are $1 per direct labor hour.

Instructions: *Prepare a monthly flexible budget at 60%, 80%, and 100% of normal capacity, showing itemized manufacturing costs, total manufacturing costs, manufacturing cost per unit, and factory overhead rate per direct labor hour, rounded to the nearest cent.*

Tijuana Taco Inc.
Monthly Flexible Manufacturing Budget

	60% of Capacity	80% of Capacity	100% of Capacity
Units.....................................			
Direct labor hours........................			
Direct materials	$	$	$
Direct labor			
Variable factory overhead:			
Supplies................................			
Indirect labor			
Other charges.........................			
Fixed factory overhead			
Total manufacturing cost	$	$	$
Manufacturing cost per unit	$	$	$
Factory overhead rate per direct labor hour ...	$	$	$

CHAPTER 18

Standard Costing: Setting Standards and Analyzing Variances

REVIEW SUMMARY

I. Purpose of the Chapter

This chapter discusses the usefulness of standard costs and the setting of standards. It explains and illustrates the computation of standard cost variances. Further, it discusses the use of standard cost variances for cost control.

II. Usefulness of Standard Costs

A **standard cost** is the predetermined cost of manufacturing a single unit or a number of units during a specific period in the immediate future. The use of standard costs for accounting purposes simplifies costing procedures through the reduction of clerical expenses. A complete standard cost file by parts and operations simplifies assigning costs to materials, work in process, and finished goods inventories.

When manufacturing budgets are based on standards for materials, labor, and factory overhead, a strong team is created for possible control and reduction of costs. Both budgets and standard costs make it possible to prepare reports that compare actual costs and predetermined costs for management. With the use of standard costs, the preparation of budgets for any volume and mixture of products is more reliably and speedily accomplished.

III. Setting Standards

A **basic standard** is a yardstick against which both expected and actual performances are compared. **Current standards** are of three types: (1) the **expected actual standard** is a standard set for an expected level of operation and efficiency; (2) the **normal standard** is a standard set for a normal level of operation and efficiency; and (3) the **theoretical standard** is a standard set for an ideal or maximum level of operation and efficiency. Standards are usually computed for a six- or twelve-month period. The success of a standard cost system depends on the reliability, accuracy, and acceptance of the standards. Standards must be set, and the

system implemented, in an atmosphere that gives full consideration to behavior characteristics of managers and workers.

IV. Materials Standards and Variances

Materials price standards should reflect current market prices and are generally used throughout the forthcoming fiscal period. The **materials purchase price variance** is computed as:

Actual quantity purchased x (Actual unit cost - Standard unit cost)

Materials quantity standards should be set after analyzing the most economical size, shape, and quantity of the product and the results expected from the use of various kinds and grades of materials. The **materials inventory variance** is computed as:

Standard unit cost x (Actual quantity purchased - Actual quantity used)

The **materials quantity variance** is computed as follows:

Standard unit cost x (Actual quantity used - Standard quantity allowed)

V. Labor Standards and Variances

Labor rate standards are based on rates established in collective bargaining agreements or as determined by agreements between the employee and the personnel department at the time of hiring. The **labor rate variance** is computed as follows:

Actual hours worked x (Actual rate - Standard rate)

Labor efficiency standards are based on the actual performance of a worker or group of workers possessing average skill and using average effort while performing manual operations or working on machines operating under normal conditions. The **labor efficiency variance** is computed as follows:

Standard rate x (Actual hours worked - Standard hours allowed)

VI.   Factory Overhead Standards and Variances

Variable overhead variances result from a comparison of actual variable costs with the flexible budget (applied) variable factory overhead. Fixed overhead variances result from a difference between budgeted fixed expenses and absorbed fixed overhead. The **standard factory overhead rate** is a predetermined rate that is based on an activity measure such as machine hours or direct labor hours at normal capacity, and it may be computed as follows:

Total factory overhead ÷ Direct labor hours, machine hours, etc.

The overall factory overhead variance is computed as follows:

Actual overhead - (Standard hours allowed for actual production x Standard overhead rate)

A.   Two-Variance Method

In the **two-variance method** of analyzing the overall overhead variance, the two variables are the (1) controllable variance and (2) volume variance. The **controllable variance** is the difference between the actual expenses incurred and the budget allowance based on standard hours allowed for the work performed. The **volume variance** is the difference between the budget allowance and the standard factory overhead charged to work in process, and it represents the cost of capacity available but not used.

B.   Three-Variance Method

In the **three-variance method**, the three variances are the (1) spending variance, (2) variable efficiency variance, and (3) the volume variance. They are computed as follows:

Spending variance = Actual factory overhead - Budget allowance based on actual hours worked

Variable efficiency variance = (Actual hours worked - Standard hours allowed) x Standard variable overhead rate

Volume variance = Budgeted fixed overhead - (Standard hours allowed x Fixed overhead rate)

VII.   Mix and Yield Variances

A **mix variance** is the result of mixing basic materials in a ratio different from standard materials specifications. The **yield variance** is the result of obtaining an amount of prime product manufactured from a given amount of materials that is different from what is expected on the basis of input. They are computed as follows:

Materials mix variance = (Actual input quantities x Individual standard materials costs) - (Actual input quantity x Weighted average standard materials input cost)

Materials yield variance = (Actual input quantity x weighted average standard materials input cost) - (Actual output quantity x Weighted average standard materials output cost)

VIII.   Causes of and Responsibility for Variances

A variance may be caused by some random event that is not expected to recur, or it may be the result of some systematic problem that can be corrected. It is also possible that the standard is simply wrong or out-of-date. The purchasing department carries the primary responsibility for materials price variances. However, economic conditions and unexpected price changes by suppliers may be outside the limits of the department's control, as well as internal factors, such as costly rush orders requiring materials shipments on short notice or in smaller than economical quantities. Materials quantity variances may result from many causes and may be the responsibility of production or purchasing depending on the circumstances. Labor rate variances tend to be fairly minor because labor rates usually are set by management for the period or by a long-term union contract. Labor efficiency variances may occur for a multitude of reasons, including a lack of materials or faulty materials, inexperienced workers and the related learning curve, badly worn or obsolete machinery, and changes in production methods. The factory overhead volume variance, which is a measure of capacity utilization, is generally the result of action taken by executive management.

Part 1 ■ True/False

Instructions: *Indicate whether each of the following statements is **True** or **False**.*

True/False

1. The use of standard costs for accounting purposes decreases the clerical labor required for costing procedures. .... _____

2. The standard cost system is more often used in job order cost accounting because of the greater practicality of setting standards for heterogeneous production. . _____

3. Over emphasis on price variances can result in a large number of low-cost vendors, high levels of inventory, and poor quality materials......................... _____

4. If standards are too tight, they are likely to reduce the worker's motivation to achieve the designated level of activity or productivity......................... _____

5. Standards are usually computed for a six- or twelve-month period, although a longer period is sometimes used. .... _____

6. A materials purchase price variance is unfavorable when the actual price paid for the materials is less than the standard price.......................... _____

7. Any difference between standard and actual labor hours results in a labor efficiency variance.. _____

8. Labor efficiency standards are usually established by industrial engineers, using time and motion studies... _____

9. The purchasing department carries the primary responsibility for the materials price variance... _____

10. The volume variance indicates the cost of capacity available but not used, and it is considered the responsibility of executive management................... _____

11. The volume variance indicates the amount of budgeted fixed overhead that is either under- or overabsorbed in a standard cost system. .... _____

12. Companies should always place primary emphasis on the elimination of all standard cost variances. .... _____

13. Although all methods of factory overhead variance analysis are commonly used, the two-variance method seems to be most popular......................... _____

14. A yield variance is the result of mixing basic materials in a ratio different from standard materials specifications. .... _____

15. Of the two labor variances, the labor efficiency variance is the more controllable by production department managers.................................... _____

Part 2 ■ Matching

Instructions: *On the line at the left of each of the following items, place the letter from the columns below that identifies the term that best matches the statement. No letter should be used more than once.*

_____ 1. The predetermined cost of manufacturing a single unit or a number of product units during a specific period in the immediate future.

_____ 2. The difference between the actual factory overhead incurred and the budget allowance based on the actual number of units of the allocation base used in actual production.

_____ 3. Emphasizes the volume of business and cost level that should be maintained if the firm is to operate as desired.

_____ 4. The difference between the budget allowance based on the actual number of units of the allocation base used in actual production and the amount of factory overhead chargeable to production in the absence of a standard cost system.

_____ 5. A standard set for an anticipated level of operation and efficiency.

_____ 6. Standard intended to represent challenging yet attainable results.

_____ 7. A standard set for an ideal or maximum level of operation and efficiency.

_____ 8. Computed by multiplying the standard unit cost by the difference between the actual quantity purchased and the actual quantity used.

_____ 9. Requires the computation of the spending variance, the volume variance, and the variable efficiency variance.

_____ 10. Should reflect current market prices and is generally used throughout the forthcoming fiscal period.

_____ 11. Computed by multiplying the actual quantity of materials purchased by the difference between the actual cost per unit and the standard cost per unit.

_____ 12. Determined by comparing the actual amount of materials used with the standard amount allowed, both priced at standard cost.

_____ 13. Determined by multiplying the actual hours worked by the difference between the actual hourly pay and the standard hourly pay.

_____ 14. Standards that include time factors for acceptable levels of fatigue and personal needs.

_____ 15. Computed at the end of any reporting period by comparing actual hours worked with standard hours allowed, but at the standard labor rate.

_____ 16. Determined by comparing the actual factory overhead incurred to the standard cost of factory overhead chargeable to work in process for the period.

_____ 17. The difference between normal factory overhead expenses incurred and the standard number of units of the allocation base allowed for actual production.

_____ 18. Indicates the cost of capacity available but not used and is generally considered the responsibility of executive management.

_____ 19. The result of blending basic materials in a ratio different from standard materials specifications.

_____ 20. The result of obtaining output different from that expected on the basis of input.

a.	expected actual standard	**k.**	net factory overhead variance
b.	materials inventory variance	**l.**	labor efficiency variance
c.	standard cost	**m.**	materials yield variance
d.	materials price standard	**n.**	materials quantity variance
e.	budget	**o.**	materials mix variance
f.	theoretical standard	**p.**	labor efficiency standards
g.	spending variance	**q.**	volume variance
h.	normal standard	**r.**	labor rate variance
i.	idle capacity variance	**s.**	controllable variance
j.	three-variance method	**t.**	materials purchase price variance

Part 3 ■ Multiple Choice

Instructions: *On the line at the left of each of the following items, place the letter of the choice that most correctly completes each item.*

_____ 1. The best basis upon which cost standards should be set in order to measure controllable production efficiencies is:

    a. theoretical standards   **d.** practical capacity

    b. expected actual standards   **e.** none of the above

    c. normal standards   *(ICMA adapted)*

_____ 2. An unfavorable factory overhead volume variance is most often caused by:

    a. actual fixed overhead incurred exceeding budgeted fixed overhead

    b. an overapplication of fixed overhead to production

    c. production levels exceeding sales levels

    d. normal capacity exceeding actual production levels

    e. none of the above   *(ICMA adapted)*

_____ 3. RDI Company uses the two-variance method for analysis of factory overhead in its standard costing system. Selected data for February follow:

Standard machine hours allowed for actual production....................	32,000
Actual machine hours...	33,000
Budgeted fixed factory overhead......................................	$ 66,000
Actual factory overhead incurred.....................................	$ 232,000
Variable factory overhead rate per machine hour........................	$ 5

    The controllable variance is:

    a. $11,000 favorable   **d.** $6,000 unfavorable

    b. $11,000 unfavorable   **e.** none of the above

    c. $6,000 favorable   *(AICPA adapted)*

_____ 4. The labor rate variance is computed as:

    a. the difference between the standard and actual rate multiplied by actual hours

    b. the difference between the standard and actual rate multiplied by standard hours

    c. the difference between the standard and actual hours multiplied by the actual rate

    d. the difference between the standard and actual hours multiplied by the difference between the standard and actual rate

    e. none of the above   *(AICPA adapted)*

_____ 5. Smoothe Company manufactures tables with vinyl tops. The standard material cost for the vinyl used per Type R table is $7.80, based on six square feet of vinyl at a cost of $1.30 per square foot. A production run of 1,000 tables in January resulted in usage of 5,800 square feet of vinyl at a cost of $1.20 per square foot, for a total cost of $6,960. The materials quantity variance resulting from this production run was:

    a. $240 favorable   **d.** $640 unfavorable

    b. $240 unfavorable   **e.** none of the above

    c. $260 unfavorable   *(AICPA adapted)*

_____ 6. Information on Dibble Company's factory overhead costs follows:

Factory overhead chargeable to work in process at standard...............	$80,000
Budgeted factory overhead based on standard direct labor hours allowed....	$84,000
Budgeted factory overhead based on actual direct hours.................	$83,000
Actual factory overhead..	$86,000

The total factory overhead variance is:

    a. $2,000 favorable   **d.** $6,000 unfavorable
    b. $6,000 unfavorable   **e.** none of the above
    c. $4,000 unfavorable   *(AICPA adapted)*

7. Actual units of direct materials used were 20,000, at an actual cost of $44,000. Standard unit cost is $2.10. The materials price usage variance is:

    a. $1,000 favorable   **d.** $2,000 unfavorable
    b. $1,000 unfavorable   **e.** none of the above
    c. $2,000 favorable

8. If the actual number of liters of materials used exceeds standard liters allowed but actual cost is less than standard cost, the materials price and usage variances, respectively, are:

    a. unfavorable, favorable   **d.** unfavorable, unfavorable
    b. favorable, favorable   **e.** none of the above
    c. favorable, unfavorable   *(AICPA adapted)*

9. If a company computes a materials price usage variance, the variance is isolated:

    a. when materials are issued
    b. when materials are purchased
    c. when materials are converted in the production process
    d. when materials are priced
    e. none of the above   *(AICPA adapted)*

10. Of the following, the most probable reason a company would experience an unfavorable labor rate variance and a favorable labor efficiency variance is that:

    a. the mix of workers assigned to the particular job was heavily weighted towards the use of higher paid, experienced individuals
    b. the mix of workers assigned to the particular job was heavily weighted towards the use of new, relatively low paid, unskilled workers
    c. because of the production schedule, workers from other production areas were assigned to assist this particular process
    d. defective materials caused more labor to be used in order to produce a standard unit
    e. none of the above   *(AICPA adapted)*

Part 4 ■ Problem

Lizard Company has a budgeted normal monthly capacity of 20,000 labor hours, with a standard production of 10,000 units at this capacity. Standard costs are:

Materials	3 lbs. @ $1
Labor	2 hrs. @ $15 per hour
Factory overhead at normal capacity:	
Fixed	$20,000
Variable	$5 per labor hour

During March, actual factory overhead totaled $112,000, and 19,500 actual labor hours cost $282,750. During the month, 9,500 units were produced using 29,200 lbs. of material at a cost of $1.10 per lb.

Instructions:

1. Compute the materials cost variances.

	Pounds	**Unit Cost**		**Amount**
Actual quantity used		$	actual	$
Actual quantity used			standard	
Materials price usage		$		$
Actual quantity used		$	standard	$
Standard quantity allowed			standard	
Materials quantity variance			standard	$

2. Compute the labor cost variances.

	Hours	**Rate**		**Amount**
Actual hours worked		$	actual	$
Actual hours worked			standard	
Labor rate variance		$		$
Actual hours worked		$	standard	$
Standard hours allowed			standard	
Labor efficiency variance			standard	$

3. Compute the factory overhead variances—two-variance method.

Actual factory overhead.		$
Budget allowance based on standard hours allowed:		
Fixed overhead budgeted.	$	
Variable overhead.		
Controllable variance		$
Budget allowance based on standard hours allowed		$
Overhead charged to production		
Volume variance		$

4. Compute the factory overhead variances—three-variance method.

Actual factory overhead.		$
Budget allowance based on actual hours worked:		
Fixed overhead budgeted.	$	
Variable overhead.		
Spending variance.		$
Budget allowance based on actual hours worked		$
Budget allowance based on standard hours allowed		
Variable efficiency variance		$
Budget allowance based on standard hours allowed		$
Overhead charged to production		
Volume variance		$

This part is based on material in the Appendix to the chapter.

5. Compute the factory overhead variances—four-variance method.

Actual factory overhead	$
Budget allowance based on actual hours worked	
Spending variance	$
Budget allowance based on actual hours worked	$
Budget allowance based on standard hours allowed	
Variable efficiency variance	$
Actual hours x fixed overhead rate	$
Standard hours allowed x fixed overhead rate	
Fixed efficiency variance	$
Normal capacity hours x fixed overhead rate	$
Actual hours worked x fixed overhead rate	
Idle capacity variance	$

Part 5 ■ Problem

Su Industries uses a standard cost card system. The standard cost card for one of its products shows the following materials standards:

Material	Pounds	x	Standard Price per Pound	=	Amount
X	20		$1.75		$35.00
Y	5		.85		4.25
Z	15		3.25		48.75
	40				$88.00

The standard 40 lb. mix average materials cost per lb. is $2.20 ($88 ÷ 40 lbs.). The standard mix should produce 32 lbs. of finished product, and the standard materials cost of finished product per lb. is $2.75 (88 ÷ 32 lbs.).

450,000 of materials were used as follows:

Material X	220,000 lbs. @	$2.00
Material Y	60,000 lbs. @	1.00
Material Z	170,000 lbs. @	3.00

The output of finished product was 375,000 lbs.

Instructions:

1. Compute the materials price usage variance.

Material	Pounds	Actual Cost per Pound	Amount
X		$	$
Y			
Z			$

Material	Pounds	Standard Cost per Pound	Amount
X		$	$
Y			
Z			$

Materials price usage variance. . . . . $ _____

2. Compute the materials mix variance.

Actual input quantities at individual standard materials cost . . . . $

Actual input quantities at weighted average standard materials cost . . . . _____

Materials mix variance . . . . $ _____

3. Compute the materials yield variance.

Actual input quantities at weighted average standard materials cost . . . . $

Actual output quantities at standard materials cost . . . . _____

Materials yield variance . . . . $ _____

Standard Costing: Incorporating Standards into the Accounting Records

REVIEW SUMMARY

I. Purpose of the Chapter

This chapter describes the accumulation of standard costs in a company's accounts and the disposition of standard cost variances. Further, the chapter illustrates the preparation of journal entries: to record the elements of cost at standard; to account for completed products in a standard cost system; and to dispose of the standard cost variances.

II. Standard Cost Accounting for Materials

The recording of materials purchased may be handled by three different methods:

1. The price variance may be recorded when materials are received and placed in the storeroom.

2. The materials may be recorded at actual cost when received, and the price variance determined when the materials are requisitioned for production.

3. The price variance may be calculated when the materials are received, but not charged to production until the materials are actually placed in process.

For control purposes, the price difference should be determined when the materials are received.

III. Standard Cost Accounting for Labor

In a standard cost system, the clock cards, job tickets, and other labor time information provide the data for the computation of the labor variances. The journal entry to distribute the payroll and set up the variance accounts should be:

Work in Process
Labor Rate Variance (assume unfavorable)
   Labor Efficiency Variance (assume favorable)
   Payroll

IV. Standard Cost Accounting for Factory Overhead

Journal entries for factory overhead, assuming the use of the two-variance method, are as follows:

1. To record actual factory overhead:

   Factory Overhead Control
      Various Credits

2. To apply overhead to work in process:

Work in Process
   Applied Factory Overhead

3. To close applied factory overhead at end of period:

   Applied Factory Overhead
      Factory Overhead Control

4. To close the factory overhead control account using the two-variance method, assuming that both controllable variance and volume variance are unfavorable:

   Factory Overhead Controllable Variance
   Factory Overhead Volume Variance
      Factory Overhead Control

5. To close the factory overhead control account using the three-variance method, assuming that all variances are favorable:

   Factory Overhead Control
      Factory Overhead Spending Variance
      Factory Overhead Variable Efficiency
        Variance
      Factory Overhead Volume Variance

V. Standard Cost Accounting for Completed Products

The completion of production requires the transfer of cost from the work in process account of one department to the work in process account of another department or to the finished goods inventory account. The cost transferred is the standard cost of the completed goods.

VI. Disposition of Variances

Variances may be disposed of either by (1) treating them as period expenses to be closed to Income Summary or (2) treating them as adjustments to Cost of Goods Sold and to inventories. If method (1) is used, unfavorable manufacturing cost variances are deducted from the gross profit at standard cost, and favorable manufacturing cost variances are added to the gross profit at standard cost. Proponents of this method believe that variances should not be treated as increases or decreases in manufacturing costs, but as deviations in contemplated costs that should be charged against income in the period incurred. Proponents of method (2) advocate that the variances should be prorated to Work in Process, Finished Goods, and Cost of Goods Sold. Cost Accounting Standards Board regulations require that significant standard cost variances be included in inventories. Current Internal Revenue Service regulations also require the inclusion of a portion of significant variances in inventories.

VII. Revision of Standard Costs

Standards should be changed only when underlying conditions change or when the standards no longer reflect the original concept. Events, rather than time, should determine whether standard costs are to be revised. When standard costs are changed, any adjustment to inventory should be made with care so that inventories are not written up or down arbitrarily.

Part 1 ■ True/False

Instructions: *Indicate whether each of the following statements is **True** or **False**.*

True/False

1. Under the method where the materials price variance is recorded when materials are received and placed into stores, the general ledger control account, Materials, is debited at actual cost. . . . . _____

2. Under the method where the materials price variance is recorded when the materials are requisitioned for production, the general ledger control account, Materials, is debited at standard cost. . . . . _____

3. For control purposes, the materials price variance should be determined when materials are used. . . . . _____

4. Under standard costing, the finished goods ledger card will show quantities only because the standard cost of the units generally remains the same during a period. _____

5. To distribute the payroll and to set up the variance accounts for labor, the journal entry includes a debit to Work in Process, a credit to Payroll, and debits or credits to Labor Rate Variance and Labor Efficiency Variance, depending upon whether the variance is unfavorable or favorable. . . . . _____

6. In a standard cost system, cost is transferred from the work in process account of one department to the work in process account of the next department at standard cost. . . . . _____

7. To avoid short-run fluctuations, variances should generally not be reported more often than every three months. . . . . _____

8. In journalizing variances, favorable variances are credited and unfavorable variances are debited. . . . . _____

9. If the entry to close the factory overhead control account includes credits to both Factory Overhead Controllable Variance and Factory Overhead Volume Variance, applied factory overhead was more than actual factory overhead. . . . . _____

10. When variances are closed to Income Summary, unfavorable variances are subtracted from the gross profit at standard cost. . . . . _____

11. The two types of labor variances are the rate variance and the efficiency variance. _____

12. When variances are closed to Cost of Goods Sold, favorable variances are added to the gross profit computed at standard cost. . . . . _____

13. Cost Accounting Standards Board regulations require that significant standard cost variances be included in inventories. . . . . _____

14. Standard costs should be changed at least once a year so that managers "keep on their toes." . . . . _____

15. Standard costing is most applicable to manufacturing situations and does not really work well in the nonprofit organization sector. . . . . _____

Part 2 ■ Matching

Instructions: *On the line at the left of each of the following items, place the letter from the columns below that identifies the term that best matches the statement. No letter should be used more than once.*

_____ **1.** Viewed as passing through the data-processing system into financial statements.

_____ **2.** Approach under which the amount of over- or underapplied factory overhead can be analyzed as volume, variable efficiency, and spending variances.

_____ **3.** Approach under which the amount of over- or underapplied overhead can be analyzed as controllable and volume variances.

_____ **4.** Variance that, for control purposes, should be determined when materials are received.

_____ **5.** Approach under which the amount of over- or underapplied factory overhead is divided into the spending, idle capacity, variable efficiency, and fixed efficiency variances.

_____ **6.** Approach under which the amount of over- or underapplied factory overhead can be analyzed as spending, idle capacity, and efficiency variances.

_____ **7.** Variance that appears on the books after the materials are issued and then only for the quantity issued.

_____ **8.** Will show quantities only because the standard cost of the units remains the same during a period unless severe cost changes occur.

_____ **9.** Approach under which the procedure for handling cost variances is to treat them as additions to or subtractions from cost of goods sold at standard.

_____ **10.** Variance that, for control purposes, should be determined when materials are used.

_____ **11.** Variance that appears on the books if the difference between the actual materials cost and the standard materials cost is recorded at the time the materials are purchased.

_____ **12.** Approach under which the procedure for handling cost variances is to consider them as profit or loss items.

_____ **13.** Approach that the Cost Accounting Standards Board requires to be used if there are significant standard cost variances.

_____ **14.** Requires the inclusion of a portion of significant variances in inventory.

_____ **15.** Requires that unplanned price or volume variances should be reported at the end of an interim period, following the same procedures used as at the end of a fiscal year.

a.	four-variance method	**i.**	alternative three-variance method
b.	three-variance method	**j.**	two-variance method
c.	materials price usage variance	**k.**	closing variances to Income Summary
d.	finished goods ledger card	**l.**	Internal Revenue Service
e.	materials quantity variance	**m.**	AICPA
f.	materials price variance	**n.**	allocating variances to Cost of Goods Sold and inventories
g.	closing variances to Cost of Goods Sold		
h.	standard costs	**o.**	materials purchase price variance

Part 3 ■ Multiple Choice

Instructions: *On the line at the left of the following items, place the letter of the choice that most correctly completes each item.*

_____ 1. A credit balance in the labor-efficiency variance account indicates that:
   a. standard hours exceed actual hours
   b. actual hours exceed standard hours
   c. standard rate and standard hours exceed actual rate and actual hours
   d. actual rate and actual hours exceed standard rate and standard hours
   e. standard rate exceeds actual rate   *(AICPA adapted)*

_____ 2. If a company follows a practice of isolating variances at the earliest point in time, the appropriate time to isolate and recognize a direct materials price variance would be:
   a. when materials are issued   d. when a purchase order is originated
   b. when materials are purchased   e. when materials leave the factory storeroom
   c. when materials are used in production   *(AICPA adapted)*

_____ 3. At the end of an accounting period, a usage variance that is significant in amount should be:
   a. reported as deferred charge or credit
   b. allocated among work in process inventory, finished goods inventory, and cost of goods sold
   c. charged or credited to cost of goods manufactured
   d. allocated among cost of goods manufactured, finished goods inventory, and cost of goods sold
   e. none of the above   *(AICPA adapted)*

_____ 4. The normal year-end treatment of immaterial variances recognized in a cost accounting system utilizing standards is:
   a. reclassified to deferred charges until all related production is sold
   b. allocated among cost of goods manufactured and ending work in process inventory
   c. closed to Cost of Goods Sold or to Income Summary in the period in which they arose
   d. capitalized as a cost of ending finished goods inventory
   e. none of the above   *(AICPA adapted)*

_____ 5. A credit balance in a direct labor efficiency variance account indicates that:
   a. the average wage rate paid to direct labor employees was less than the standard rate
   b. the standard hours allowed for the units produced were greater than actual direct labor hours used
   c. actual total direct labor costs incurred were less than standard direct labor costs allowed for the units produced
   d. the number of units produced was less than the number of units budgeted for the period
   e. all of the above   *(AICPA adapted)*

_____ 6. According to IRS regulations, at the end of an accounting period a usage variance that is significant in amount should be:
   a. reported as a deferred charge or credit
   b. allocated among Work in Process, Finished Goods, and Cost of Goods Sold
   c. charged or credited to cost of goods manufactured
   d. allocated among cost of goods manufactured, Finished Goods, and Cost of Goods Sold
   e. none of the above   *(AICPA adapted)*

_____ 7. Information on Red Company's direct labor costs for the month of January is as follows:

Actual direct labor hours 34,500
Standard direct labor hours 35,000
Total direct labor payroll $241,500
Direct labor efficiency variance—favorable .... $ 3,200

What is Red's direct labor rate variance?

a. $17,250 unfavorable   **d.** $21,000 favorable
b. $20,700 unfavorable   **e.** none of the above
c. $21,000 unfavorable

(AICPA adapted)

_____ 8. The following journal entry has been recorded:

Work in Process 7,560
Factory Overhead Variable Efficiency Variance.............. 950
    Factory Overhead Control 8,510

This entry indicates that the:

a. two-variance method is in use and the variance is unfavorable
b. three-variance method is in use and the variance is favorable
c. four-variance method is in use and the variance is unfavorable
d. three-variance method is in use and the variance is unfavorable
e. none of the above

_____ 9. Which of the following organizations utilizes standard costs?

a. construction contractors
b. hospitals
c. charitable organizations
d. governments
e. all of the above

_____ 10. If standard costs represent conditions that are expected to prevail in the coming period but that have not affected costs in the past period, then ending inventories are costed at:

a. the new standard
b. actual cost
c. the contra amount carried in cost of sales
d. the old standard
e. fifo

Part 4 ■ Problem

Jeffries Corp. determines that the following variances arose in production during June:

Variance	Amount	
Materials purchase price	$ 900	fav.
Materials quantity................................	750	unfav.
Labor efficiency	1,000	fav.
Labor rate.......................................	600	fav.
Variable efficiency	750	fav.
Volume..	1,500	unfav.
Spending...	500	fav.

Materials purchases totaled $90,000 at standard cost. Materials issued to the factory totaled $75,000 at standard cost. Labor payroll totaled $80,000, while actual overhead incurred was $60,000.

Instructions: *Prepare the journal entries to record the variances listed on page 179. (Credit Factory Overhead Control when applying factory overhead to production.)*

JOURNAL   PAGE

	DESCRIPTION	DEBIT	CREDIT	
1				1
2				2
3				3
4				4
5				5
6				6
7				7
8				8
9				9
10				10
11				11
12				12
13				13
14				14
15				15
16				16
17				17
18				18
19				19
20				20
21				21
22				22
23				23
24				24
25				25
26				26
27				27
28				28
29				29
30				30

Note: The part of this problem related to factory overhead is based on material in the Appendix to the chapter.

Part 5 ■ Problem

Kriss Kross Company makes a product for which the following standards have been set:

Materials: 3 square yards @ $4.95	$ 14.85
Direct labor: 2 hours @ $8	16.00
Variable factory overhead: 2 hours @ $1.50	3.00
Fixed factory overhead: 2 hours @ $2	4.00
	$ 37.85
Normal output	5,000 units

Actual data for March:

Production (no work in process inventories)	4,000	units
Sales at $50 per unit	3,000	units
Materials purchased (inventoried at standard cost), actual cost, $5.20 per square yard	15,000	square yards
Materials used	12,500	square yards
Direct labor @ $8.25 per hour	8,500	hours
Factory overhead	$ 32,100	

It was decided that all variances—two variances each for materials and direct labor, four variances for factory overhead—should be closed to Cost of Goods Sold.

Work in Process is charged with standard costs for actual production.

Instructions:

1. Complete the schedules below.

	Square Yards	Unit Cost		Amount
Actual quantity purchased		$	actual	$
Actual quantity purchased			standard	
Materials purchase price variance .		$		$
Actual quantity used		$	standard	$
Standard quantity allowed			standard	
Materials quantity variance				$

	Time	Rate		Amount
Actual hours worked		$	actual	$
Actual hours worked			standard	
Labor rate variance		$		$
Actual hours worked		$	standard	$
Standard hours allowed			standard	
Labor efficiency variance				$

Actual factory overhead . . . . $
Budget allowance based on actual hours worked:
    Fixed overhead budgeted . . . . $
    Variable overhead . . . . _____
Spending variance . . . . $
Budget allowance based on actual hours worked . . . . $
Budget allowance based on standard hours allowed:
    Fixed overhead budgeted . . . . $
    Variable overhead . . . . _____
    Variable efficiency variance . . . . $
Actual hours x fixed overhead rate . . . . $
Standard hours allowed x fixed overhead rate . . . .
Fixed efficiency variance . . . . $
Budget allowance based on actual hours worked . . . . $
Actual hours worked x factory overhead rate . . . .
Idle capacity variance . . . . $

2. Prepare the appropriate journal entries.

JOURNAL   PAGE

	DESCRIPTION	DEBIT	CREDIT	
1				1
2				2
3				3
4				4
5				5
6				6
7				7
8				8
9				9
10				10
11				11
12				12
13				13
14				14
15				15
16				16

JOURNAL

	DESCRIPTION	DEBIT	CREDIT	
1				1
2				2
3				3
4				4
5				5
6				6
7				7
8				8
9				9
10				10
11				11
12				12
13				13
14				14
15				15
16				16
17				17
18				18
19				19
20				20
21				21
22				22
23				23
24				24
25				25
26				26
27				27
28				28
29				29
30				30
31				31
32				32

Part 6 ■ Problem

The management of Peterson Products Inc. was presented with the following distribution of materials, labor, and overhead costs in inventories and cost of goods sold:

	Materials Costs	Direct Labor Costs	Overhead Costs
Materials—ending inventory	$ 25,000		
Work in process—ending inventory	40,000	$ 35,000	$ 62,000
Finished goods—ending inventory	35,000	35,000	88,000
Cost of goods sold	300,000	680,000	450,000
Total	$ 400,000	$ 750,000	$ 600,000

During the year, the following variances were noted:

Materials purchase price variance	$ (7,000)	fav.
Materials price usage variance	9,240	unfav.
Labor rate variance	(12,160)	fav.
Labor efficiency variance	6,340	unfav.
Overhead variances	9,790	unfav.

Instructions:

1. Allocate the variances to inventories and cost of goods sold, using the following schedule.

Materials purchase price variance to:

Materials	$
Work in process	
Finished goods	
Cost of goods sold	
Total	$

Materials price usage variance to:

Work in process	$
Finished goods	
Cost of goods sold	
Total	$

Labor rate variance to:

Work in process	$
Finished goods	
Cost of goods sold	
Total	$

Labor efficiency variance to:

Work in process	$
Finished goods	
Cost of goods sold	
Total	$

Overhead variances to:

Work in process . . . . $

Finished goods . . . .

Cost of goods sold . . . .

Total . . . . $

2. Compute the cost of goods sold after the variance allocation.

Standard:

Materials . . . . $

Labor . . . .

Overhead . . . .

Standard cost of goods sold . . . . $

Add unfavorable variances:

_____ $

_____

_____

$

Less favorable variances:

_____ $

_____

Actual cost of goods sold . . . . $

Direct Costing and Cost-Volume-Profit Analysis

REVIEW SUMMARY

I. Purpose of the Chapter

This chapter distinguishes direct costing from absorption costing, computes income on a direct costing basis and reconciles it with absorption costing income. In addition, the chapter lists the uses of and arguments for and against direct costing. Also, the chapter illustrates the computation of the level of sales in dollars and units required to break even or to achieve a target profit level, the preparation of a break-even chart, and the computation of the margin of safety and the margin of safety ratio.

II. Absorption Costing vs. Direct Costing

Absorption costing assigns direct materials and direct labor costs and a share of both fixed and variable factory overhead to units of production. However, in **direct costing** (also referred to as **variable costing** or **marginal costing**) only direct materials, direct labor, and variable factory overhead are charged to the product and are referred to as product costs. Fixed manufacturing costs are totally expensed in the period incurred and are called period costs.

III. Internal Uses of Direct Costing

Executive management generally has praised the planning, control, and analytical potentialities of direct costing. With its separation of variable and fixed costs and the calculation of the **contribution margin** or **marginal income**, direct costing facilitates analysis of cost-volume-profit relationships. A knowledge of variable costs, fixed costs, and the contribution margin provides guidelines for the selection of the most profitable products, customers, and territories.

Direct costing can serve as a guide in making pricing decisions because the direct-cost segment of unit cost consists of those cost elements that are comparable among firms in the same industry. Direct costing also provides a basis for the study of con-templated changes in production levels or proposed actions concerning new markets, plant expansion, or special promotional activities. Reports constructed on the direct costing basis become valuable control tools by reminding management of the profit objective for the period.

IV. External Uses of Direct Costing

Proponents of direct costing for external reporting purposes believe that the separation of fixed and variable expenses, and the accounting for each under some direct costing plan, simplifies both the understanding of the income statement and the assignment of costs to inventories. To keep fixed overhead out of reported product costs, variable and fixed expenses should be recorded in separate accounts.

A. Effects of Direct Costing on the Income Statement

If the number of units produced differs from the number sold, reported net income under absorption costing will differ from reported net income under direct costing. The difference is caused by the elimination of fixed manufacturing expenses from inventories in direct costing. In direct costing, fixed factory overhead is charged to period expense and does not become a part of the product's cost. Generally, when production exceeds sales, absorption costing shows a higher profit than does direct costing; and, when sales exceed production, the reverse occurs. The difference in operating income under the two methods can be reconciled as follows:

Difference in operating income = (Units produced - Units sold) x Fixed factory overhead rate for absorption costing

Managers prefer income statements prepared using direct costing because the variable cost of goods sold varies directly with sales volume, and the influence of production on profit is eliminated.

B. Positions on Direct Costing for Financial Reporting

The use of direct costing for financial reporting is not accepted by the accounting profession, the Internal Revenue Service, or the Securities and Exchange Commission. The position of these groups is generally based on their opposition to excluding fixed costs from inventories. Companies using direct costing internally adjust to absorption costing when preparing income tax returns and when reporting externally.

V. Cost-Volume-Profit Analysis

Break-even analysis indicates the point at which the company neither makes a profit nor suffers a loss. A **break-even chart** is a graphic analysis of the relationship of costs and sales to profit. **Cost-volume-profit analysis** is concerned with determining the optimal level and mix of output to be produced with available resources.

Break-even analysis may be based on historical data, past operations, or future sales and costs. The data in a flexible budget can be used directly and without refinement for break-even analysis; or, it can be converted into a break-even chart. The contribution margin ratio is determined by dividing the contribution margin (sales minus variable costs) by sales revenue. The contribution margin per unit is the difference between the sales price per unit and the variable costs per unit. Formulas for break-even computations are as follows:

$$\text{Break-even sales volume in dollars} = \frac{\text{Fixed costs}}{1 - \left(\dfrac{\text{Variable costs}}{\text{Sales}} \right)}$$

$$\text{Break-even sales volume in units} = \frac{\text{Fixed costs}}{\text{Contribution margin per unit}}$$

VI. Constructing a Break-Even Chart

In the conventional break-even chart, the fixed cost line is parallel to the x-axis, and the variable cost is plotted above the fixed cost. Many analysts prefer an alternative chart in which the variable cost is drawn first and the fixed cost is plotted above the variable cost line. A break-even chart can be constructed in even greater detail by breaking down fixed and variable costs into subclassifications.

VII. Break-Even Analysis for Decision Making

The break-even chart is fundamentally a static analysis. The amount of fixed and variable costs, as well as the slope of the sales line, is meaningful only in a defined range of activity and must be redefined for activity outside the relative range. In using break-even analysis, management should understand that:

1. A change in per-unit variable cost or in sales price changes the contribution margin ratio and the break-even point.

2. A change in fixed cost changes the break-even point but not the contribution margin figure.

3. A combined change in fixed and variable costs in the same direction causes an extremely sharp change in the break-even point.

A. Multiple Products and Sales Mix

When firms produce more than one product, the variable costs per dollar of sales revenue may be different for different products; thus, the contribution margin ratio, the break-even point, and the level of sales required to achieve targeted profit levels also would be different. Computations of the above items in the multiple-product case are essentially the same as those in the single-product case, except that the results are valid only for one specific sales mix. Rather than performing multiple-product analysis, a separate break-even analysis may be prepared for each product. However, if arbitrarily allocated common or joint costs are included, the results are of limited value.

B. Margin of Safety

The **margin of safety** indicates how much sales may decrease from a selected sales figure before the company will incur a loss. The margin of safety expressed as a percentage of sales is called the **margin of safety ratio** and is computed as follows:

$$\text{Margin of safety ratio (MIS)} = \frac{\text{Selected sales figure} - \text{Break-even sales}}{\text{Selected sales figure}}$$

Part 1 ■ True/False

Instructions: *Indicate whether each of the following statements is **True** or **False**.*

	True/False

1. Absorption costing assigns direct materials, direct labor costs, and a share of both fixed and variable factory overhead to units of production.................... _____

2. Direct costing charges variable costs to the product and expenses fixed manufacturing costs in the period in which they are incurred...................... _____

3. Contribution margin is the result of subtracting all variable costs from sales revenue. _____

4. A profit plan covers all phases of future operations to attain a stated profit goal. _____

5. Absorption costing is quite useful in planning for short periods, in pricing special orders, or in making current operating decisions........................ _____

6. In direct costing, there are no variances in fixed expenses because all fixed costs are charged currently against revenue......................... _____

7. Generally, when sales exceed production, absorption costing shows a higher profit than direct costing........................... _____

8. Gross contribution margin is sales less variable costs of goods sold.......... _____

9. The major objection of the accounting profession to direct costing is its exclusion of fixed costs from inventory........................... _____

10. In filing reports with the SEC, a firm that uses direct costing must adjust its inventories and reported net income to what they would have been had absorption costing been used. .... _____

11. The purpose of break-even analysis is to determine the optimal level and mix of output to be produced with available resources........................ _____

12. Break-even analysis is generally accomplished with the aid of a break-even chart because it is a compact, readable reporting device. .... _____

13. Data for break-even analysis can be taken directly from the conventional or full-cost income statement............................ _____

14. The contribution margin ratio is determined by dividing sales minus variable costs by sales revenue. .... _____

15. Break-even sales volume in dollars is computed by dividing fixed costs by the contribution margin ratio........................... _____

16. The break-even chart is fundamentally a static analysis since the amount of fixed and variable costs as well as the slope of the sales line are only meaningful for a certain range of activity........................... _____

17. In using break-even analysis, management should understand that a change in fixed cost changes the break-even point but not the contribution margin figure..... _____

18. One problem in a multiproduct firm is that it is not possible to prepare a separate break-even analysis for each product or product line. .... _____

19. The margin of safety expressed as a percentage of sales is called the contribution margin ratio. .... _____

20. If the contribution margin ratio and the profit percentage are known, the margin of safety ratio can be computed........................... _____

Part 2 ■ Matching

Instructions: *On the line at the left of each of the following items, place the letter from the columns below that identifies the term that best matches the statement. No letter should be used more than once.*

_____ 1. Costing method that assigns a portion of both fixed and variable factory overhead to production.

_____ 2. Costing method that charges units of product with only those manufacturing costs that vary directly with volume.

_____ 3. Costs that are more closely associated with the passage of time than with production activity.

_____ 4. Costs that are more closely associated with production activity than with the passage of time.

_____ 5. Difference between sales revenue and variable cost.

_____ 6. Point at which the company neither makes a profit nor suffers a loss.

_____ 7. Concerned with determining the optimal level and mix of output to be produced with available resources.

_____ 8. A graphic analysis of the relationship of costs and sales to profit.

_____ 9. Result of dividing the contribution margin by sales revenue.

_____ 10. Result of dividing fixed costs by the contribution margin ratio.

_____ 11. Result of dividing fixed costs by the contribution margin per unit.

_____ 12. Where the amount of fixed and variable costs as well as the slope of the sales line is meaningful.

_____ 13. When a shift in this occurs, a change in profit can also be expected unless the same contribution margin ratio is realized on all products.

_____ 14. Another term for absorption costing.

_____ 15. Result of multiplying the margin of safety ratio times the contribution margin ratio.

_____ 16. The margin of safety expressed as a percentage of sales.

_____ 17. Products make a favorable contribution as long as the sales revenue exceeds this.

_____ 18. When these are arbitrarily allocated in break-even analysis, the results are of limited value.

_____ 19. Indicates how much sales may decrease before the company will break even.

_____ 20. Another term for direct costing.

a.	direct costing	k.	break-even point
b.	product costs	l.	margin of safety ratio
c.	absorption costing	m.	profit ratio
d.	contribution margin	n.	contribution margin ratio
e.	period costs	o.	sales mix
f.	relevant range	p.	break-even point in dollars
g.	conventional costing	q.	break-even point in units
h.	cost-volume-profit analysis	r.	variable costing
i.	related variable cost	s.	margin of safety
j.	break-even chart	t.	common costs

Part 3 ■ Multiple Choice

Instructions: *On the line at the left of each of the following items, place the letter of the choice that most correctly completes each item.*

_____ **1.** Direct costing is not in accordance with generally accepted accounting principles because:

      a. it assumes fixed manufacturing costs to be period costs

      b. its procedures are not well known in industry

      c. net earnings are always overstated when using it

      d. it ignores the concept of lower of cost or market when valuing inventory

      e. none of the above   *(AICPA adapted)*

_____ **2.** A tenet of direct costing is that period costs should be expensed currently. The rationale behind this procedure is that:

      a. period costs are uncontrollable and should not be charged to a specific product

      b. period costs are generally immaterial in amount, and the cost of assigning the amounts to specific products would outweigh the benefits

      c. allocation of period costs is arbitrary at best and could lead to erroneous decisions by management

      d. period costs will occur whether or not production occurs, and so, it is improper to allocate these costs to production and thus defer a current cost of doing business

      e. none of the above   *(AICPA adapted)*

_____ **3.** For manufacturing costs, operating income computed using absorption costing or using direct costing differ because:

      a. absorption costing considers all costs in the determination of operating income, whereas direct costing considers only direct costs

      b. absorption costing inventories all direct costs, but direct costing considers direct costs to be period costs

      c. absorption costing inventories all fixed manufacturing costs for the period in ending finished goods inventory, but direct costing expenses all fixed manufacturing costs

      d. absorption costing allocates fixed costs between cost of goods sold and inventories, while direct costing considers all fixed costs to be period costs

      e. none of the above   *(AICPA adapted)*

_____ **4.** Jorge, Inc. manufactured 700 units of Product A, a new product, in 19A. Product A's variable and fixed manufacturing costs per unit were $6 and $2, respectively. There was no inventory of Product A on January 1, 19A. The inventory on December 31, 19A, consisted of 400 units. The difference between the dollar amount of inventory on December 31, 19A, using the direct costing method and the dollar amount using the absorption costing method would be:

      a. $1,600 decrease   **d.** $400 increase

      b. $400 decrease   **e.** none of the above

      c. $1,200 decrease   *(AICPA adapted)*

_____ **5.** A company has operating income of $50,000 using direct costing for a given period. Beginning and ending inventories for that period were 18,000 units and 13,000 units, respectively. If the fixed factory overhead application rate is $4 per unit, the operating income using absorption costing is:

      a. $40,000   **d.** $30,000

      b. $60,000   **e.** not determinable from the information given

      c. $50,000   *(AICPA adapted)*

_____ **6.** Bright Company, a lamp manufacturer, made available to its customers a new line called "Twilight." The break-even point for sales of Twilight is $400,000, with a contribution margin of 40%. If the operating income for the Twilight line for 19A amounted to $200,000, total sales for 19A were:

a. $600,000   d. $950,000

b. $900,000   e. none of the above

c. $840,000   *(AICPA adapted)*

_____ **7.** The Altimeter Company is planning to produce two products, Alt and Tude. Altimeter is planning to sell 100,000 units of Alt at $4 a unit and 200,000 units of Tude at $3 a unit. At the break-even point, variable costs are 70% of sales for Alt and 80% of sales for Tude. Fixed costs are $250,000. What is the break-even number of units?

a. 312,500   d. 253,333

b. 200,000   e. none of the above

c. 300,000   *(AICPA adapted)*

_____ **8.** The following data pertain to two types of products manufactured by Douglass Corp.:

	Per Unit	
	Sales Price	**Variable Costs**
Product Y......................................	$120	$ 70
Product Z......................................	$500	$200

Fixed costs total $300,000 annually. The expected mix in units is 60% for Product Y and 40% for Product Z. How much is Douglass's break-even sales in units?

a. 857   d. 2,459

b. 1,111   e. none of the above

c. 2,000

_____ **9.** If the fixed cost for a product increases and the variable cost (as a percentage of sales dollars) increases, what will be the effect on the contribution margin ratio and the break-even point, respectively?

	Contribution Margin Ratio	**Break-Even Point**
a.	Decreased	Increased
b.	Increased	Decreased
c.	Decreased	Decreased
d.	Increased	Increased

(AICPA adapted)

_____ **10.** To obtain the break-even point stated in units, the total fixed cost is divided by:

a. variable cost per unit

b. (sales price per unit - variable cost per unit) ÷ sales price per unit

c. fixed cost per unit

d. sales price per unit - variable cost per unit

e. none of the above

(AICPA adapted)

Part 4 ■ Problem

The following information is available for Bowe Corporation's new product line:

Sales price per unit.. $30
Variable manufacturing cost per unit of production $15
Total annual fixed manufacturing cost $60,000
Variable general and administrative cost per unit of production $5
Total annual fixed marketing and administrative expenses $25,000

There was no inventory at the beginning of the year. During the year, 30,000 units were produced (normal capacity) and 25,000 units were sold.

Instructions:

1. Determine the cost of the ending inventory, using direct costing.

2. Determine the cost of the ending inventory, using absorption costing.

3. Using direct costing, determine the total variable cost charged to expense for the year.

4. Using absorption costing, determine the total fixed cost charged to expense for the year.

5. Using direct costing, determine the total fixed cost charged to expense for the year.

Part ■ 5 Problem

Franchi Corporation produced 50,000 units (normal capacity) of product during the second quarter of the year; 40,000 units were sold at $25 per unit. The costs of this production were:

Materials	$100,000
Direct labor	250,000
Factory overhead:	
Variable cost	125,000
Fixed cost	150,000

Marketing and administrative expenses for the quarter total $350,000; $100,000 of which are variable.

Instructions:

1. Prepare an income statement using absorption costing.

Franchi Corporation
Income Statement—Absorption Costing
For Quarter Ended June 30, 19--

2. Prepare an income statement using direct costing.

Franchi Corporation
Income Statement—Direct Costing
For Quarter Ended June 30, 19--

Part 6 ■ Problem

Trenton Toothbrush Co. manufactures one style of deluxe toothbrush. The following information was received by management, covering the past three months:

	October	November	December
Sales (at $10 per unit)	$5,000	$2,000	$20,000
Beginning inventory	0	$2,500	$ 6,500
Cost of goods manufactured in month	$5,000	5,000	5,000
Costs of goods available for sale.	$5,000	$7,500	$11,500
Ending inventory.	2,500	6,500	1,500
Cost of goods sold	$2,500	$1,000	$10,000
Gross profit	$2,500	$1,000	$10,000

Supplementary information:
  Sales price per unit: $10
  Units manufactured per month: 1,000
  Standard cost per unit at normal volume: $5
  Total manufacturing cost at normal volume:
    Variable. $3,000
    Fixed.   2,000
The Cost Department believes that a direct standard costing system may be more helpful for management purposes than the standard absorption system presently in use.

Instructions:

1. Prepare income statements for each of the three months on the direct standard cost basis.

Trenton Toothbrush Co.
Comparative Income Statements for October, November, and December
Direct Costing Method

	October	November	December
Sales	$	$	$
Beginning inventory..............................	$	$	$
Variable cost of goods manufactured (variable costs) ..			
Variable cost of goods available for sale	$	$	$
Ending inventory			
Variable cost of goods sold	$	$	$
Gross contribution margin..........................	$	$	$
Less fixed factory overhead			
Gross profit (loss)	$	$	$

2. Show computations explaining the differences in gross profit for each month.

	October	November	December
Gross profit—absorption costing....................	$	$	$
Gross profit—direct costing........................			
Difference	$	$	$
Inventory change—absorption costing	$	$	$
Less inventory change—direct costing			
Difference	$	$	$

Part 7 ■ Problem

The following data of Wiz Co. are given for March:

Plant capacity....................................	1,600 units for the month
Fixed cost.......................................	$80,000 per month
Variable cost	$90 per unit
Sales price	$150 per unit

Instructions:

1. Determine the break-even point in dollars.

2. Determine the break-even point in units.

3. Prepare a conventional break-even chart, using the accompanying form. Label and identify each element of the chart.

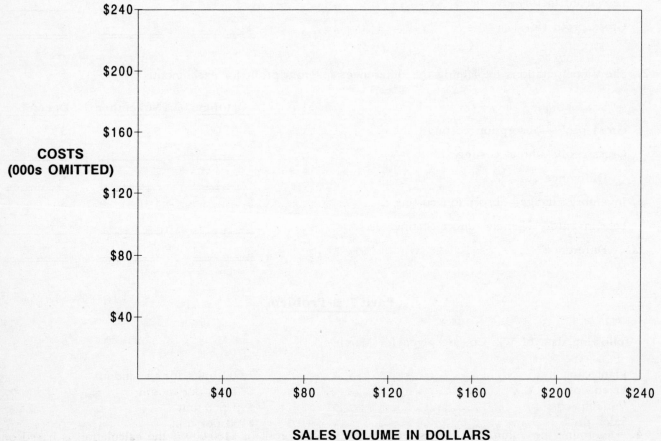

**COSTS
(000s OMITTED)**

**SALES VOLUME IN DOLLARS
(000s OMITTED)**

Part 8 ■ Problem

Tecumseh Teflon Company provides the following data:

Normal plant capacity	3,000 units
Fixed cost	$600,000
Variable cost	$140 per unit
Sales price	$400 per unit

Instructions: *Determine each of the following items, rounding all dollar amounts to the nearest whole dollar and rounding all percentages to two decimal places.*

1. Compute the break-even point in:

   (a) Dollars

   (b) Number of units

2. When operating at normal capacity, compute the:

   (a) Margin of safety in dollars

   (b) Margin of safety ratio

3. Determine the new break-even point in dollars if the sales price is reduced to $350 and other data remain the same.

4. Determine the volume in dollars required to yield a profit of $100,000 if the calculation is based on:

   (a) The data in 1 above

(b) The data in 3 on page 197

5. Determine the expected profit if budgeted sales of $1,200,000 are realized, and costs and selling price are the same as at the beginning of the problem.

Part 9 ■ Problem

Alphabet Company manufactures two products, P and Q. P sells for $25 and Q for $10. Variable costs per unit are $18 and $6 for P and Q, respectively. Total fixed cost is $435,000. Alphabet management has targeted profit for the coming period at $75,000. Three units of P are expected to sell for every two units of Q sold during the period.

Instructions:

1. Compute the contribution margin per hypothetical package:

	Product P	Product Q
Sales price per unit.............................	$	$
Variable cost per unit...........................		
Unit contribution margin	$	$
Expected sales mix..............................		
Contribution margin per hypothetical package........	$	+ $

2. Compute the break-even point in units of product and in sales dollars.

3. Compute the level of sales in units and dollars necessary to achieve Alphabet's profit goal.

Differential Cost Analysis

REVIEW SUMMARY

I. Purpose of the Chapter

This chapter: defines differential cost studies and relates them to short-term decision making; distinguishes costs that are relevant to short-term decision making from those that are not; lists several examples of short-term decision problems; and illustrates the computation of differential costs and their use in making short-term decisions. It also defines linear programming and illustrates its use in solving problems.

II. Differential Cost Studies

Differential cost, often referred to as **marginal** or **incremental cost**, is the difference in the cost of alternative choices. Differential cost studies deal with the determination of incremental revenues, costs, and margins with regard to alternative uses of fixed facilities or available capacity. Variable costs usually represent the differential costs, although additional fixed costs may be incurred. To enable management to have useful and meaningful cost data with which to maximize long-run profits, several other cost terms, concepts, and classifications, in addition to differential cost, must be incorporated in the decision-making process. **Opportunity costs** are the measurable value of an opportunity by-passed by rejecting an alternative use of resources. Imputed costs are hypothetical costs representing the cost or value of a resource measured by its use value. **Out-of-pocket costs** are the cash outlays required by any decision. **Sunk costs** are past costs that are irrelevant to a future decision.

A. Accepting Additional Orders

If available capacity is not fully used, a differential cost analysis might indicate the possibility of selling additional output at a figure lower than the existing average unit cost. The new or additional business can be accepted as long as the variable cost is recovered, since any contribution to the recovery of fixed costs and profit is desirable. Whenever a differential cost analysis leads management to accept a special order at or above the differential cost, it is assumed that the order is not going to disturb the market for the other products being offered. The firm must also be careful not to violate the Robinson-Patman Act and other governmental pricing restrictions.

B. Make-or-Buy Decisions

The problem of whether to make or buy an item arises particularly in connection with the use of idle equipment, idle space, or idle labor. The accountant should prepare a statement presenting the differential costs of making the item—including a share of existing fixed expense and a profit figure that places the total cost of "make versus buy" on a comparable basis. A cost study with only the differential costs and with no allocation of existing fixed expenses or profit may indicate possible cost savings in the short run, but in the long run, the full cost must be covered and a reasonable profit achieved.

C. Facilities Shutdown and Product Discontinuance

In the short run, a firm is better off operating than to shut down facilities, as long as the products or services sold recover the variable cost and make a contribution to the recovery of fixed costs that continue during periods of inactivity. Decisions to discontinue individual products require careful analysis of relevant differential cost and revenue data through a structured and continuous product evaluation program. Studies have shown that firms do a poor job of identifying products that are in difficulty and that should be eliminated, mainly due to the lack of relevant data.

The following notes are based upon the Appendix to the chapter.

III. Linear Programming

Differential cost studies must often determine the profitability of the short-run use of available capacity. **Linear programming** allows the accountant to determine the optimum course of action when the resource allocation problem is complex and its solution is neither obvious nor feasible by trial and error.

A. Maximization of Contribution Margin

Linear programming may be used to solve contribution margin maximization problems. For example, assume that management is trying to decide how much of each of two products to produce, given different contribution margins and hours required for production of each product. To maximize the total contribution margin, management must decide on (1) the allocation of available production capacity to each product and (2) the number of units of each product to produce. This type of problem may be solved by two basic linear programming techniques: the **graphic method** or the **simplex method**. These methods may also be used to solve cost minimization problems.

B. Graphing Linear Programming Problems

When a linear programming problem involves only two variables, a two-dimensional graph can be used to determine the optimal solution. In the example mentioned above, the maximum number of units of each product that can be produced would be determined by dividing the hours of productive capacity available in each department by the number of departmental hours required to complete each product unit. To determine the combination of production levels in order to maximize the contribution margin, all the constraints would be plotted on a graph. The best feasible solution, according to mathematics, is at one of the four corner points on the graph. Consequently, all four corner-point-variables must be examined to find the combination that maximizes the contribution margin.

Part 1 ■ True/False

Instructions: *Indicate whether each of the following statements is **True** or **False**.*

True/False

1. Historical costs drawn from accounting records generally give management the differential cost information needed to evaluate alternatives. . . . .   _____

2. The term "marginal cost" is widely used by economists. . . . .   _____

3. In differential cost studies, variable costs are significant because they usually represent the differential cost. . . . .   _____

4. If one alternative in a differential cost study requires the addition of new equipment, the related fixed costs are differential costs. . . . .   _____

5. If available capacity is not fully used, new or additional business can be accepted as long as all variable costs are recovered. . . . .   _____

6. Whenever a differential cost analysis leads management to accept an additional order at above the differential cost, the Robinson-Patman Act and other government pricing restrictions may be applicable. . . . .   _____

7. A shutdown of facilities eliminates all fixed costs in the short run. . . . .   _____

8. In decisions to discontinue a product, management must consider not only the profitability of the product but also the extent to which sales of other products will be adversely affected when the product is removed. . . . .   _____

9. Studies have shown that the lack of timely, relevant data is a major reason why firms do a poor job of identifying products that are in difficulty. . . . .   _____

10. Linear programming is used when the resource allocation problem is simple and its solution is fairly obvious. . . . .   _____

11. The undepreciated book value of an old asset is a sunk cost and is irrelevant in deciding whether to keep or replace the asset. . . . .   _____

12. Linear programming is a valuable aid to management because it provides a systematic and efficient procedure that can be used as a guide in decision making.   _____

13. When the total contribution margin is maximized, management's profit objective should be satisfied. . . . .   _____

14. When a linear programming problem involves more than two variables, the graphic method must be used to determine the optimal solution. . . . .   _____

15. In a make-or-buy decision, the full absorption cost is usually equal to the differential cost. . . . .   _____

Part 2 ■ Matching

Instructions: *On the line at the left of each of the following items, place the letter from the columns below that identifies the term that best matches the statement. No letter should be used more than once.*

_____ **1.** The difference in the cost of alternative choices.

_____ **2.** A synonym for differential cost that is widely used by economists.

_____ **3.** A term used by engineers to describe the added cost incurred when a project is extended beyond its originally intended goal.

_____ **4.** Arises particularly in connection with the possible use of idle equipment, idle space, and even idle labor.

_____ **5.** Departmental flexible budgets that state the amount for each class of expense at each production level.

_____ **6.** Allows the accountant to determine the optimum course of action when the resource allocation problem is complex and its solution is not obvious by trial and error.

_____ **7.** The required cash outlay in a differential cost study.

_____ **8.** The measurable value of sacrifices associated with alternatives.

_____ **9.** Hypothetical costs representing the cost or value of a resource measured by its use value.

_____ **10.** Past costs that are irrelevant to future decisions.

_____ **11.** When this is maximized, management's profit objective should be satisfied.

_____ **12.** Used to determine the optimal solution when a linear programming problem involves only two variables.

_____ **13.** An expenditure that does not have to be incurred after abandoning an activity.

_____ **14.** An iterative, stepwise process that approaches an optimum solution in order to reach an objective function of maximization or minimization.

_____ **15.** Provides for an increment or addition to the company's total revenue for the period.

a.	marginal cost	**i.**	sunk costs
b.	out-of-pocket cost	**j.**	imputed costs
c.	incremental cost	**k.**	two-dimensional graph
d.	linear programming	**l.**	marginal revenue
e.	differential cost	**m.**	simplex method
f.	cost analysis budgets	**n.**	avoidable cost
g.	make-or-buy decision	**o.**	contribution margin
h.	opportunity costs		

Part 3 ■ Multiple Choice

Instructions: *On the line at the left of each of the following items, place the letter of the choice that most correctly completes each item.*

_____ 1. The opportunity cost of making a component part in a factory with excess capacity for which there is no alternative use is:

    a. the variable manufacturing cost of the component
    b. the total manufacturing cost of the component
    c. the total variable cost of the component
    d. the fixed manufacturing cost of the component
    e. zero   *(ICMA adapted)*

_____ 2. A sunk cost is a cost that:

    a. may be saved by adopting an alternative
    b. may be shifted to the future with little or no effect on current operations
    c. cannot be avoided because it has already been incurred
    d. does not entail any dollar outlay but is relevant to the decision-making process
    e. none of the above   *(ICMA adapted)*

_____ 3. An imputed cost is:

    a. the difference in total costs that results from selecting one alternative instead of another
    b. a cost that may be shifted to the future with little or no effect on current operations
    c. a cost that cannot be avoided because it has already been incurred
    d. a cost that does not entail any dollar outlay but is relevant to the decision-making process
    e. none of the above   *(ICMA adapted)*

_____ 4. In considering a special order situation that will enable a company to make use of present idle capacity, a cost that would be irrelevant is:

    a. direct materials   **d.** variable factory overhead
    b. depreciation   **e.** none of the above
    c. direct labor   *(AICPA adapted)*

_____ 5. Barkley Company budgeted sales of 400,000 calculators at $40 per unit for the year. Variable manufacturing costs were budgeted at $16 per unit and fixed manufacturing costs at $10 per unit. In March, Barkley received a special order offering to buy 40,000 calculators for $18 each. Barkley has sufficient plant capacity to manufacture the additional quantity; however, the production would have to be done on an overtime basis at an estimated additional cost of $3 per calculator. Acceptance of the special order would not affect Barkley's normal sales, and no selling expenses would be incurred. What would be the effect on operating profit if the special order were accepted?

    a. $120,000 decrease   **d.** $80,000 increase
    b. $40,000 decrease   **e.** none of the above
    c. $140,000 decrease   *(AICPA adapted)*

_____ 6. Haywood Company's regular selling price for its product is $10 per unit. Variable costs are $6 per unit. Fixed costs total $1 per unit based on 100,000 units and remained unchanged within the relevant range of 50,000 units to total capacity of 200,000 units. After sales of 80,000 units were projected for the year, a special order was received for an additional 10,000 units. To increase its operating income by $10,000, what price per unit should Haywood charge for this special order?

    a. $10   **d.** $7.11
    b. $8   **e.** none of the above
    c. $7.13   *(AICPA adapted)*

7. Nugget Inc. has been manufacturing 5,000 units of Part 10541, which is used in the manufacture of one of its products. At this level of production, the cost per unit of manufacturing Part 10541 is as follows:

Direct materials . . . . $ 2
Direct labor 8
Variable overhead 4
Applied fixed overhead 6
   Total $20

Wynn Company has offered to sell Nugget 5,000 units of Part 10541 for $19 a unit. Nugget has determined that it could use the facilities presently used to manufacture Part 10541 to manufacture product RAC and generate an operating profit of $4,000. Nugget has also determined that two-thirds of the applied fixed overhead will continue even if Part 10541 is purchased from Wynn. To determine whether to accept Wynn's offer, the net relevant cost to Nugget of continuing to manufacture Part 10541 is:

a. $70,000
d. $84,000
b. $80,000
e. none of the above
c. $90,000
(AICPA adapted)

8. As part of the data presented in support of a proposal to increase the production of videogames, the sales manager of Katsaumi Products reported the total additional cost required for the proposed increased production level. The increase in total cost is known as:

a. controllable cost
d. out-of-pocket cost
b. differential cost
e. none of the above
c. opportunity cost
(AICPA adapted)

9. Faced with a make-or-buy decision, management should consider all of the following, *except*:

a. the quantity, quality, and dependability of supply of the items
b. the cost of making the items with the cost of buying them
c. more profitable alternative uses of the firm's own facilities
d. customer and supplier reactions
e. all of the above should be considered

10. Letter Company manufactures two products, Q and P, in a small building with limited capacity. The sales price, cost data, and production time are given below:

	Product Q	**Product P**
Sales price per unit.	$20	$17
Variable cost of producing and selling a unit	$13	$12
Hours to produce a unit	3	1

Based on this information, the contribution margin maximization objective function for a linear programming solution may be stated as:

a. 20Q + 17P
d. $4 \frac{1}{3}$ Q + 12P
b. 13Q + 12P
e. 7Q + 5P
c. 3Q + 1P
(AICPA adapted)

Part 4 ■ Problem

Although Sesame Company has the capacity to produce 10,000 units per month, current plans call for monthly production sales of only 8,000 units at $15 each. Costs per unit at the 8,000 unit level are as follows:

Direct materials	$ 4.00
Direct labor	2.50
Variable factory overhead	2.00
Fixed factory overhead	1.75
Variable marketing expense	.50
Fixed administrative expense	1.25
	$12.00

Instructions:

1. Determine whether the company should accept a special order for 1,000 units @ $9.50.

2. Determine the maximum unit price that the company should be willing to pay an outside supplier to manufacture 10,000 units of this product, assuming that $2,500 of fixed factory overhead would not be incurred if the product were made outside.

Part 5 ■ Problem

Studley Company manufactures Nerds for use in its assembly operation. Costs per unit for 1,000 units of Nerds are:

Direct materials	$ 5
Direct labor	17
Variable factory overhead	10
Fixed factory overhead	12
Total unit cost	$44

Collins Company has offered to sell Studley 1,000 units of Nerds for $45 each. If Studley accepts, some of the facilities presently used to manufacture Nerds could be used to help with the manufacture of Geeks, resulting in an additional contribution margin of $10,000 and eliminating two-thirds of the fixed factory overhead incurred in making Nerds.

Instructions: *Prepare a make-or-buy decision analysis.*

Part 6 ■ Problem

From a particular joint process, Roman Company produces three products—Anthony, Brutus, and Cassius. Each product may be sold at the point of split-off or processed further. Additional processing requires no special facilities, and production costs of further processing are entirely variable and traceable to the products involved. During the past year, these products were processed beyond split-off. The joint production cost for the year was $100,000. Sales value and costs needed to evaluate Roman's current production policy follow:

| | | | If Processed Further | |
Product	Units Produced	Sales Value at Split-Off	Sales Value	Added Cost
Anthony	10,000	$75,000	$90,000	$15,000
Brutus	8,000	60,000	72,000	20,000
Cassius	5,000	43,000	58,000	10,000

The joint cost is allocated to the products in proportion to the relative physical volume of output.

Instructions:

1. Determine the unit production cost most relevant to a sell-or-process further decision for units of Cassius.

2. Complete the following schedule for purposes of determining the products that the company should process further in order to maximize profits.

	Anthony	Brutus	Cassius
Sales value if processed further	$	$	$
Sales value at split-off.............................			
Added sales value	$	$	$
Added cost.......................................			
Difference in favor (against) processing further ...	$	$	$

Part 7 ■ Problem

Franklin-Gluck Company sells two products with the following characteristics:

	Cassette	Disk
Quantity sold..................................	50,000 units	25,000 units
Standard cost per unit:		
Fixed......................................	$ 5	$10
Variable...................................	12	18
	$17	$28
Sales price per unit.............................	$25	$26

Instructions:

1. Compute the profit per unit and the total, assuming that the firm operates at normal capacity and that the standard cost and the actual cost are the same.

2. Recommend whether the firm should continue its sale of both products, assuming that the fixed cost will remain the same in total whether either or both are produced and that more of one product cannot be sold in lieu of the other.

3. Decide whether it would be more profitable to drop Disk and add Super Disk, assuming that the same facilities can be used for the production of either and that Super Disk cost data are:

Quantity sold...	12,500 units
Standard cost per unit:	
Fixed..	$12
Variable...	20
	$32
Sales price per unit....................................	$50

Computations:

4. Compute the opportunity cost of producing Super Disk rather than Disk.

Part 8 ■ Problem
(The following problems are based on material in the Appendix.)

Planet Company produces two products, Apollos and Lunars, in two departments, Mixing and Molding. The mixing machines can be operated 80 hours per week, and the molding machines 60 hours per week. Each Apollo requires twice as much mixing time as a Lunar but requires only one-half as much molding time. Each Lunar requires one hour of work in each process. The contribution margin on each Apollo is $100,000, and on each Lunar is $80,000.

Instructions:

1. Complete the schedule below and draw the graph on the form provided to determine the product mix that the Planet Company should maintain to maximize the total contribution margin. (Round answers to the nearest whole unit.)

Department	Hours Available	Hours Required Per Apollo	Hours Required Per Lunar	Maximum Units Apollo	Maximum Units Lunar
Mixing........					
Molding.......					

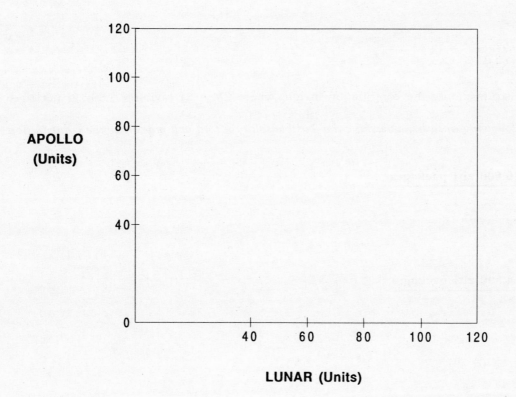

2. Determine the maximum weekly contribution margin figure. (Round all computations to the nearest whole number.)

Part 9 ■ Problem

Casa Roma Enterprises Inc. manufactures two products, ravioli and ziti. Each product must be processed in each of three departments: Mixing, Stuffing, and Cooking. The minutes needed to produce one bag of ravioli and one bag of ziti per department and the maximum possible minutes per department are:

Department	Production Minutes per Ravioli	Ziti	Maximum Capacity in Minutes
Mixing	3	4	48,000
Stuffing	4	3	45,000
Cooking	3	2	34,500

Other restrictions:
Ravioli   2,400 packages
Ziti   2,400 packages

The objective function is to maximize the contribution margin where CM = $1 ravioli + $.50 ziti package.

Instructions: *From the following answers, determine the feasible solution that will maximize the contribution margin:*

6,000 ravioli and 6,000 ziti packages

Mixing . . . .
Stuffing . . . .
Cooking . . . .

7,200 ravioli and 4,800 ziti packages

Mixing . . . .
Stuffing . . . .
Cooking . . . .

8,400 ravioli and 3,600 ziti packages

Mixing . . . .
Stuffing . . . .
Cooking . . . .

9,600 ravioli and 2,400 ziti packages

Mixing . . . .
Stuffing . . . .
Cooking . . . .

Conclusion:

Planning for Capital Expenditures

REVIEW SUMMARY

I.   Purpose of the Chapter

This chapter explains the need for a structured framework for planning capital expenditures, cites examples of ethical problems in capital budgeting, and lists different objectives for capital expenditures. It also clarifies capital expenditure projects, identifies the amount and timing of cash flows, adjusts cash flows for anticipated inflation and the expected effect of income taxes, and lists the steps in controlling capital expenditures.

II.   Planning for Capital Expenditures

Capital budgeting is the process of planning the continuing investment of an organization's resources and the monitoring of that investment. **Capital expenditures** involve long-term commitments of resources to realize future benefits. Planning for capital expenditures consists of relating plans to objectives, structuring the framework, searching for proposals, budgeting the expenditures, and requesting authority for the expenditures. The management accountant has an ethical responsibility to make sure that the company's policies and procedures are not circumvented and to make sure that the data used in the evaluation of capital projects are reliable and realistic.

III.   Evaluating Capital Expenditures

Evaluating capital expenditures refers to the basic theory, techniques, and procedures for the appraisal and reappraisal of projects throughout the course of their development. Capital expenditure projects can be classified as (1) equipment replacement expenditures, (2) expansion investments, and (3) improvements of existing products or additions of new products.

IV.   Estimating Cash Flows

The amount and timing of cash inflows and outflows over the life of the capital project must be estimated. The **initial cash outflow** usually consists of the purchase price of one or more assets (or a down payment) and the cost of installing the property and getting it ready for use. In addition, operating cash outflows are incurred each period in the operation of the project, plus annual payments if purchased on installment or leased. **Cash inflows** received over the life of a project include revenues from the additional business generated by the project and/or cost savings. At the end of the life of a capital project, a cash inflow, known as a **salvage value**, may be generated from the sale of the property used in the project. The estimated cash inflows from the acquisition of an advanced technology should include an estimate of the net cash inflows that are likely to be lost if the technology is not adopted.

V.   Inflationary Considerations in Estimating Cash Flows

If inflation is expected to occur during the life of the project, the cash inflows should be adjusted to reflect the anticipated effect of changing prices. Unless the cash flows of a capital expenditure proposal are adjusted for the expected effects of inflation, the cash inflows over the life of the project would be understated. If the impact of inflation is expected to be different for the cash inflows and outflows, separate inflation adjustments must be made for each.

VI.   Income Tax Considerations in Estimating Cash Flows

The effect of income taxes on cash flows is an important consideration in planning and evaluating capital expenditures. Depreciation allowed for income tax purposes reduces taxable income and, consequently, tax liability, which directly affects cash flow. For federal income tax purposes, gain recognized on the disposal of depreciable property (other than buildings) is treated as ordinary income to the extent of tax depreciation prior to disposal. Gain is generally not recognized on the trade-in of used business property in exchange for replacement property. Although the **investment tax credit** has not been a stable feature of income tax law, it is an important capital expenditure consideration during periods when it is available because it reduces income tax expense at the end of the project's first year.

VII. Controlling Capital Expenditures

When a project or a series of projects has been approved, methods, techniques, and procedures must be set in motion to permit the control and review of all project elements until completion. PERT/cost uses the network scheme to show the relationships of the multiple activities required to complete the average to large-scale project. A follow-up or postcompletion audit involves comparing and reporting results as related to the outcome predicted when the investment project was evaluated and approved. It affords a test of the existing planning and control procedure and allows for the possibility of reinforcing successful projects, salvaging or terminating failing projects, and improving upon future investment proposals and decisions.

Part 1 ■ True/False

Instructions: *Indicate whether each of the following statements is **True** or **False**.*

True/False

1. Capital expenditures have a significant long-term effect on the economic well-being of the firm. . . . . _____

2. The higher the level at which a capital expenditure decision is authorized, the greater the need for guidelines extending to detailed procedures and standards. _____

3. The capital expenditures budget is typically prepared for a one-year period. . _____

4. Authority to commit funds to a capital project should be formally documented. _____

5. Accelerated depreciation increases the impact of inflation by slowing the recovery of capital expenditures. . . . . _____

6. In equipment replacement decisions, the original cost of the present facility is a cost that is relevant to the decision. . . . . _____

7. The degree of uncertainty in an equipment replacement decision is much smaller than in a decision to enlarge an existing plant. . . . . _____

8. An ethical consideration for the accountant in capital budgeting is that the economic benefits of capital projects may be exaggerated to increase the likelihood of approval. . . . . _____

9. In most cases, the accountant should first discuss a perceived ethical problem with the individuals involved. . . . . _____

10. Strategic consideration and managerial intuition often drive investment decisions rather than evaluations of the results of analytical techniques applied to quantitative data. . . . . _____

11. The movement toward CIM, robotics, and FMS is motivated primarily by cost savings. _____

12. The amount of accounting income to be generated from a capital expenditure is not relevant to the investment decision. . . . . _____

13. The estimated cash inflows from the acquisition of an advanced technology should include an estimate of the net cash inflows that are likely to be lost if the technology is not adopted. . . . . _____

14. Unless the cash flows of a capital expenditure proposal are adjusted for the expected effects of inflation, the cash inflows over the life of the project would be overstated. _____

15. The use of PERT/cost is appropriate for evaluating capital expenditures where more than one estimate is needed due to risk and uncertainty. . . . . _____

Part 2 ■ Matching

Instructions: *On the line at the left of each of the following items, place the letter from the columns below that identifies the term that best matches the statement. No letter should be used more than once.*

_____ 1. The process of planning the continuing investment of an organization's resources and the monitoring of that investment.

_____ 2. Involve long-term commitments of resources to realize future benefits.

_____ 3. Involves plant enlargements for the purpose of enhancing existing markets or invading new markets.

_____ 4. Typically prepared for a one-year period.

_____ 5. May require development of new processes or modernization of facilities, or both.

_____ 6. Include revenues from the additional business generated by the capital project and/or the cost savings from the project.

_____ 7. Uses the network scheme to show the relationships of the multiple activities required to complete the average to large-scale project.

_____ 8. Made to the cash flows to reflect the anticipated effect of changing prices.

_____ 9. Represents the amount of cash inflow expected from the final sale of the property.

_____ 10. Prescribes the capitalization of interest costs incurred in acquiring assets that require a period of time to be made ready for their intended use.

_____ 11. A system for recovering the cost of capital expenditures required for federal income taxes for tangible, depreciable property placed in service after 1980.

_____ 12. Increased the number of property classes and lengthened the recovery periods of most kinds of depreciable assets under the Tax Reform Act of 1986.

_____ 13. An unstable feature of the income tax law; but when available, an important capital expenditure consideration because it reduces income tax expense in a project's first tax year.

_____ 14. Involves comparing and reporting results as related to the outcome predicted when the investment was evaluated and approved.

_____ 15. Usually consists of the purchase price of one or more assets and the cost of installing the property and getting it ready for use.

a.	salvage value	**i.**	MACRS
b.	capital expenditures	**j.**	cash inflows
c.	ACRS	**k.**	capital expenditures budget
d.	investment tax credit	**l.**	SFAS No. 34
e.	initial cash outflow	**m.**	inflation adjustment
f.	expansion investment	**n.**	PERT/cost
g.	postcompletion audit	**o.**	improvement expenditures
h.	capital budgeting		

Part 3 ■ Multiple Choice

Instructions: *On the line at the left of each of the following items, place the letter of the choice that most correctly completes each item.*

_____ 1. In selecting the purchase of one of two machines to replace an old machine, the management of Niles Company should consider as relevant:

   a. historical costs associated with the old machine
   b. future costs that will be classified as variable rather than fixed
   c. future costs that will be different under the two alternatives
   d. future costs that will be classified as fixed rather than variable
   e. none of the above   *(AICPA adapted)*

_____ 2. Common problems related to ethical considerations in the capital budgeting process include all of the following, *except*:

   a. superiors and associates sometimes apply pressure to circumvent the approval process
   b. pressure may exist to write-off or devalue assets below their true value to justify replacement
   c. the economic benefit of capital projects may be exaggerated to increase the likelihood of approval
   d. the accountant may mistakenly go to the accounting supervisor first, rather than first discussing it with individuals involved in the capital budgeting decision
   e. all of the above are ethical problems related to the capital budgeting process

_____ 3. The acquisition of new machinery to take the place of obsolete assets is an example of a(n):

   a. replacement expenditure   d. improvement expenditure
   b. allowance expenditure   e. none of the above
   c. expansion expenditure

_____ 4. Plant enlargement for the purpose of enhancing existing markets or invading new markets is an example of a(n):

   a. replacement expenditure   d. improvement expenditure
   b. allowance expenditure   e. none of the above
   c. expansion expenditure

_____ 5. Changing product quality or design to counter the actions of competitors is an example of a(n):

   a. replacement expenditure   d. improvement expenditure
   b. allowance expenditure   e. none of the above
   c. expansion expenditure

_____ 6. Primary motivations for computer integrated manufacturing, robotics, and flexible manufacturing systems include all of the following, *except*:

   a. the need to improve product quality in the face of increasing competition
   b. the desire to be able to adjust production output quantity quickly to satisfy changing consumer demand
   c. cost savings
   d. the desire to be able to adjust production output variety quickly to satisfy changing consumer demand
   e. all of the above are primary motivations

_____ 7. All of the following are common cash inflows related to capital expenditure proposals, *except*:

  a. additional revenues from increased sales
  b. computer programming and fine tuning
  c. reduction in inventory carrying costs
  d. salvage value at the end of the project
  e. all of the above are cash inflows

_____ 8. The system for recovering the cost of capital expenditures through federal income tax deductions that was required for tangible, depreciable property placed in service after 1980 is known as:

  a. MACRS   **d.** 150% declining balance
  b. 200% declining balance   **e.** none of the above
  c. ACRS

_____ 9. A machine that cost $100,000 and is fully depreciated is sold for $25,000. It is then used as a down-payment on the purchase of a new machine costing $150,000. Assuming a 30% tax rate, the out-of-pocket cost of the new machine would be:

  a. $132,500   **d.** $75,000
  b. $150,000   **e.** none of the above
  c. $125,000

_____ 10. A machine that cost $100,000 and is fully depreciated is allowed a $25,000 trade-in on a replacement machine costing $150,000. Assuming a 30% tax rate, the out-of-pocket cost of the new machine would be:

  a. $132,500   **d.** $75,000
  b. $150,000   **e.** none of the above
  c. $125,000

Part 4 ■ Problem

England Corporation is considering purchasing a new machine to be used to manufacture a new product, called Brits, which will sell for $50 a unit. Variable manufacturing cost is expected to be $20 for each unit of Brits manufactured, and variable marketing cost, $5 for each unit sold. The machine being considered could produce 15,000 units a year, all of which the Marketing Department believes could be sold for $50 a unit. The proposed machine would cost $1,000,000. Although the machine would probably last 10 years, management believes that the product's life cycle would be only 5 years. The salvage value of the new machine at the end of the product's 5 year life cycle is expected to be $200,000. Management does not believe the machine could be used to manufacture any of the company's other products.

Instructions: *Using the schedule appearing on page 217, compute the pretax net cash inflows expected from the capital expenditure proposal for each year, and ignoring the effect of income taxes, determine the excess of cash inflows from all sources over the cost of the machine.*

Year	Estimated Demand in Units	Unit Sales Price	Unit Variable Cost	Unit Contribution Margin	Net Pretax Cash Inflows From Sales
1					
2					
3					
4					
5					

Total net pretax cash inflows from sales. . . . . _____

Initial cash outflow (cost of asset). . . . .

Less pretax estimated salvage value. . . . .   _____   _____

Excess of net pretax cash inflows over cost. . . . .   _____

Part 5 ■ Problem

Skippy Corporation is considering a capital expenditure proposal which will require an initial cash outlay of $100,000. The project life is expected to be 5 years. The estimated salvage value for the equipment (based on today's market price for similar used 5-year old equipment) is $10,000. Estimated annual net cash inflows from operations during the life of the project will follow:

Year	Estimated Annual Cash Inflow
1	$20,000
2	25,000
3	25,000
4	25,000
5	15,000

Instructions: *Compute the excess of cash inflows over cash outflows assuming management expects a constant 6% rate of inflation during the 5-year period. (Round your price level index to three decimal places.)*

Year		Estimated Net Pretax Cash Inflows	6% Annual Price-level Adjustment	Price-level Adjusted Net Cash Inflows
1				
2				
3				
4				
5				

Total price-level adjusted net pretax cash inflows
    from operations. . . . .   _____

Plus cash inflows from salvage. . . . .   _____

Price-level adjustment . . . .   _____

Total price level adjusted net pretax cash inflows over initial
    cash outflow . . . .

Less initial cash outflow . . . .   _____

Excess of net pretax cash inflows over initial cash outflow . . . . . .   _____

Part 6 ■ Problem

Autry Company is considering a capital expenditure with the following estimated net cash inflows:

Year	Estimated Pretax Inflation Adjusted Net Cash Inflow
1	$50,000
2	60,000
3	70,000
4	80,000
5	50,000
6	35,000
7	20,000

The equipment required for the project would have an initial cost of $300,000, and it is not expected to have any salvage value at the end of the life of the project. The equipment will be depreciated using the straight-line method over its economic life of 7 years for book purposes; however, it qualifies as 5-year property for tax purposes. The company's effective tax rate is 40%.

Instructions: *Determine the estimated after-tax net cash inflows for each of the project's 7 years, and the total excess of cash inflows over the life of the project over cash outflows. (Use the MACRS rates provided to compute tax depreciation.)*

Year	(1) Estimated Inflation Adjusted Net Cash Inflows	(2) Tax Depreciation*	(3) Taxable Income (Loss) (1) - (2)	(4) Tax Liability With 40% Tax Rate 40% x (3)	(5) Net After-tax Cash Inflows (1) - (4)
1					
2					
3					
4					
5					
6					
7					

Total net after-tax cash inflows . . . .

Less initial cash outflow to purchase system . . . .

Excess of net after-tax cash inflows over initial cash outflow . . . .

*

Year	MACRS 5-year Recovery Rate	Depreciable Basis	Tax Depreciation
1	0.200		
2	0.320		
3	0.192		
4	0.115		
5	0.115		
6	0.058		
	1.000		

Economic Evaluation of Capital Expenditures

REVIEW SUMMARY

I.   Purpose of the Chapter

The purposes of this chapter include defining and computing the cost of capital, illustrating the computation of the payback period, and computing the accounting rate of return for a capital expenditure proposal. Additionally, the concept of time value of money is explained, and the computation of the net present value and the internal rate of return for a capital expenditure is illustrated.

II.   The Cost of Capital

The **cost of capital** represents the expected return that investors demand for a given level of risk. If a company obtains funds by some combination of bonds, preferred and common stock, retained earnings, and bank loans to achieve or maintain a particular capital structure; then the cost of capital is the weighted-average cost of each money source. The cost of bonds is the after-tax rate of interest; preferred stock is the dividend per share divided by the current market price per share; common stock and retained earnings are the expected earnings per common share divided by the current market price of the stock.

III.   Economic Evaluation Techniques

The following four capital expenditure evaluation techniques are in current usage: (1) the payback (payout) period method, (2) accounting rate of return method, (3) the net present value method, and (4) the internal rate of return method.

A.   Payback Period Method

The payback period method measures the length of time required by a project to recover its initial outlay. The calculated payback period is then compared to the payback period acceptable to management for that particular type of project.

B.   Accounting Rate of Return Method

Under the accounting rate of return method, an investment proposal is evaluated by comparing the accounting rate of return on the original investment with a target rate of return. The accounting rate of return on original investment is computed as follows:

$$\frac{\text{Net income}}{\text{Economic life}} + \text{Original investment}$$

Another approach is to divide the average annual net income by the average investment rather than the original investment.

C.   Net Present Value Method

Using the net present value method, the estimated results of an investment proposal can be stated at its cash equivalent at the present time. It is preferable to discount all proposals at a constant rate, the cost of capital. If the true rate of return is greater than the cost of capital discount rate, then the net present value will be positive and the project should be accepted.

D.   Internal Rate of Return Method

In the internal rate of return method, the discount rate is not known but is defined as the rate at which the sum of positive present values equals the sum of negative present values. The internal rate of return can be determined by trial and error by computing net present value at various discount rates to find the rate at which the net present value is zero. The internal rate of return method permits management to maximize corporate profits by selecting proposals with the highest rates of return as long as the rates are higher than the company's own cost of capital.

IV.   The Error Cushion

A project whose estimated desirability is near a cutoff point for the type of project being evaluated affords little cushion for errors. A higher degree of sophistication in evaluating a project, at a higher cost of obtaining the data, may be necessary to add confidence when the evaluation is close to a cutoff point or when two or more project alternatives yield about the same "best" answer.

V. Purchase Versus Leasing

The possibility of a lease arrangement as an alternative to purchasing a capital asset can be evaluated by determining the incremental annual cost of leasing versus purchasing. Generally the capital expenditure or investment decision is first justified, followed by the lease or financing decision. Usually the lease is the more expensive alternative because a lease avoids some ownership risks for which a price must be paid.

Part 1 ■ True/False

Instructions: *Indicate whether each of the following statements is* ***True*** *or* ***False***.

	True/False

1. The specific cost of financing a specific project often is called the weighted-average cost of capital. . . . . _____

2. The cost of capital for preferred stock is the dividend per share divided by the current market price per share. . . . . _____

3. An advantage of the payback period method is that it considers the time value of money. . . . . _____

4. An advantage of the accounting rate of return method is that it considers income over the entire life of the project. . . . . _____

5. A net present value of zero would indicate that a project's rate of return was exactly equal to the cost of capital rate for that type of project. . . . . _____

6. A disadvantage of the net present value method is that management must determine, in advance, the discount rate to be used. . . . . _____

7. An advantage of the internal rate of return method is that it is more easily interpreted by managers than the net present value or the net present value index. . . . . . . _____

8. The cost of capital for bonds is the after-tax rate of interest. . . . . _____

9. A disadvantage of the payback period method is that it excludes cash flows that may occur beyond the payback period. . . . . _____

10. A disadvantage of the accounting rate of return method is that it ignores the time value of money. . . . . _____

11. An advantage of the net present value method is that it allows for different discount rates over the life of the project. . . . . _____

12. A disadvantage of the internal rate of return method is that the percentage figures computed do not lend themselves to a generally sound, uniform ranking of projects. _____

13. Discounting using the net present value method implies that cash inflows can be reinvested to earn the rate earned by the investment being evaluated. . . . . _____

14. When one alternative is clearly superior to others, there is a smaller error cushion than when two or more of the best alternatives indicate approximately the same expected results. . . . . _____

15. In a purchase versus leasing decision, the investment decision should be made first, followed by the lease or financing decision. . . . . _____

Part 2 ■ Matching

Instructions: *On the line at the left of each of the following items, place the letter from the columns below that identifies the term that best matches the statement. No letter should be used more than once.*

_____   **1.** The specific cost of financing a specific project.

_____   **2.** Technique that measures the length of time required by the project to recover the initial cash outlay.

_____   **3.** Computes an average annual return on a project by dividing annual net income by the original investment.

_____   **4.** The cash equivalent at the current time of cash flows to be received or paid in the future.

_____   **5.** Includes the cost of capital rate plus an additional component to compensate for risk.

_____   **6.** Computed to overcome the problem of comparing projects that require different initial increments, replacing the net present value dollar figure.

_____   **7.** Represents the estimated value of a project at the end of its expected useful life.

_____   **8.** Represents the expected return investors demand for a given level of risk.

_____   **9.** Computed on the basis of proportions and rates for bonds, preferred stock, common stock, and retained earnings.

_____   **10.** Is usually the more expensive alternative because it avoids some ownership risks for which a price must be paid.

_____   **11.** Presence indicates that the true rate of return is greater than the cost of capital discount rate.

_____   **12.** When this method of evaluating capital expenditures is used, the discount rate is not known but is defined as the rate at which the sum of positive present values equals the sum of negative present values.

_____   **13.** Virtually nonexistent when a project's estimated desirability is near a cutoff point for that particular type of project.

_____   **14.** Should be made prior to the lease or financing decision.

_____   **15.** Enables management to determine the minimum life for a project necessary to recover the original investment and earn a desired rate of return on the investment.

a.	weighted-average cost of capital	**i.**	internal rate of return
b.	payback period method	**j.**	net present value index
c.	positive net present value	**k.**	present value
d.	error cushion	**l.**	leasing
e.	present value payback method	**m.**	cost of capital
f.	accounting rate of return method	**n.**	terminal value
g.	capital expenditure decision	**o.**	hurdle rate
h.	marginal cost of capital		

Part 3 ■ Multiple Choice

Instructions: *On the line at the left of each of the following items, place the letter of the choice that most correctly completes each item.*

_____ **1.** The specific cost of financing a specific project often is called the:

  a. cost of capital   **d.** hurdle rate
  b. marginal cost of capital   **e.** discount rate
  c. weighted-average cost of capital

_____ **2.** For a project such as a plant investment, the return that investors demand for investing in a firm is known as:

  a. internal rate of return   **d.** cost of capital
  b. net present value   **e.** accounting rate of return
  c. payback   *(AICPA adapted)*

_____ **3.** Danny Company is planning to purchase a new machine. The payback period is estimated to be six years. After-tax cash flow is estimated to be $2,000 yearly for the first three years and $3,000 yearly for the next three years of the payback period. Annual depreciation of $1,500 will be charged to income for each of the six years of the payback period. The machine will cost:

  a. $15,000   **d.** $6,000
  b. $12,000   **e.** none of the above
  c. $9,000   *(AICPA adapted)*

_____ **4.** An advantage of using the payback method is that the method is:

  a. precise in estimates of profitability
  b. used to select investments yielding a quick return of cash
  c. based on discounted cash-flow data
  d. sensitive to the life of the project being evaluated
  e. all of the above   *(AICPA adapted)*

_____ **5.** The net present value and internal rate of return methods of evaluating capital expenditure proposals are superior to the payback method because they:

  a. are easier to implement
  b. consider cash flow over the entire life of the project
  c. require less input
  d. reflect the effects of depreciation and income tax
  e. all of the above   *(AICPA adapted)*

_____ **6.** A planned factory expansion project has an estimated initial cost of $800,000. Using a 20% discount rate, the present value of future cost savings from the expansion is $843,000. To yield exactly a 20% internal rate of return, the actual investment cost cannot exceed the $800,000 estimate by more than:

  a. $160,000   **d.** $1,075
  b. $20,000   **e.** $0
  c. $43,000   *(AICPA adapted)*

_____ 7. On January 1, a company invested in an asset with a useful life of three years. The company's expected rate of return is 10%. The cash flow and present and future value factors for the three years are as follows:

Year	Cash Inflow From the Asset	Present Value of $1 at 10%	Future Value of $1 at 10%
1	$ 8,000	.91	1.10
2	$ 9,000	.83	1.21
3	$10,000	.75	1.33

All cash inflows are assumed to occur at year end. If the asset generates a positive net present value of $2,000, what was the amount of the original investment?

a. $20,250
b. $22,250
c. $30,991

d. $33,991
e. none of the above

_____ 8. The effectiveness of the net present value method has been appropriately questioned as a capital expenditure evaluation technique because:

a. it does not consider the relative size of computing projects
b. the average return on investment method is usually more accurate and useful
c. the payback method is theoretically more reliable
d. the computation involves some difficult mathematical applications that most accountants cannot perform
e. all of the above

(AICPA adapted)

_____ 9. Jarvis Inc., a calendar year company, purchased a new machine for $28,000 on January 1. The machine has an estimated useful life of eight years with no salvage value and is being depreciated on the straight-line basis. The accounting rate of return is expected to be 15% on the initial investment. On the assumption of a uniform cash inflow, this investment is expected to provide annual cash flow from operations, net of income taxes, of:

a. $3,500
b. $4,025
c. $4,200

d. $7,700
e. none of the above

(AICPA adapted)

_____ 10. Two projects have an initial outlay of $497, and each has an income stream lasting three years. Project A returns $200 per year for the three years. Project B returns $200 for the first two years and $248 for the third year.

Present Value - Amount

n	8%	10%	12%	14%
1	.9259	.9091	.8929	.8772
2	.8575	.8264	.7972	.7695
3	.7938	.7513	.7118	.6750

The internal rate of return for Project B is:

a. 14%
b. 12%
c. 10%

d. 8%
e. none of the above

Part 4 ■ Problem

Regis Company wishes to compute a weighted-average cost of capital for use in evaluating capital expenditure proposals. Earnings, capital structure, and current market prices of the company's securities are:

Earnings:

Earnings before interest and tax	$ 300,000
Interest expense on bonds	75,000
Pretax earnings	$ 225,000
Income tax (assume 30% tax rate)	67,500
After-tax earnings	$ 157,500
Preferred stock dividends.	36,000
Earnings available to common stockholders.	$ 121,500
Common stock dividends.	25,000
Retained earnings	$ 96,500

Capital structure:

Mortgage bonds, 15%, 20 years.	$ 500,000
Preferred stock, 12%, $100 par	250,000
Common stock, no par, 50,000 shares	300,000
Retained earnings (equity of common stockholders).	450,000
	$1,500,000

Market price of the company's securities:

Preferred stock	$96
Common stock	15

Instructions: *Determine the company's cost of capital. (Round all computations to three decimal places.)*

Funds	Proportion of Funds	After-Tax Cost	Weighted Cost
Bonds			
Preferred Stock.			
Common stock and retained earnings	_____		_____
	==========		==========

Computations:

Part 5 ■ Problem

Rocky Ridge Amusement Park is considering the purchase of a new ride costing $100,000. The ride is to be depreciated using the MACRS recovery percentages for five-year property. The salvage value is zero. Assume a 30% tax rate, a cost of capital of 12%, and an economic life of six years. The estimated cash benefit before taxes is given in the table below. MACRS rates are:

Year	Rate
1	20.0%
2	32.0%
3	19.2%
4	11.5%
5	11.5%
6	5.8%

Instructions:

1. Complete the table.

Year	Pretax Cash Benefit	Annual Depreciation*	Taxable Income	Federal Income Tax	Net After-tax Cash Inflow
1	$45,000	$	$	$	$
2	50,000				
3	44,000				
4	38,000				
5	34,000				
6	10,000				

Computations: $_____

2. Determine the following:

(a) The payback period. (Round to the nearest tenth of a year.)

Year	Cash Flow	Needed	Balance	Payback Years Required
1	$	$	$	
2				
3				
4				
5				
6				
Total payback period in years				

(b) The accounting rate of return on original investment. (Round to the nearest tenth of a percent.)

(c) The accounting of rate return on average investment. (Round to the nearest tenth of a percent.)

(d) The net present value assuming that all cash inflows occur at year end. (Use the present value tables on pages 230 and 231, and round all computations to the nearest dollar.)

Year	Cash (Outflow) Inflow	Present Value of $1 @ 12%	Net Present Value of Cash Flow
0	$		$
1			
2			
3			
4			
5			
6			
Net present value			$

(e) The internal rate of return. (Round to the nearest tenth of a percent. Use the present value tables on pages 230 and 231, and round all computations to the nearest dollar.)

Year	Cash (Outflow) Inflow	Present Value of $1	Net Present Value of Cash Flow @ 25%	Present Value of $1	Net Present Value of Cash Flow @ 26%
0	$		$		$
1					
2					
3					
4					
5					
6					
			$		$

Internal rate of return:

Part 6 ■ Problem

Buffet Enterprises plans to operate a sight-seeing boat in Montego Bay. In negotiating the purchase of a new boat from Parrot Inc., Buffet learned that Parrot would lease the boat to them as an alternative to selling it outright. Through such an arrangement, Buffet would not pay the $300,000 purchase price but would lease it for $70,000 annually. Buffet expects the boat to last for ten years, after which its value would be $30,000.

The annual net cash flow, excluding any consideration of lease payments and income tax, is expected to be $100,000. The company's income tax rate is 40%, and its cost of capital is 12%. The straight-line depreciation method is to be used and salvage value may be ignored for tax purposes. Assume that all cash inflows and outflows other than the initial purchase of the boat occur at year end.

Instructions:

1. Use the net present value method to evaluate each alternative. (Use the present value tables on pages 230 and 231.)

    (a) Purchase:

(b) Lease:

2. Give your decision.

PRESENT VALUE OF $1

Future Years	1%	2%	4%	6%	8%	10%	12%	14%	15%	16%	18%	20%	22%	24%	25%	26%	28%	30%	35%	40%	45%	50%
1	.990	.980	.962	.943	.926	.909	.893	.877	.870	.862	.847	.833	.820	.806	.800	.794	.781	.769	.741	.714	.690	.667
2	.980	.961	.925	.890	.857	.826	.797	.769	.756	.743	.718	.694	.672	.650	.640	.630	.610	.592	.549	.510	.476	.444
3	.971	.942	.889	.840	.794	.751	.712	.675	.658	.641	.609	.579	.551	.524	.512	.500	.477	.455	.406	.364	.328	.296
4	.961	.924	.855	.792	.735	.683	.636	.592	.572	.552	.516	.482	.451	.423	.410	.397	.373	.350	.301	.260	.260	.198
5	.951	.906	.822	.747	.681	.621	.567	.519	.497	.476	.437	.402	.370	.341	.328	.315	.291	.269	.223	.186	.156	.132
6	.942	.888	.790	.705	.630	.564	.507	.456	.432	.410	.370	.335	.303	.275	.262	.250	.227	.207	.165	.133	.108	.088
7	.933	.871	.760	.665	.583	.513	.452	.400	.376	.354	.314	.279	.249	.222	.210	.198	.178	.159	.122	.095	.074	.059
8	.923	.853	.731	.627	.540	.467	.404	.351	.327	.305	.266	.233	.204	.179	.168	.157	.139	.123	.091	.068	.051	.039
9	.914	.837	.703	.592	.500	.424	.361	.308	.284	.263	.225	.194	.167	.144	.134	.125	.108	.094	.067	.048	.035	.026
10	.905	.820	.676	.558	.463	.386	.322	.270	.247	.227	.191	.162	.137	.116	.107	.099	.085	.073	.050	.035	.024	.017
11	.896	.804	.650	.527	.429	.350	.287	.237	.215	.195	.162	.135	.112	.094	.086	.079	.066	.056	.037	.025	.017	.012
12	.887	.788	.625	.497	.397	.319	.257	.208	.187	.168	.137	.112	.092	.076	.069	.062	.052	.043	.027	.018	.012	.008
13	.879	.773	.601	.469	.368	.290	.229	.182	.163	.145	.116	.093	.075	.061	.055	.050	.043	.033	.020	.013	.008	.005
14	.870	.758	.577	.442	.340	.263	.205	.160	.141	.125	.099	.078	.062	.049	.044	.039	.032	.025	.015	.009	.006	.003
15	.861	.743	.555	.417	.315	.239	.183	.140	.123	.108	.084	.065	.051	.040	.035	.031	.025	.020	.011	.006	.004	.002
16	.853	.728	.534	.394	.292	.218	.163	.123	.107	.093	.071	.054	.042	.032	.028	.025	.019	.015	.008	.005	.003	.002
17	.844	.714	.513	.371	.270	.198	.146	.108	.093	.080	.060	.045	.034	.026	.023	.020	.015	.012	.006	.003	.002	.001
18	.836	.700	.494	.350	.250	.180	.130	.095	.081	.069	.051	.038	.028	.021	.018	.016	.012	.009	.005	.002	.001	.001
19	.828	.686	.475	.331	.232	.164	.116	.083	.070	.060	.043	.031	.023	.017	.014	.012	.009	.007	.003	.002	.001	.001
20	.820	.673	.456	.312	.215	.149	.104	.073	.061	.051	.037	.026	.019	.014	.012	.010	.007	.005	.002	.001	.001	
21	.811	.660	.439	.294	.199	.135	.093	.064	.053	.044	.031	.022	.015	.011	.009	.008	.006	.004	.002	.001		
22	.803	.647	.422	.278	.184	.123	.083	.056	.046	.038	.026	.018	.013	.009	.007	.006	.004	.003	.001	.001		
23	.795	.634	.406	.262	.170	.112	.074	.049	.040	.033	.022	.015	.010	.007	.006	.005	.003	.002	.001			
24	.788	.622	.390	.247	.158	.102	.066	.043	.035	.028	.019	.013	.008	.006	.005	.004	.003	.002	.001			
25	.780	.610	.375	.233	.146	.092	.059	.038	.030	.024	.016	.010	.007	.005	.004	.003	.002	.001	.001			
26	.772	.598	.361	.220	.135	.084	.053	.033	.026	.021	.014	.009	.006	.004	.003	.002	.002	.001				
27	.764	.586	.347	.207	.125	.076	.047	.029	.023	.018	.011	.007	.005	.003	.002	.002	.001	.001				
28	.757	.574	.333	.196	.116	.069	.042	.026	.020	.016	.010	.006	.004	.002	.002	.002	.001	.001				
29	.749	.563	.321	.185	.107	.063	.037	.022	.017	.014	.008	.005	.003	.002	.002	.001	.001	.001				
30	.742	.552	.308	.174	.099	.057	.033	.020	.015	.012	.007	.004	.003	.002	.001	.001	.001					
40	.672	.453	.208	.097	.046	.022	.011	.005	.004	.003	.001	.001										
50	.608	.372	.141	.054	.021	.009	.003	.001	.001	.001												

PRESENT VALUE OF $1 RECEIVED OR PAID ANNUALLY FOR EACH OF THE NEXT N YEARS

Future Years	1%	2%	4%	6%	8%	10%	12%	14%	15%	16%	18%	20%	22%	24%	25%	26%	28%	30%	35%	40%	45%	50%
1	.990	.980	.962	.943	.926	.909	.893	.877	.870	.862	.847	.833	.820	.806	.800	.794	.781	.769	.741	.714	.690	.667
2	1.970	1.942	1.886	1.833	1.783	1.736	1.690	1.647	1.626	1.605	1.566	1.528	1.492	1.457	1.440	1.424	1.392	1.361	1.289	1.224	1.165	1.111
3	2.941	2.884	2.775	2.673	2.577	2.487	2.402	2.322	2.283	2.246	2.174	2.106	2.042	1.981	1.952	1.923	1.868	1.816	1.696	1.589	1.493	1.407
4	3.902	3.808	3.630	3.465	3.312	3.170	3.037	2.914	2.855	2.798	2.690	2.589	2.494	2.404	2.362	2.320	2.241	2.166	1.997	1.849	1.720	1.605
5	4.853	4.713	4.452	4.212	3.993	3.791	3.605	3.433	3.352	3.274	3.127	2.991	2.864	2.745	2.689	2.635	2.532	2.436	2.220	2.035	1.876	1.737
6	5.795	5.601	5.242	4.917	4.623	4.355	4.111	3.889	3.784	3.685	3.498	3.326	3.167	3.020	2.951	2.885	2.759	2.643	2.385	2.168	1.983	1.824
7	6.728	6.472	6.002	5.582	5.206	4.868	4.564	4.288	4.160	4.039	3.812	3.605	3.416	3.242	3.161	3.083	2.937	2.802	2.508	2.263	2.057	1.883
8	7.652	7.325	6.733	6.210	5.747	5.335	4.968	4.639	4.487	4.344	4.078	3.837	3.619	3.421	3.329	3.241	3.076	2.925	2.598	2.331	2.108	1.922
9	8.566	8.163	7.435	6.802	6.247	5.759	5.328	4.946	4.772	4.607	4.303	4.031	3.786	3.566	3.463	3.366	3.184	3.019	2.665	2.379	2.144	1.948
10	9.471	8.983	8.111	7.360	6.710	6.145	5.650	5.216	5.019	4.833	4.494	4.192	3.923	3.682	3.571	3.465	3.269	3.092	2.715	2.414	2.168	1.965
11	10.368	9.787	8.760	7.887	7.139	6.495	5.988	5.453	5.234	5.029	4.656	4.327	4.035	3.776	3.656	3.544	3.335	3.147	2.752	2.438	2.185	1.977
12	11.255	10.575	9.385	8.384	7.536	6.814	6.194	5.660	5.421	5.197	4.793	4.439	4.127	3.851	3.725	3.606	3.387	3.190	2.779	2.456	2.196	1.985
13	12.134	11.348	9.986	8.853	7.904	7.103	6.424	5.842	5.583	5.342	4.910	4.533	4.203	3.912	3.780	3.656	3.427	3.223	2.799	2.468	2.204	1.990
14	13.004	12.106	10.563	9.295	8.244	7.367	6.628	6.002	5.724	5.468	5.008	4.611	4.265	3.962	3.824	3.695	3.459	3.249	2.814	2.477	2.210	1.993
15	13.865	12.849	11.118	9.712	8.559	7.606	6.811	6.142	5.847	5.575	5.092	4.675	4.315	4.001	3.859	3.726	3.483	3.268	2.825	2.484	2.214	1.995
16	14.718	13.578	11.652	10.106	8.851	7.824	6.974	6.265	5.954	5.669	5.162	4.730	4.357	4.033	3.887	3.751	3.503	3.283	2.834	2.489	2.216	1.997
17	15.562	14.292	12.166	10.477	9.122	8.022	7.120	6.373	6.047	5.749	5.222	4.775	4.391	4.059	3.910	3.771	3.518	3.295	2.840	2.492	2.218	1.998
18	16.398	14.992	12.659	10.828	9.372	8.201	7.250	6.467	6.128	5.818	5.273	4.812	4.419	4.080	3.928	3.786	3.529	3.304	2.844	2.494	2.219	1.999
19	17.226	15.678	13.134	11.158	9.604	8.365	7.366	6.550	6.198	5.877	5.316	4.844	4.442	4.097	3.942	3.799	3.539	3.311	2.848	2.496	2.220	1.999
20	18.046	16.351	13.590	11.470	9.818	8.514	7.469	6.623	6.259	5.929	5.353	4.870	4.460	4.110	3.954	3.808	3.546	3.316	2.850	2.497	2.221	1.999
21	18.857	17.011	14.029	11.764	10.017	8.649	7.562	6.687	6.312	5.973	5.384	4.891	4.476	4.121	3.963	3.816	3.551	3.320	2.852	2.498	2.221	2.000
22	19.660	17.658	14.451	12.042	10.201	8.772	7.645	6.743	6.359	6.011	5.410	4.909	4.488	4.130	3.970	3.822	3.556	3.323	2.853	2.498	2.222	2.000
23	20.456	18.292	14.857	12.303	10.371	8.883	7.718	6.792	6.399	6.044	5.432	4.925	4.499	4.137	3.976	3.827	3.559	3.325	2.854	2.499	2.222	2.000
24	21.243	18.914	15.247	12.550	10.529	8.985	7.784	6.835	6.434	6.073	5.451	4.937	4.507	4.143	3.981	3.831	3.562	3.327	2.855	2.499	2.222	2.000
25	22.023	19.523	15.622	12.783	10.675	9.077	7.843	6.873	6.464	6.097	5.467	4.948	4.514	4.147	3.985	3.834	3.564	3.329	2.856	2.499	2.222	2.000
26	22.795	20.121	15.983	13.003	10.810	9.161	7.896	6.906	6.491	6.118	5.480	4.956	4.520	4.151	3.988	3.837	3.566	3.330	2.856	2.500	2.222	2.000
27	23.560	20.707	16.330	13.211	10.935	9.237	7.943	6.935	6.514	6.136	5.492	4.964	4.524	4.154	3.990	3.839	3.567	3.331	2.856	2.500	2.222	2.000
28	24.316	21.281	16.663	13.406	11.051	9.307	7.984	6.961	6.534	6.152	5.502	4.970	4.528	4.157	3.992	3.840	3.568	3.331	2.857	2.500	2.222	2.000
29	25.066	21.844	16.984	13.591	11.158	9.370	8.022	6.983	6.551	6.166	5.510	4.975	4.531	4.159	3.994	3.841	3.569	3.332	2.857	2.500	2.222	2.000
30	25.808	22.396	17.292	13.765	11.258	9.427	8.055	7.003	6.566	6.177	5.517	4.979	4.534	4.160	3.995	3.842	3.569	3.332	2.857	2.500	2.222	2.000
40	32.835	27.355	19.793	15.046	11.925	9.779	8.244	7.105	6.642	6.234	5.548	4.997	4.544	4.166	3.999	3.846	3.571	3.333	2.857	2.500	2.222	2.000
50	39.196	31.424	21.482	15.762	12.234	9.915	8.304	7.133	6.661	6.246	5.554	4.999	4.545	4.167	4.000	3.846	3.571	3.333	2.857	2.500	2.222	2.000

Decision Making Under Uncertainty

REVIEW SUMMARY

I. Purpose of the Chapter

This chapter defines probability and explains how probabilities can be obtained and used in decision making. It illustrates the use of payoff tables and decision trees to determine the best strategy under uncertainty. It also demonstrates the use of normal distribution in evaluating the riskiness of short-term projects. Finally, it explains Monte Carlo simulations and discusses and illustrates the use of normal distribution to evaluate the riskiness of capital expenditure proposals and the use of the multi-attribute decision model to incorporate both quantitative and nonquantitative factors into the analysis.

II. Using Probabilities in Decision Making

Probability analysis is an application of statistical decision theory that, under certain conditions of uncertainty, leads to more consistent and reliable decisions than single best guesses. As long as the underlying process that generates the decision variable is not expected to change in the future, historical data can be used to model the probability distribution. The **variance** of a probability distribution, σ^2, and the **standard deviation**, which is the squareroot of the variance σ, are measures of dispersion that are commonly used as measures of risk. The problem of comparing the relative riskiness of alternatives can be resolved by computing the **coefficiency of variation**, a measure that relates the standard deviation of a probability distribution to its expected value:

$$\text{Coefficient of variation} = \frac{\text{Standard deviation}}{\text{Expected value (contribution margin) } E(x)}$$

III. Determining the Best Strategy Under Uncertainty

There may be an opportunity to acquire additional information that will be useful in selecting the best decision alternative. The cost of the additional information should be weighted against the increase in the expected value that can be obtained by using the information. The maximum increase in the expected value that could be obtained from additional information is the expected value of **perfect information** and, consequently, the maximum amount one would be willing to pay for additional information.

IV. Revising Probabilities

Probabilities should be revised as new information becomes available. One approach to probability revision is an application of Bayes' theorem. Bayes' theorem can be used to revise the original probability estimates for two or more events when new information becomes available about additional events. The revised probability estimate is referred to as **posterior probability**. The estimates made before the new information became available are referred to as **prior probabilities**.

V. Decision Trees, Continuous Probability Distributions, and Monte Carlo Simulations

A **decision tree** is a graphic representation of the decision points, the alternative actions available to the decision maker, the possible outcomes and the related probabilities for each decision alternative, and the expected values of each event. When possible outcomes can take on any value within a defined range, a **continuous probability distribution** may provide a better description of the nature of the variable and be a better basis for prediction. The normal distribution is the most frequently applied continuous distribution because it is symmetrical, and it has only one mode. **Monte Carlo simulation** is a computer-oriented procedure that uses statistical sampling techniques to obtain probabilistic approximation of some mathematical or physical problem.

VI. Uncertainty in Capital Expenditure Evaluation

One way to evaluate the potential effects of uncertainty on proposed capital expenditures is to consider the effect of the distribution of probable outcomes on the expected cash flows and the relative risk of available capital projects. Probabilistic estimates are most frequently used with the present value method, where the expected value of the net cash flow in each period, rather than the single most likely net cash flow, is discounted to present value. If a probability distribution is not symmetrical, the use of expected values rather than estimates of the most likely events will result in a different net present value.

A.   Independent, Perfectly Correlated, and Mixed Cash Flows

The procedure for computing the variance and the standard deviation for the expected net present value varies, depending upon whether the cash flows in each of the periods are independent, perfectly correlated, or partially independent and partially correlated. If the cash flows in each period are independent, the standard deviation of the expected net present value is computed by taking the square root of the sum of the discounted periodic variances. If the cash flows in each of the periods are perfectly correlated, the standard deviation of the expected net present value is determined by summing the discounted standard deviations for each period over the life of the project. If the period cash flows are neither independent nor perfectly correlated, the cash flows may be treated as if they contain a mixture of independent and dependent period cash flows. The expected periodic cash flows are simply divided into the two components, a separate expected value and variance is then computed for each, and finally the standard deviation of the expected net present value is determined by computing the square root of the sum of the variances of the independent cash flows and the dependent cash flows.

B.   Evaluating Investment Risk

Once the standard deviation of the expected net present value has been determined, it can be used to evaluate the riskiness of the proposed capital investment. Alternatives with the smallest coefficients of variation are the least risky. Areas of the normal distribution can be related to deviations from the mean expressed in terms of standard deviations to indicate to management the range of return, measured in terms of net present value likely to occur at some level of probability. The reliability of the estimated range for the net present value and the probability of achieving a positive net present value are highly dependent upon the accuracy of the estimates of the expected values of the annual cash flows and their estimated standard deviations.

VII.   Incorporating Nonquantitative Factors

The **multiattribute decision model (MADM)** is an expenditure evaluation tool that explicitly incorporates both quantitative and nonquantitative factors into decision analysis. The factors are the important benefits that management expects from the investment. When the relative importance of the factors has been determined, each alternative is rated on the basis of how well management believes it will satisfy each factor. The alternative with the highest composite score best satisfies the multiattribute objectives of management and is selected for implementation.

Part 1 ■ True/False

Instructions: *Indicate whether each of the following statements is **True** or **False**.*

True/False

1. In applying probability distributions to cost studies, the smaller the standard deviation, the smaller the risk that the actual cost will differ from the expected cost. _____

2. The value of perfect information is the maximum amount that management would be willing to pay to improve its information. . . . . _____

3. Decision trees are especially useful when sequential decisions are involved. . . . _____

4. Monte Carlo simulation models are computer-oriented because without the speed of the computer they would be impractical to solve. . . . . _____

5. In practice, most decisions are based on management's best guess of the single most likely result for each period. . . . . _____

6. Probabilistic estimates are most frequently used with the payback method of capital expenditure evaluation. . . . . _____

7. If a probability distribution is symmetrical, the use of expected value rather than estimates of the most likely events will result in a different net present value. _____

8. The least risky investment is the one with the smallest standard deviation. . . . . _____

9. Perfectly correlated cash flows might occur if the capital expenditure relates to the production of a new product or entrance into a new market. . . . . _____

10. In practice, independent cash flows could occur when the capital expenditure relates to the production of an established product and the demand for it is expected to vary in response to temporary changes in consumer tastes. . . . . _____

11. Investment alternatives with the largest coefficient of variation would be the least risky. . . . . _____

12. If the expected values of the annual cash flows and their estimated standard deviations are based upon historical data rather than subjective estimates, greater reliance can be placed on the results. . . . . _____

13. All future events that affect cash flows follow the pattern of random variables drawn from a normal distribution. . . . . _____

14. If two events are related, the probability that one event will occur given that the other event has occurred is called conditional probability. . . . . _____

15. The multiattribute decision model is an expenditure evaluation tool that incorporates only nonquantitative factors into the decision analysis. . . . . _____

Part 2 ■ Matching

Instructions: *On the line at the left of each of the following items, place the letter from the columns below that identifies the term that best matches the statement. No letter should be used more than once.*

_____ 1. A procedure that uses statistical sampling techniques in order to obtain a probabilistic approximation of some mathematical or physical problem.

_____ 2. Graphic portrayal of alternatives and their expected results.

_____ 3. Provides a numerical measure of the scatter of the possible values around the average value.

_____ 4. Based on quantification of the likelihood of the occurrence of possible events.

_____ 5. The difference between the average profit under conditions of certainty and the average expected profit using the best strategy under uncertainty.

_____ 6. An expenditure evaluation tool that explicitly incorporates both quantitative and nonquantitative factors into the decision analysis.

_____ 7. Using these rather than estimates of the most likely events will result in a different net present value if a probability distribution is not symmetrical.

_____ 8. Procedure used to revise the original probability estimates for events when new information becomes available.

_____ 9. A measure of the relative variability of a distribution determined by dividing the standard deviation by the expected value.

_____ 10. Situation where the magnitude of cash flows in subsequent periods is not affected by the magnitude of cash flows that occurs in earlier periods.

_____ 11. Situation where the magnitude of cash flows in later periods depends upon the magnitude of cash flows in earlier periods.

_____ 12. Presents the conditional value of each event that can occur for each course of action being considered and the expected value of each alternative based on the probabilities of the events that can occur.

_____ 13. Because it is symmetrical and has only one mode, the expected value is not only the mean of the probability distribution, but it is also the mode.

_____ 14. When future events that affect cash flows do not follow a pattern of random variables, it may be necessary to construct this using historical data or subjective estimates based on informed business judgment.

_____ 15. If two events are related, the probability that one event will occur given that the other event has occurred is called this.

a. value of perfect information	**i.** normal distribution
b. probability distribution	**j.** payoff table
c. standard deviation	**k.** multiattribute decision model
d. decision tree	**l.** nonnormal distribution
e. Monte Carlo simulation	**m.** coefficient of variation
f. Bayes' theorem	**n.** independent cash flows
g. expected values	**o.** conditional probability
h. perfectly correlated cash flows	

Part 3 ■ Multiple Choice

Instructions: *On the line at the left of each of the following items, place the letter of the choice that most correctly completes each item.*

_____ **1.** Of the following, the one that is generally viewed as a measure of investment risk is the:
    a. expected value   **d.** coefficient of determination
    b. conditional value   **e.** none of the above
    c. standard deviation

_____ **2.** These are apt to occur when the capital expenditure relates to the production of a new product or the entrance into a new market:
    a. perfectly correlated cash flows   **d.** mixed cash flows
    b. positive cash flows   **e.** none of the above
    c. independent cash flows

_____ **3.** Because the normal distribution is symmetrical and has only one mode, this is not only the mean of the probability distribution, but it is also the mode:
    a. coefficient of variance   **d.** variance
    b. standard deviation   **e.** expected value
    c. coefficient of determination

_____ **4.** This would be the same when a normal probability distribution is used in the analysis as it would when the probability distribution of future cash flows is ignored:
    a. net present value   **d.** internal rate of return
    b. time adjusted rate of return **e.** accounting rate of return
    c. payback

_____ **5.** The standard deviation of the expected net present value is computed by taking the square root of the sum of the discounted periodic variances when the cash flows of each period are:
    a. perfectly correlated   **d.** independent
    b. mixed   **e.** negative
    c. positive

_____ **6.** Not all future events that affect cash flows follow the pattern of random variables drawn from:
    a. payoff tables   **d.** joint probabilities
    b. conditional probabilities   **e.** none of the above
    c. a normal distribution

_____ **7.** This is sometimes used to determine the best choice of action in a decision-tree analysis:
    a. induction   **d.** backward induction
    b. random scheduling   **e.** queuing theory
    c. subjective judgment

_____ **8.** The technique that is especially useful in evaluating problems that contain numerous stochastic variables is:
    a. sensitivity analysis   **d.** linear programming
    b. Monte Carlo simulation   **e.** learning theory
    c. queuing theory

_____ 9. The variance of the net present value for dependent cash flows is $500,000 and for independent cash flows is $150,000. The variance of the total net present value of the investment would be computed as:

a. $500,000 x $150,000

b. $500,000 + $150,000

c. $500,000 - $150,000

d. $500,000 ÷ $150,000

e. none of the above

_____ 10. The variance of the net present value for dependent cash flows is $500,000 and for independent cash flows is $150,000. The standard deviation of the total net present value of the investment would be computed as:

a. $650,000^2$

b. $\sqrt{500,000^2 + 150,000^2}$

c. $\sqrt{650,000}$

d. $\sqrt{350,000}$

e. none of the above

Part 4 ■ Problem

1. Compute the expected contribution margin for a product of the Simi Valley Company by completing the schedule below:

Units Demanded	Probability of Unit Demand	Total Contribution Margin of Units Demanded	Expected Contribution Margin
0	.05	0	$
5	.10	$1,500	
10	.40	3,000	
15	.20	4,500	
20	.15	6,000	
25	.10	7,500	
			$

2. Compute the variance and standard deviation of the expected value. (Round to the nearest whole dollar.)

(1) Contribution Margin (Conditional Value)	(2) Difference From Expected Value	(3) (2) Squared	(4) Probability	(5) Variance (3) x (4)
$	$			$

Standard deviation =

3. Compute the coefficient of variation.

Part 5 ■ Problem

Milton Inc. is considering an investment in new machinery with a five-year estimated useful life, which has an estimated net present value of $15,000. The cash inflows are expected to be normally distributed; however, 40% of each period's cash inflow is expected to be independent, and the remaining 60% is expected to be perfectly correlated. Cash inflows are expected to be $12,000 each period. The independent cash inflows have a standard deviation of $1,000, and the perfectly correlated (dependent) cash inflows have a standard deviation of $2,000. The initial cash outflow has a standard deviation of zero. The corporation's weighted-average cost of capital is 10%.

1. Determine the variance of the net present value for the independent cash flows.

(1) Year	(2) Periodic Standard Deviation	(3) Periodic Variance $(2)^2$	(4) Present Value of $1 @10%	(5) Present Value of $1 @10% Squared $(4)^2$	(6) Present Value of Variance (3) x (5)
0	$				$
1					
2					
3					
4					
5					

Variance of the net present value for the independent cash flows $\underline{\underline{\$\qquad}}$

2. Determine the standard deviation of the net present value for the perfectly correlated cash flows.

(1) Year	(2) Periodic Standard Deviation	(3) Present Value of $1 @ 10%	(4) Present Value of Standard Deviation (2) x (3)
0	$		$
1			
2			
3			
4			
5			

Standard deviation of the net present value
   for dependent cash flows $\underline{\underline{\$\qquad}}$

3. Compute the variance of the total net present value of the investment.

Variance of net present value for dependent cash flows. . . . . $ _____

Variance of net present value for independent cash flows . . . .   _____

Variance of total net present value of investment . . . . $ _____

4. Determine the standard deviation of the total net present value of the investment. (Round to the nearest whole dollar.)

Part 6 ■ Problem

Wallbanger Inc. is considering constructing a racquetball facility in a suburb that does not have one. The following data are relevant to the decision.

Annual Demand (Number of One-hour Time Slots)	Probability of Demand	Annual After-Tax Net Cash Inflows	Cost of Building With Capacity to Meet Demand
60,000	.30	$200,000	$1,500,000
80,000	.40	300,000	2,000,000
100,000	.20	400,000	2,500,000
120,000	.10	500,000	3,000,000

The present value of an annuity of $1 discounted at the company's weighted-average cost of capital (10%) over an investment horizon of 20 years is 8.514, and the present value of $1 received at the end of 20 years is .149.

1. Construct a payoff table to determine the expected value of the annual after-tax net cash inflows for each size of racquetball facility.

Potential Action (Racquetball Facility Capacity to Be Built)	Annual After-Tax Net Cash Inflows From Different Levels of Demand				Expected Value of After-Tax Net Cash Inflows
	60,000	80,000	100,000	120,000	
60,000					
80,000					
100,000					
120,000					

2. Determine the expected net present value of each alternative racquetball facility size and indicate which size Wallbanger should build.

(1) Possible Action (Racquetball Facility Capacity to Be Built)	(2) Expected Value of Annual After-Tax Net Cash Inflows	(3) Present Value of 20-Year Annuity of $1 @ 10%	(4) Present Value of Annual After-Tax Net Cash Inflows (2) x (3)	(5) Initial Cash Outflow	(6) Expected Net Present Value (4) - (5)
60,000					
80,000					
100,000					
120,000					

Marketing Expense and Profitability Analysis

REVIEW SUMMARY

I. Purpose of the Chapter

This chapter discusses the scope of marketing activities, including a comparison of expenses incurred to market a product with those incurred to manufacture it. Also, it describes how manufacturing cost control techniques can be applied to control marketing expenses. It explains and illustrates marketing profitability analysis and discusses product pricing.

II. Scope of Marketing Activities

Marketing is the matching of a company's products with markets for the satisfaction of customers at a reasonable profit to the firm. Management requires meaningful marketing expense information in order to determine and analyze the profitability of territories, classes of customers, product lines or brands, and promotional efforts. Control of marketing expenses begins with their assignment to various expense groups such as territories, customers, and products.

III. Comparison of Marketing Expenses with Manufacturing Costs

Major differences between manufacturing expenses and marketing expenses include the following:

1. Manufacturing techniques seldom change to any great extent once the factory is set up; whereas, changes in market conditions often necessitate changes in channels of distribution.

2. Management can control manufacturing factors such as labor cost and number of machines operated; whereas, customer resistance is the enigma in marketing expense analysis.

3. Factory managers measure their accomplishments in terms of reduced costs per unit; whereas, sales managers consider sales the yardstick for measuring their efficiency.

4. The effect of manufacturing changes is usually felt quickly; whereas, many promotional expenditures are incurred for future results.

IV. Marketing Expense Control

Recognition of the fixed-variable expense classification is valuable in controlling marketing expenses and in decision making. Fixed marketing expenses, also called **capacity costs**, include items such as salaries of executive and administrative sales staffs, as well as rent and depreciation on marketing facilities. Variable marketing expenses, also called **volume costs**, include the expense of handling, warehousing, and shipping that tends to vary with sales volume.

Marketing expenses may be directly identifiable with functional classifications, although indirectly identifiable with respect to other classifications such as territories or products, or the expense may be indirect both as to function as well as to other classifications. Expenses that can not be assigned directly are recorded in total and then allocated by appropriate bases to various activities.

V. Allocating Marketing Expenses

The assignment of functional marketing expenses as percentages of actual sales or manufacturing costs does not offer reliable results. The determination of a functional standard unit costing rate is a more dependable solution. The total expense of each marketing function should be divided by the activities that drive these expenses (e.g., number of salespersons' calls, relative media circulation, etc.). Detailed analysis of marketing activities and the expenses created by those activities provide a basis for controlling and improving efficiency and is called **activity-based management (ABM)**.

VI. Marketing Profitability Analysis

When marketing activities are organized on a territorial basis, each identifiable geographical unit can be charged directly with the expenses incurred within its area, thereby minimizing the proration of expenses. Since the large number of customers makes the allocation and analysis of marketing expenses by customers cumbersome, customers are grouped according to the following characteristics to make the analysis more meaningful: (1) territories, (2) amount of average order, (3) customer-volume groups, or (4) kinds of customers. Just as customers are grouped for purposes of analysis, products sold can be grouped according to product lines or brands possessing common characteristics. **Activity-based costing** helps to improve product profitability analysis by charging costs to products based on the resources they actually consume.

VII.   Gross Profit Analysis

A careful analysis of unexpected changes in gross profit is useful to a company's management. Such changes may result from changes in (1) sales prices of products, (2) number of physical units sold, (3) types of products sold, or (4) materials, labor, and overhead costs.

Gross profit analysis may be based on a company's sales and cost data. The budgeted sales and costs are accepted as the basis for all comparisons. A sales price variance and a sales volume variance are computed first, followed by a cost price variance and a cost volume variance. The computations are as follows:

1.   Sales price variance = Actual sales - (Actual unit sales x Budgeted prices)

2.   Sales volume variance = (Actual unit sales x Budgeted prices) - Budgeted dollar sales

3.   Cost price variance = Actual cost of goods sold - (Actual unit sales x Budgeted unit costs)

4.   Cost volume variance = (Actual unit sales x Budgeted unit costs) - Budgeted cost of goods sold

The net volume variance is a composite of the sales volume and cost volume variances. It should be analyzed further to determine the sales mix and final sales volume variances. These are computed as follows:

1.   Sales mix variance = [Actual unit sales x (Budgeted prices - Budgeted costs)] - (Actual unit sales x Budgeted average gross profit per unit)

2.   Final sales volume variance = Budgeted average gross profit per unit x (Actual unit sales - Budgeted unit sales)

Gross profit analysis based on budgets and standard costs depicts the weak spots in a period's performance. For example, gains due to higher prices may be more than offset by increased costs, shifts to less profitable products, and decreases in units sold. Planned gross profit is the responsibility of both the marketing and manufacturing functions.

The marketing function must explain the changes in sale prices, the shifts in sales mix, and the changes in units sold; whereas, the production function must account for changes in costs.

VIII.   Contribution Margin Analysis

For more effective marketing expense analysis, it has been suggested that only the variable manufacturing cost be subtracted from each segment's sales, thus arriving at a figure called "gross contribution margin." Proponents of the contribution margin approach point out that only specific and direct costs, whether fixed or variable, should be assigned to territories, customers, product groups, or salespersons, with a clear distinction as to their fixed and variable characteristics.

IX.   Product Pricing

Under the **profit maximization method** of price setting, the price that yields the largest profit at a certain volume is the price to be charged to a consumer. Some companies set prices based on a **return-on-capital-employed method**, using a formula such as the following:

$$\text{Price} = \frac{\text{Total cost} + (\text{Desired rate of return} \times \text{Total capital employed})}{\text{Sales volume in units}}$$

Conversion cost pricing attempts to direct management's attention to the amount of labor and factory overhead that products require. Using the **contribution margin approach** to pricing, the cost of additional units is accepted as a basis for pricing them, and any price over and above total differential cost is acceptable. The use of standard costs for pricing purposes makes cost figures more readily available and reduces clerical detail. **Life cycle costs** include all the costs that the manufacturer will incur over the life of the product, including product design and development costs, manufacturing cost, selling and distribution expenses, and service expenses after the sale. Prices based on life cycle costing are set at each stage of the product's life cycle with a view toward recovering total life cycle costs and achieving an acceptable long-run profit.

X.   Effect of Robinson-Patman Act on Pricing

The **Clayton Act** prohibited price discrimination only where it had a serious effect on competition in general, and it contained no other provisions for the control of price discrimination. At the core of the **Robinson-Patman Act** is the provision that differential prices granted must not exceed differences in the cost of serving different customers. To avoid litigation, a firm should establish records that show that price differentials are extended only to the extent justified by allowable cost savings.

Part 1 ■ True/False

Instructions: *Indicate whether each of the following statements is True or False.*

	True/False

1. Life cycle costing includes only the manufacturing costs incurred over a product's life. . . . . _____

2. A meaningful comparison of the marketing expense of one company with another is not always possible. . . . . _____

3. Marketing expense analysis is not easy to perform because the customer is a controlling rather than a controllable factor. . . . . _____

4. It is easy to identify quantities or units of activity with the cost incurred and results achieved for marketing expenses. . . . . _____

5. Using budgets, the final sales volume variance may be computed by comparing the budgeted gross profit of actual units sold with the budgeted gross profit. . . . . _____

6. Order-filling expenses are the expenses of activities carried on to bring in the sales orders and include selling and advertising. . . . . _____

7. To obtain the sales mix variance, the budgeted gross profit of actual units sold is subtracted from the difference between actual sales at budgeted prices and the budgeted cost of actual units sold. . . . . _____

8. The number of customers' orders, transactions, or invoice lines would serve as reasonable activity bases for the credit and collection function . . . . _____

9. The number, weight, or size of the shipping units would be logical activity bases for the packing and shipping function. . . . . _____

10. Capacity costs is another term for fixed marketing expenses, such as salaries, rent, and depreciation. . . . . _____

11. Unlike production costs, it is not important to establish flexible budgets and standards for marketing expenses. . . . . _____

12. Companies sometimes set minimum dollar values or quantities for orders to eliminate the situation where marketing expenses exceed the gross profit from the order. _____

13. Proponents of the contribution margin approach point out that only specific and direct marketing expenses should be assigned to territories, customers, product groups, or salespersons. . . . . _____

14. The Robinson-Patman Act prohibited price discrimination only where it had a serious effect on competition in general. . . . . _____

15. The use of standard costs for pricing makes cost figures more difficult to obtain and increases clerical detail. . . . . _____

Part 2 ■ Matching

Instructions: *On the line at the left of each of the following items, place the letter from the columns below that identifies the term that best matches the statement. No letter should be used more than once.*

_____ 1. Matching of a company's products with markets for the satisfaction of customers at a reasonable profit for the firm.

_____ 2. Expenses that can be identified with a territory, customer, product, or definite type of sales outlet.

_____ 3. Attempts to direct management's attention to the amount of labor and factory overhead that products require.

_____ 4. Attempts to charge marketing expenses to territories, customers, products, or salespersons, based on their consumption of resources that cause these expenses to occur.

_____ 5. Established by central management at a level considered best for overall company interests.

_____ 6. Approach to pricing in which any price over and above the total differential cost would be acceptable.

_____ 7. A product costing approach that assigns a share of all of the costs that will be incurred in connection with a product.

_____ 8. Expenses incurred for more than one function or classification and hence must be allocated.

_____ 9. Expense of activities carried on to bring in the sales orders.

_____ 10. Expenses of warehousing, packing and shipping, credit and collection, and general accounting.

_____ 11. Process of analyzing marketing activities and expenses created by those activities as a basis for controlling and improving efficiency.

_____ 12. Marketing function for which size, weight, or number of products shipped or handled would be appropriate activity bases.

_____ 13. Marketing function for which quantity of product units sold, relative media circulation, or cost of space directly assignable would be appropriate activity bases.

_____ 14. Influences the thinking of the volume-minded sales manager who must recognize that profit is more beneficial than volume.

_____ 15. Another term for fixed marketing expenses that include such items as sales salaries, rent, and depreciation.

_____ 16. Another term for variable marketing expenses that include the expenses of handling, warehousing, and shipping that tend to vary with sales volume.

_____ 17. Difference between actual sales at budgeted prices and at budgeted costs, and actual sales at budgeted average gross profit.

_____ 18. Approach to pricing in which the product is priced as if its market share were larger than it actually is.

_____ 19. States that price differentials granted to various customers must not exceed differences in the cost of serving such customers.

_____ 20. Sales mix variance plus or minus final sales volume variance.

a.	order-filling expense	k.	contribution margin analysis
b.	direct expenses	l.	activity-based costing
c.	activity-based management	m.	order-getting expenses
d.	capacity costs	n.	warehousing
e.	Robinson-Patman Act	o.	marketing
f.	net volume variance	p.	volume costs
g.	target pricing	q.	indirect expenses
h.	life cycle costing	r.	advertising
i.	sales mix variance	s.	profit maximization pricing
j.	contribution margin pricing	t.	conversion cost pricing

Part 3 ■ Multiple Choice

Instructions: *On the line at the left of each of the following items, place the letter of the choice that most correctly completes each item.*

_____ 1. Budgeting of order-getting costs will *not* be affected by:
   a. policies and actions of competitors
   b. sales promotion policies
   c. general economic conditions
   d. location of distribution warehouses
   e. any of the above

   (ICMA adapted)

_____ 2. The control of order-filling costs:
   a. can be accomplished through the use of flexible budget standards
   b. requires a budget that shows budgeted expenses for the average level of activity
   c. is related to pricing decisions, sales promotion, and customer reaction
   d. is not crucial because the order-filling routine is entrenched and external influences are minimal
   e. none of the above

   (ICMA adapted)

_____ 3. Potash Company, which sells a single product, provided the following data from its income statement for the calendar years 19X4 and 19X3:

	19X4		19X3 (Base Year)	
Sales	$750,000	(150,000 units)	$720,000	(180,000 units)
Cost of goods sold	525,000		575,000	
Gross profit	$225,000		$145,000	

In an analysis of variation in gross profit between the two years, what would be the effects of changes in sales price and sales volume?

	Sales Price	Sales Volume
a.	$150,000 favorable	$120,000 unfavorble
b.	$150,000 unfavorable	$120,000 favorable
c.	$180,000 favorable	$150,000 unfavorable
d.	$180,000 unfavorable	$150,000 favorable

(AICPA adapted)

_____ 4. A single-product company's total cost is $200,000, total capital employed is $500,000, the sales volume is 50,000 units, and the desired rate of return on capital employed is 15%. The product's sales price should be:
   a. $4
   b. $10
   c. $5.50
   d. $7.50
   e. none of the above

_____ 5. The process of analyzing marketing activities and the expenses created by those activities to provide a basis for controlling and improving efficiency is known as:
   a. activity-based costing
   b. life cycle management
   c. differential costing
   d. activity-based management
   e. none of the above

_____ 6. All the costs that the manufacturer will incur for the product, including product design and development costs, manufacturing costs, selling and distribution expenses, and service after the sale are called:
   a. standard costs
   b. differential costs
   c. life cycle costs
   d. indirect costs
   e. fixed costs

7-9. The standard billing rate per invoice line in the Billing Department was $.40 per line, consisting of $3,000 of fixed expense and $.30 per invoice line of variable expense at a normal capacity of 30,000 invoice lines. Actual sales required 32,000 lines for a month at a total of $12,700.

_____ 7. Based on the above information, the budget allowance for the 32,000 lines billed would be:

    a. $12,700   **d.** $12,500
    b. $12,800   **e.** none of the above
    c. $12,600

_____ 8. Based on the above information, the spending variance for the Billing Department would be:

    a. $200 unfavorable   **d.** $200 favorable
    b. $100 unfavorable   **e.** none of the above
    c. $100 favorable

_____ 9. Based on the above information, the idle capacity variance for the Billing Department would be:

    a. $200 unfavorable   **d.** $200 favorable
    b. $100 unfavorable   **e.** none of the above
    c. $100 favorable

_____ 10. An approach to pricing that accepts any price over and above the total differential cost to produce and sell the product is known as:

    a. contribution margin pricing   **d.** profit maximization pricing
    b. target pricing   **e.** none of the above
    c. life cycle pricing

Part 4 ■ Problem

Pacer Company of Indianapolis markets a single product in Indianapolis and Fort Wayne. Marketing expenses for the past year were:

Sales salaries	$108,000
Salespersons' expenses	50,000
Advertising	63,000
Delivery expense	33,000
Credit investigation expense	5,000
Collection expense	12,000
Total	$271,000

Additional information:

(a) The company has six salespersons, two in Fort Wayne and four in Indianapolis, and each is paid the same salary.

(b) The salespersons receive equal allowances for expenses, except that the Fort Wayne salespersons each receive $1,000 per year extra for turnpike toll fees.

(c) All advertising is placed according to the number of subscribers to the Indianapolis and Fort Wayne daily newspapers, 500,000 and 130,000 respectively.

(d) Delivery is made by an outside agency that charges a flat annual fee. The agency made 3,000 deliveries (2,500 in Indianapolis, 500 in Fort Wayne) from a centrally located warehouse.

(e) A total of 500 new customers were obtained: 400 in Indianapolis, 100 in Fort Wayne.

(f) A total of 4,000 customers' remittances were received: 3,200 from Indianapolis, 800 from Fort Wayne.

Instructions: *Prepare a marketing expense analysis for the two territories, using the schedule below.*

	Total	Territory Indianapolis	Fort Wayne
Sales salaries	$	$	$
Salespersons' expenses			
Advertising			
Delivery expense			
Credit investigation expense			
Collection expense.....................			
Total	$	$	$

Part 5 ■ Problem

Durango Company sells various products through selected retail outlets. Data relative to standard selling costs for one of the company's salespersons show:

Standard sales for the year..................................	$400,000
Standard selling costs for the year...........................	50,000
Sales for June...	35,000
Selling costs for June:	
Actual cost	4,100
Budgeted costs for $35,000 sales	4,300

1. Determine the standard selling cost, rounded to the nearest whole dollar, to be charged if the salesperson reported $7,500 sales in the first week of June.

2. Determine the spending variance for the salesperson's June sales.

3. Determine the June idle capacity variance for the salesperson.

Part 6 ■ Problem

ACR assembles a large-screen TV that is sold to three classes of customers. The data with respect to these customers are shown below:

Customer Class	Sales	Gross Profit	Number of Sales Calls	Number of Orders	Number of Invoice Lines
Department stores ...	$ 280,000	$100,000	360	240	1,050
Retail appliance stores	525,000	200,000	480	1,160	2,300
Wholesalers	300,000	75,000	600	600	1,650
Total	$1,105,000	$375,000	1,440	2,000	5,000

The company uses an activity-based costing system for marketing expenses as well as for manufacturing costs. Actual marketing costs for the year are:

Function	Costs	Activity Base
Selling.....................	$115,200	Salespersons' calls
Packing and shipping	16,000	Customers' orders
Advertising	50,000	Dollar sales
Credit and collection..........	20,000	Invoice lines
General accounting	22,000	Customers' orders

Instructions: *Prepare an income statement by customer class, with distribution of marketing expenses, using activity-based costing principles. (Round to the nearest dollar.)*

ACR
Income Statement
For the Year Ended December 31, 19--

	Department Stores	Retail Appliance Stores	Wholesalers	Total
Sales	$	$	$	$
Cost of goods sold				
Gross profit	$	$	$	$
Less marketing expenses:				
Selling	$	$	$	$
Packing and shipping.......				
Advertising				
Credit and collection				
General accounting.........				
Total.................	$	$	$	$
Operating income (loss)	$	$	$	$

Part 7 ■ Problem

Sigma Co. prepared the following income statements by product:

	Product Delta	Product Gamma	Total
Sales	$550,000	$100,000	$650,000
Cost of goods sold	200,000	62,000	262,000
Gross profit	$350,000	$ 38,000	$388,000
Marketing expenses:			
Advertising	$ 20,000	$ 4,000	$ 24,000
Commissions	27,500	5,000	32,500
Shipping and packing	10,000	10,000	20,000
Administrative sales salaries	8,000	8,000	16,000
Total	$ 65,500	$ 27,000	$ 92,500
General administrative expenses	60,000	12,000	72,000
Total expenses	$125,500	$ 39,000	$164,500
Net income (loss)	$224,500	$ (1,000)	$223,500

Management is considering the elimination of Product Gamma. Additional data for products Delta and Gamma are as follows:

	Product Delta	Product Gamma
Commissions	5% of sales	5% of sales
Variable cost of goods sold	15% of sales	25% of sales
Number of orders processed	1,000	250
Lines of advertising devoted to product	674	--
Variable general and administrative expenses	15% of gross profit	15% of gross profit

All expenses other than those listed above are fixed and no attempt is made to allocate them to products. Management has determined that the number of orders processed would be a good basis for allocating shipping and packing expenses. Management also notes that advertising has been devoted entirely to promoting Product Delta and is considered variable. Finally, no unallocated fixed cost would be eliminated by dropping Product Gamma.

1. Prepare an income statement showing the contribution by product, using the schedule below.

	Product Delta	Product Gamma	Total
Sales	$	$	$
Less variable costs and expenses:			
Cost of goods sold	$	$	$
Advertising			
Commissions			
Shipping and packing			
General and administrative expenses			
Total variable costs and expenses	$	$	$
Contribution margin	$	$	$
Fixed costs and expenses:			
Manufacturing costs			$
Administrative sales salaries			
General and administrative expenses			
Total fixed costs and expenses			$
Net income			$

2. Compute the change in net income resulting from the elimination of Product Gamma.

Part 8 ■ Problem

Actual sales and budget data for 19-- for Lonestar Outfitters Inc. are:

	Product X	Product Y	Total
Actual sales	50,000 units @ $8.00	24,000 units @ $7.00	$568,000
Actual cost of goods sold	50,000 units @ $6.80	24,000 units @ $5.85	480,000
Budgeted sales	40,000 units @ $8.25	25,000 units @ $7.50	517,500
Budgeted cost of goods sold	40,000 units @ $7.00	25,000 units @ $6.00	430,000

1. Compute the following variances:

(a) Actual sales .... $

Actual sales at budgeted prices:

X .... $

Y ....

Sales price variance.............................. $

(b) Actual sales at budgeted prices .... $

Budgeted sales....................................

Sales volume variance............................. $

(c) Cost of goods sold—actual .... $

Budgeted cost of actual units sold:

X .... $

Y ....

Cost price variance .... $

(d) Budgeted cost of actual units sold .... $

Budgeted cost of budgeted units sold...............

Cost volume variance .... $

Sales volume variance............................. $

Cost volume variance ....

Net volume variance .... $

2. Determine the sales mix and final sales volume variances. (Round computations to three decimal places.)

Actual sales at budgeted prices .... $

Budgeted cost of actual units sold ....

Difference.. $

Budgeted gross profit of actual units sold ....

Sales mix variance................................ $

Budgeted gross profit of actual units sold .... $

Budgeted sales.................................... $

Budgeted cost of budgeted units sold...............

Budgeted gross profit ....

Final sales volume variance .... $

Part 9 ■ Problem

Sneaker Company is considering changing its sales price of Glider, presently $25. Increases and decreases of both 10% and 20%, as well as changes in advertising and promotion expenditures, are being considered, with the following estimated results for 19A and 19B:

Price	Estimated Unit Sales		Estimated Advertising and Promotion Expenditures	
	19A	19B	19A	19B
-20%	225,000	245,000	$ 550,000	$ 600,000
-10%	210,000	230,000	700,000	725,000
No change	200,000	230,000	750,000	750,000
+10%	190,000	210,000	800,000	825,000
+20%	175,000	195,000	1,000,000	1,200,000

The company has the necessary flexibility in its production capacity to meet these volume levels. The variable manufacturing cost per unit of Glider is estimated to be $15 in 19A and $17 in 19B.

Instructions: *Determine the recommended sales price for 19A and 19B, using the schedule provided on page 253.*

Alternate Sales Price	Variable Manufacturing Cost per Unit	Contribution Margin per Unit	Unit Sales	Total Contribution Margin	Additional Advertising and Promotion Expenditures	Contribution to Other Fixed Costs
19A:						
$	$	$		$	$	$
19B:						
$	$	$		$	$	$

Part 10 ■ Problem

Gimmicks Inc. sells one of its products at a price of $25 each, with total costs at $20 per unit. The company has $5,000,000 in capital employed. Unit sales amounted to 200,000 units.

1. Determine the return on capital presently employed by the company.

2. Determine the minimum selling price, rounded to the nearest cent, at which the company could sell its product and still maintain the same return on capital, assuming a 10% increase in sales volume, with constant costs and capital employed.

CHAPTER 26

Profit Performance Measurements and Intracompany Transfer Pricing

REVIEW SUMMARY

I. Purpose of the Chapter

This chapter explains and illustrates the concept of the return on capital employed, distinguishes between using it to evaluate profitability and using it to evaluate the performance of division managers, and discusses its advantages and limitations. The chapter also discusses intracompany transfer pricing alternatives and identifies when each should be used.

II. Rate of Return on Capital Employed

In equation form, the rate of return on capital employed may be expressed as follows:

$$\frac{\text{Profit}}{\text{Sales}} \times \frac{\text{Sales}}{\text{Capital Employed}} = \frac{\text{Rate of Return}}{\text{on Capital Employed}}$$

The **percentage of profit to sales** measures the ability to maintain satisfactory control over costs. The **capital-employed turnover rate** reflects the speed with which committed assets are employed in the operations. There is no single rate of return on capital employed that is satisfactory for all companies.

III. The Formula's Underlying Data

A rate of return on capital employed is computed by using figures from the balance sheet and income statement. Operating income is the preferred profit figure for measuring divisional or departmental performance because nonoperating items are usually the responsibility of the entire company. Capital employed refers to total assets (the sum of current assets and noncurrent assets). The amount of capital employed should be averaged over the fiscal period, if possible.

The determination of divisional return on capital is a matter of relating performance to assets placed at the disposal of divisional management. The best approach is to calculate a rate of return based on sales, costs, and capital employed specific to the division, followed by a rate of return calculation that includes a full allocation of total company sales, costs, and capital employed, so that both rates of return are clearly presented. Divisional return-on-capital-employed measures have been criticized as a motivational tool because a division may seek to maximize relative profits rather than absolute profits. A possible solution is to use a **residual income** figure that emphasizes marginal profit dollars above the cost of capital, rather than the rate of return on capital employed.

IV. Using the Rate of Return on Capital Employed

The real purpose of the return-on-capital-employed ratio is for internal profit measurement and control, with trends more meaningful than single ratios. Executive management of many companies has shown a growing acceptance of the rate-of-return-on-capital-employed concept as a tool in planning, in establishing sales prices, and in measuring operational profitability. Advantages of the use of the rate of return on capital employed are that it:

1. Focuses management's attention upon earning the best profit possible on the capital available.

2. Serves as a yardstick for measuring management's efficiency and effectiveness for the company as a whole and its divisions.

3. Ties together the many phases of financial planning, sales objectives, cost control, and the profit goal.

4. Affords a comparison of managerial results both internally and externally.

5. Develops a keener sense of responsibility and team effort in divisional managers.

6. Aids in detecting weakness with respect to the use or nonuse of individual assets.

Limitations of the use of the return-on-capital-employed ratio include:

1. The frequent use of a single acceptable rate of return for all divisions.

2. The lack of data as to sales, costs, and assets by division.

3. The valuation of assets of different vintages in different divisions might give rise to comparison difficulties.

4. Making decisions that are not in the best long-run interest of the firm for the sake of making current period returns look good.

5. The focus on a single measure of performance may result in the neglect of other activities, such as research and development or personnel training.

Many well-managed companies use multiple performance measures to overcome the limitations of a single measure.

V.   Management Incentive Compensation Plans

Incentive compensation plans are used by top managements and boards of directors to encourage managers to pursue company goals.   Incentive compensation changes often in response to top management turnover and to changes in the company's environment.   The performance measures selected for use in the plan are crucial to the long-run success of the company.   To be effective, the performance measures selected must be controllable by the managers who are to be evaluated and clearly understood and accepted by all parties involved.

VI.   Intracompany Transfer Pricing

When transfers of goods or services are made between autonomous divisions, a portion of the revenue of one segment becomes a portion of the cost of another, and the price at which transfers are made influences the earnings reported by each profit center. A transfer pricing system must satisfy these three fundamental criteria:

1. Allow central management to judge as accurately as possible the performance of the divisional profit center in terms of its separate contribution to the total corporate profit.

2. Motivate the division manager to pursue the division's profit goal in a manner conducive to the success of the company as a whole.

3. Stimulate the manager's efficiency without losing the division's autonomy as a profit center.

VII.   Types of Transfer Prices

A **cost-based transfer price** may be sufficient in a totally centralized firm or in a firm where there are few intracompany transfers. The **market-based transfer price** is usually identical with the one charged to outside customers. It is the best profitability and performance measurement because it is objective. A **cost-plus transfer price** includes the cost to manufacture plus a normal mark-up and is often used when a market price is not available. A **negotiated transfer price** is sometimes used because it is felt that the setting of the price by negotiations between buying and selling divisions allows unit managers the greatest degree of authority and control over the profit of their units. An **arbitrary transfer price** is established by central management and is at a level considered best for overall company interests, with neither the buying nor selling units having any control over the final decision. Under a **dual transfer pricing** system, a producing division would have a profit inducement to expand sales and production both internally and externally, but the consuming division's costs would not include an artificial profit.

Part 1 ■ True/False

Instructions: *Indicate whether each of the following statements is **True** or **False**.*

True/False

1. The rate of return on capital employed may be expressed as the product of two factors: the percentage of profit to sales and the capital-employed turnover rate.   _____

2. The capital-employed turnover rate reflects the speed with which committed assets are used in the operations. . . . .   _____

3. There is a single rate of return on capital employed that all companies' performances may be measured against. . . . .   _____

4. In measuring divisional performance, operating income is the most appropriate figure to use. . . . .   _____

5. Total assets used in the business are the assets included in the capital-employed computation. . . . .   _____

6. The residual income figure emphasizes marginal profit dollars above the cost of capital. . . . .   _____

7. The rate of return on capital employed is not a good measure of profitability for the company as a whole. . . . .   _____

8. An advantage of the use of the rate of return on capital employed is that it focuses management's attention upon earning the best profit possible on the total assets available. . . . .   _____

9. A disadvantage of the use of the rate of return on capital employed is that management may be influenced to make decisions to enhance short-run profits that are not best for the long-run profitability of the firm.   _____

10. Multiple performance measurement means that different divisions use different standards. . . . .   _____

11. Today, transfer pricing plays a major role in cost control. . . . .   _____

12. A transfer pricing system should stimulate the manager's efficiency without losing the division's autonomy as a profit center. . . . .   _____

13. A market-based transfer price is most appropriate for use in a totally decentralized firm. . . . .   _____

14. A market-based transfer price is the worst profitability and performance measurement because it is not objective. . . . .   _____

15. The best thing about an arbitrary transfer price is that it is established by the division involved. . . . .   _____

Part 2 ■ Matching

Instructions: *On the line at the left of each of the following items, place the letter from the columns below that identifies the term that best matches the statement. No letter should be used more than once.*

_____ **1.** The percentage of profit to sales times the capital-employed turnover rate.

_____ **2.** Sales divided by capital employed.

_____ **3.** Measures the degree of success in maintaining satisfactory control over costs.

_____ **4.** Provides central management with a more comprehensive picture of divisional performance by considering a wider range of management responsibility.

_____ **5.** Sum of current assets and noncurrent assets.

_____ **6.** Accountants who favor this method of valuing noncurrent assets argue that it enables the gross assets of one plant to be compared better with those of another plant, where depreciation practices or the age of assets may be different.

_____ **7.** Accountants who favor this method of valuing noncurrent assets state that cash built up via a depreciation allowance, if added to gross assets, amounts to overstating the investment.

_____ **8.** Accountants who favor this method of valuing noncurrent assets believe that a company receiving a satisfactory return based on book values should recognize the situation as being out of step with actual conditions.

_____ **9.** A division's income less an amount representing the company's cost of capital employed by the division.

_____ **10.** Established by central management at a level considered best for overall company interests.

_____ **11.** A transfer pricing method that has the disadvantage of inflating inventories with intracompany profits that must be eliminated from consolidated financial statements.

_____ **12.** A transfer pricing method that is the best profitability and performance measurement because it is objective.

_____ **13.** A transfer pricing method that may allow unit managers the greatest degree of authority and control over the profit of their units.

_____ **14.** Method of transfer pricing under which a producing division would have a profit inducement to expand sales and production, while the cost to consuming divisions would be the firm's actual costs and would not include an artificial profit.

_____ **15.** A management philosophy that attempts to make each division of the business as autonomous as possible.

a. percentage of profit to sales	**i.** negotiated transfer pricing
b. capital employed	**j.** dual transfer pricing
c. depreciated cost method	**k.** arbitrary transfer price
d. residual income	**l.** multiple performance measurements
e. capital-employed turnover rate	**m.** cost-plus transfer pricing
f. original cost method	**n.** inflation accounting method
g. rate of return on capital employed	**o.** decentralization
h. market-based transfer pricing	

Part 3 ■ Multiple Choice

Instructions: *On the line at the left of each of the following items, place the letter of the choice that most correctly completes each item.*

_____ 1. A major problem in comparing profitability measures among companies is:

   a. lack of general agreement over which profitability measure is best
   b. differences in the size of the companies
   c. differences in the accounting methods used by the companies
   d. differences in the dividend policies of the companies
   e. effect of interest rates on net income   *(ICMA adapted)*

_____ 2. A company's return on investment is affected by a change in:

	Capital Turnover	Profit Margin on Sales
a.	Yes	Yes
b.	Yes	No
c.	No	No
d.	No	Yes

(AICPA adapted)

_____ 3. To evaluate the performance of each department, interdepartmental transfers of a product preferably should be made at prices:

   a. equal to the market price of the product
   b. set by the receiving department
   c. equal to fully allocated costs to the producing department
   d. equal to variable costs to the producing department   *(AICPA adapted)*

_____ 4. A management decision may be beneficial for a given profit center, but not for the entire company. From the overall company viewpoint, this decision would lead to action referred to as:

   a. suboptimization   **c.** goal congruence
   b. centralization   **d.** maximization   *(AICPA adapted)*

_____ 5. Zee Company has two decentralized divisions, X and Y. Division X has always purchased certain units from Division Y at $75 per unit. Because Y plans to raise the price to $100 per unit, X wants to purchase these units from outside suppliers for $75 per unit. Y's costs are as follows:

Variable cost per unit	$70
Unavoidable annual fixed cost	$15,000
Annual production of these units for X	1,000 units

   If X buys from an outside supplier, the facilities Y uses to manufacture these units would remain idle. If Zee enforces a transfer price of $100 per unit between Divisions X and Y, the result would be:

   a. suboptimization for the company, because X should buy from outside suppliers for $75 per unit
   b. a lower overall company net income than a transfer price of $75 per unit
   c. a higher overall company net income than a transfer price of $75 per unit
   d. more profitable for the company than allowing X to buy from outside suppliers at $75 per unit

(AICPA adapted)

_____ **6.** Assuming that sales and net income remain the same, a company's return on investment will:

    a. increase if invested capital increases
    b. decrease if invested capital decreases
    c. decrease if the capital-employed turnover rate decreases
    d. decrease if the capital-employed turnover rate increases
    e. none of the above
                                                                   (AICPA adapted)

_____ **7.** In a decentralized company in which divisions may buy goods from one another, the transfer pricing system should be designed primarily to:

    a. increase the consolidated value of inventory
    b. prevent division managers from buying from outsiders
    c. minimize the degree of autonomy of division managers
    d. aid in the appraisal and motivation of managerial performance   *(AICPA adapted)*

_____ **8.** If profits are $25,000, sales are $150,000, and capital employed is $100,000, the rate of return on investment would be:

    a. 16%   **d.** 25%
    b. 150%   **e.** none of the above
    c. 66%

_____ **9.** If profits are $10,000, sales are $100,000, and capital employed is $100,000, the capital-employed turnover rate would be:

    a. 1   **d.** 0
    b. 0.1   **e.** none of the above
    c. 10

_____ **10.** Residual income is the:

    a. contribution margin of an investment center less the imputed interest on the invested capital used by the center
    b. contribution margin of an investment center plus the imputed interest on the invested capital used by the center
    c. income of an investment center less the imputed interest on the invested capital used by the center
    d. income of an investment center plus the imputed interest on the invested capital used by the center
    e. none of the above
                                                                     (AICPA adapted)

Part 4 ■ Problem

The management of Kittyhawk Company has been using the return-on-capital-employed method of measuring performance by division and product managers. Recently the management decided to apply the concept to three product groups. The Cost Department assembled the following data from the annual financial statements:

Item	Product Orville	Product Wilbur	Product Amelia
Capital employed..............................	$750,000	$500,000	$12,000,000
Sales volume in dollars.........................	1,500,000	1,000,000	6,000,000
Operating profit................................	75,000	200,000	1,200,000

1. For each product, determine the (1) capital-employed turnover rate, (2) percentage of profit to sales, and (3) rate of return on capital employed.

Product	(1) Capital-Employed Turnover Rate	(2) Percentage of Profit to Sales	(3) Rate of Return on Capital Employed
Orville			
Wilbur			
Amelia			

2. Since Orville and Amelia have the same low rate of return on capital employed, do they have the same problems? Explain what measures you would take to improve the rate of return for each product.

Part 5 ■ Problem

Cannes Chemical Products sells 20,000 gallons of chemical Ennui each year at $30 per gallon. Its plant has a capacity to produce 25,000 gallons per year. Fixed costs related to the plant amount to $200,000 a year. Variable costs per gallon are $18. Paris Industrial Products, a subsidiary located in another city, uses Ennui to produce an industrial resin. One-half gallon of Ennui is needed for each pound bag of resin. At present, the resin sells for $50 per bag and costs $40 per bag (all variable costs, including Ennui). The subsidiary sells 10,000 bags per year and at present purchases its Ennui from an outside supplier at $27 per gallon. Cannes Chemical Products asks its subsidiary to buy 5,000 gallons at the $30 price—an offer which is refused by Paris.

Instructions:

1. Prepare a comparison of gross profits under the present market-based transfer pricing system for Cannes Chemical Products, its subsidiary, and the corporation as a whole with the gross profits if the transfer pricing system were based on standard costs for a production level of 25,000 gallons of Ennui, using the schedule below:

System	Cannes	Paris	Corporation as a Whole
Market-based transfer pricing:			
Sales to outsiders	$	$	$
Cost of goods sold......................			
Gross profit.............................	$	$	$
Standard costing (using 25,000 gallons as a basis for allocating fixed costs):			
Sales to outsiders	$	$	$
Intracompany sales			
Cost of goods sold......................			
Gross profit	$	$	$

2. How should this transfer pricing dispute be resolved?

Part 6 ■ Problem

Oslo Co's industrial photo-finishing division, Rho, incurred the following costs and expenses in 1994.

	Variable	Fixed
Direct materials	$200,000	
Direct labor	150,000	
Factory overhead	70,000	$42,000
General, selling, and administrative	30,000	48,000
Totals	$450,000	$90,000

During 1994, Rho produced 300,000 units of industrial photo-prints, which were sold for $2.00 each. Oslo's investment in Rho was $500,000 and $700,000 at January 1, 1994 and December 31, 1994, respectively. Oslo normally imputes interest on investments at 8% of average invested capital.

1. Compute Rho's return on average investment for the year ended December 31, 1994.

2. Compute Rho's residual income (loss) for the year ended December 31, 1994.

3. Compute Rho's contribution margin for the year ended December 31, 1994.

SOLUTIONS

CHAPTER 1

Part 1 ■ True/False

1.	T	6.	F	11.	F
2.	T	7.	T	12.	T
3.	F	8.	T	13.	T
4.	F	9.	T	14.	F
5.	T	10.	T	15.	T

Part 2 ■ Matching

1.	a	8.	h	15.	d
2.	p	9.	g	16.	f
3.	o	10.	s	17.	q
4.	n	11.	i	18.	l
5.	m	12.	k	19.	t
6.	c	13.	j	20.	r
7.	e	14.	b		

Part 3 ■ Multiple Choice

1. d They are examples of non-value-added activities that result from the complexity that becomes embedded in the production setting rather than from the production effort itself.

2. a Accountability is the reporting of results to higher authority. It is important because it makes possible the measurement of the extent to which objectives have been achieved. Authority is the power to command others to perform or not to perform activities. Responsibility originates particularly in the superior-subordinate relationship because the superior has the authority to require specific work from other people.

3. d The line makes decisions and performs the true management function; whereas, the staff gives advice and performs technical functions.

4. e The human interrelations function directs the company's efforts in relation to the behavior of people inside and outside the company. The resources function involves the acquisition, disposal, and prudent management of a wide variety of resources. The processes function deals with activities such as product design, research and development, and purchasing.

5. a Operating management is primarily concerned with short-range decisions, middle management with medium-range decisions, and executive management with strategic planning.

6. a During its existence, the CASB issued a series of Cost Accounting Standards that govern the determination and allocation of specific costs relative to federal contracts.

7. e All terms are examples of systems or processes used in the new manufacturing environment.

8. c The CMA designation is formal recognition of professional competence and educational achievement in the field of management accounting.

9. d Standard costs are predetermined costs that are established by using information accumulated from past experience and from scientific research. Budgets should be based on standard costs.

10. d A budget is a quantified, written expression of management's plans for the future. It aids in: (1) setting goals; (2) informing individuals as to what they must do to contribute to the achievement of these goals; (3) motivating desired performance; (4) evaluating performance; and (5) suggesting corrective action.

Part 4 ■ Problem

1. The five tasks are:
   (1) To create and execute plans and budgets for operating under expected competitive and economic conditions.
   (2) To establish costing methods that permit control of activities, reductions of cost, and improvements of quality.
   (3) To create inventory values for costing and pricing purposes, and, at times, to control physical quantities.
   (4) To determine company costs and profit for an annual accounting period or a shorter period.
   (5) To choose from among two or more alternatives that might increase revenues or decrease costs.

2. The four standards are: CAS 409, which requires contractors to depreciate their assets for contract costing purposes over lives that are based on documenting historical usefulness, irrespective of the lives used for either financial or income tax purposes; CASs 414 and 417, which recognize as a contract cost the imputed cost of capital committed to facilities, thereby overturning the government's long-standing practice of disallowing interest and other financing-type costs; and CAS 416 which recognizes a cost for self-insurance.

3. The line-staff concept of management is based on the fundamental assumption that all positions or functional divisions can be categorized into two groups: the line, which makes decisions and performs the true management functions; and the staff, which gives advice and performs technical functions.

4. Strategic plans are formulated at the highest levels of management, make the broadest view of the company, are the least quantifiable, and are formulated at irregular intervals by an unsystematic process. Short-range plans, called budgets, are prepared through a systematized process, are highly quantified, are expressed in financial terms, and are usually prepared for periods of a quarter or a year. Long-range plans typically extend three to five years into the future, may culminate in a highly summarized set of financial statements or financial targets, and serve as a starting point for each set of short-range plans.

5. The five ways are:
   (1) Setting goals.
   (2) Informing individuals about what they should contribute to the accomplishment of the goals.
   (3) Motivating desirable performance.
   (4) Evaluating performance.
   (5) Suggesting when corrective action should be taken.

6. The accountant should go to each superior level of management and to the board of directors, if necessary, until the matter is resolved. The accountant may clarify relevant concepts and possible courses of action by going to an objective advisor. The accountant should resign if no internal resolution is achieved.

CHAPTER 2

Part 1 ■ True/False

1. F	6. T	11. T
2. T	7. T	12. F
3. T	8. T	13. T
4. T	9. F	14. T
5. T	10. F	15. F

Part 2 ■ Matching

1. t	8. f	15. n
2. r	9. d	16. i
3. p	10. b	17. g
4. k	11. s	18. e
5. l	12. q	19. c
6. j	13. o	20. a
7. h	14. m	

Part 3 ■ Multiple Choice

1. b Factory overhead consists of indirect materials, indirect labor, and all other indirect manufacturing costs.

2. c The characteristics of fixed costs are: (1) fixed total amount within a relevant output range; (2) decrease in unit cost as volume increases; (3) assignable to departments on the basis of arbitrary cost allocation methods; and (4) controllable by executive management.

3. e All four items are reasons why increased attention is being given to nonfinancial performance measures.

4. c Conversion cost represents the cost of converting direct materials into finished products and consists of direct labor and factory overhead.

5. e All four items are fixed costs (for example, they do not vary with the level of production).

6. d Fuel cost would vary with the level of production; whereas, the other costs are either fixed or semivariable.

7. b Power is an indirect factory overhead cost (for example, it is a manufacturing cost but it cannot be identified with specific jobs); whereas, the other three items are commercial expenses.

8. a Repairs and maintenance would be an example of a semivariable cost because a certain amount of maintenance would be required regardless of the level of activity; however, the more production that takes place the greater the repairs expense would be.

9. d Auditing is a typical administrative expense; whereas, the other three items are marketing expenses.

10. b Entertainment is a typical marketing expense; whereas, the other three items are administrative expenses.

Part 4 ■ Problem

1. Variable	6. Variable	11. Semivariable	16. Variable
2. Variable	7. Variable	12. Semivariable	17. Variable
3. Fixed	8. Semivariable	13. Fixed	18. Variable
4. Variable	9. Fixed	14. Fixed	19. Fixed
5. Semivariable	10. Fixed	15. Fixed	20. Semivariable

Part 5 ■ Problem

1. Admin. Expenses	6. Admin. Expenses	11. Indirect Labor	16. Market. Expenses
2. Other Indir. Costs	7. Market. Expenses	12. Indirect Labor	17. Admin. Expenses
3. Indirect Materials	8. Market. Expenses	13. Indirect Materials	18. Admin. Expenses
4. Indirect Labor	9. Other Indir. Costs	14. Indirect Materials	19. Indirect Labor
5. Admin. Expenses	10. Other Indir. Costs	15. Market. Expenses	20. Indirect Labor

Part 6 ■ Problem

	Estimated Unit Cost
1. Direct labor	$ 6
Variable factory overhead	9
Fixed factory overhead	15
Conversion cost	$30
2. Direct material	$25
Direct labor	6
Prime cost	$31
3. Direct material	$25
Direct labor	6
Variable factory overhead	9
Variable manufacturing cost	$40
4. Direct material	$25
Direct labor	6
Variable factory overhead	9
Variable marketing	3
Total variable cost	$43

5. Total Cost = Variable Manufacturing Cost + Variable Marketing Cost + Fixed Cost
   = [5,000 x ($25 + $6 + $9)] + (4,500 x $3) + [5,000* x ($15 + $5)]
   = $200,000 + $13,500 + $100,000 = $313,500

*Because this was the volume level used to compute the unit fixed costs that were given.

6. Total Cost = Variable Manufacturing Cost + Variable Marketing Cost + Fixed Cost
   = [5,000 x ($25 + $6 + $9)] + (5,500 x $3) + [5,000 x ($15 + $5)]
   = $200,000 + $16,500 + $100,000 = $316,500

CHAPTER 3

Part 1 ■ True/False

1. T	6. T	11. T
2. T	7. F	12. F
3. T	8. T	13. T
4. F	9. F	14. F
5. T	10. F	15. F

Part 2 ■ Matching

1. r	8. a	15. p
2. q	9. l	16. k
3. b	10. t	17. j
4. i	11. g	18. e
5. d	12. n	19. f
6. o	13. s	20. h
7. m	14. c	

Part 3 ■ Multiple Choice

1. b Fixed costs remain the same, in total, within a relevant range of activity and decrease per unit as the activity level increases.

2. a The scattergraph method is used for analyzing semivariable expenses by plotting various costs (e.g., electricity expense) on the y-axis and measurement figures (e.g., direct labor dollars) on the x-axis, and then fitting a line to the data points by visual inspection.

3. b A variable expense is expected to increase or decrease proportionally, in total, to an increase or decrease in activity, and to remain constant on a per-unit basis within a relevant range.

4. b The method of least squares involves the use of two variables: (1) an independent variable representing a measure of activity, such as machine hours; and (2) a dependent variable representing expense, such as repairs and maintenance.

5. a The coefficient of determination represents the percentage of variance in the dependent variable explained by the independent variable.

6. a

High	$2,252	5,200
Low	2,000	4,300
Difference	$ 252	900

Variable Rate = $\dfrac{\$252}{900}$ = $.28

$2,252 = 5,200(.28) + Fixed Cost

Fixed Cost = $2,252 − $1,456 = $796

7. c When $r = 0$, there is no correlation; and when $r = +1$, the correlation is perfect. As r approaches $+1$, the correlation is positive; and as r approaches -1, the correlation is negative and the regression line slopes downward to the right.

8. e $480 + $.50(20,000) = $10,480

9. c Fixed expenses, such as depreciation or a long-term lease agreement, commit management for a long period of time; therefore, they are called committed fixed costs.

10. a The high and low method is the alternative that least precisely separates fixed and variable costs because it only has two data points.

Part 4 ■ Problem

1.

Production costs:		
Direct labor		$250,000
Direct materials		300,000
Overhead to be incurred:		
Supervision	$40,000	
Power [$1,000 + ($1 x 10,000 units) + ($2 x 1,000 machine hours)]	13,000	
Factory supplies [$1,750 + ($.50 x 10,000 units)]	6,750	
Depreciation—equipment	7,000	
Depreciation—building	80,000	146,750
Total production costs		$696,750

Part 5 ■ Problem

1.

(a)

	Cost	Activity Level		High	Low
High	$1,667	350	Total repairs and maintenance	$1,667	$1,405
			Variable cost	841*	579 **
Low..............	1,405	241	Fixed cost..........	$ 826	$ 826
Difference........	$ 262	109			

Variable Rate = $\dfrac{\$262}{109}$ = $2.404 per machine hour

* $2.404 x 350

** $2.404 x 241

(b)

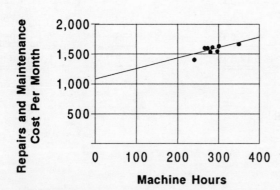

Average cost ($12,602÷8)	$1,575
Less fixed cost	1,050
Variable cost...	$ 525

Variable cost per machine hour: $\dfrac{\$525}{2,294 \div 8}$ = $1.831

(c)

Month	(1) Repairs and Maintenance Costs	(2) Difference from Average Cost	(3) Machine Hours	(4) Difference from Average Hours	(5) $(4)^2$	(6) (4) x (2)	(7) $(2)^2$
January	$ 1,548	$ (27)	297	10	100	$ (270)	$ 729
February	1,667	92	350	63	3,969	5,796	8,464
March	1,405	(170)	241	(46)	2,116	7,820	28,900
April	1,534	(41)	280	(7)	49	287	1,681
May	1,600	25	274	(13)	169	(325)	625
June.........	1,600	25	266	(21)	441	(525)	625
July	1,613	38	285	(2)	4	(76)	1,444
August	1,635	60	301	14	196	840	3,600
Total	$ 12,602	$ 2*	2,294	(2)*	7,044	$ 13,547	$46,068

Average machine hours (x): $\dfrac{2,294}{8}$ = 287

Average repairs and maintenance cost (y): $\dfrac{\$12,602}{8}$ = $1,575

Variable rate (b): $\dfrac{\$13,547}{7,044}$ = $1.923

Fixed cost per month: $y = a + bx$

$1,575 = a + ($1.923 x 287)$

$a = \$1,575 - \$552 = \$1,023$

2.

Month	(1) Machine Hours	(2) Factory Repairs and Maintenance Cost	(3) Predicted Repairs and Maintenance Cost	(4) Prediction Error (2) - (3)	(5) Prediction Error^2 [(4)^2]
January	297	$ 1,548	$ 1,594	(46)	2,116
February	350	1,667	1,696	(29)	841
March	241	1,405	1,486	(81)	6,561
April	280	1,534	1,561	(27)	729
May	274	1,600	1,550	50	2,500
June	266	1,600	1,535	65	4,225
July	285	1,613	1,571	42	1,764
August	301	1,635	1,602	33	1,089
Total	2,294	$ 12,602	$ 12,595	7**	$19,825

$$\sqrt{\frac{\sum\left(y_i - y_i^1\right)^2}{n-2}} = \sqrt{\frac{Col.5}{8-2}} = \sqrt{\frac{\$19,825}{6}} = \sqrt{\$3,304} = \$57.48$$

* $1,923 x + $1,023
** rounding difference

3.

$$y_1 = t_{95}\% \; s^1 \sqrt{1 + \frac{1}{n} + \frac{\left(x_i - \bar{x}\right)^2}{\sum\left(x_i - \bar{x}\right)^2}} = \$1.600 \pm (1.943)(\$57.58)(1.072)^{**}$$

$$= \$1,600 \pm \$120$$

$$** \sqrt{1 + \frac{1}{8} + \frac{\left(300 - 287\right)^2}{7,044}} = 1.072$$

4.

$$r = \frac{\sum(x - \bar{x})(y - \bar{y})}{\sqrt{\sum(x - \bar{x})^2 (y - \bar{y})^2}} = \frac{\$13,547}{\sqrt{(7,044)(\$46,068)}} = .7520$$

$$r^2 = .5655$$

CHAPTER 4

<table>
<tr><td colspan="3">Part 1 ■ True/False</td><td colspan="3">Part 2 ■ Matching</td></tr>
<tr><td>1. F</td><td>6. T</td><td>11. F</td><td>1. i</td><td>6. o</td><td>11. m</td></tr>
<tr><td>2. T</td><td>7. F</td><td>12. T</td><td>2. c</td><td>7. d</td><td>12. h</td></tr>
<tr><td>3. T</td><td>8. T</td><td>13. F</td><td>3. f</td><td>8. l</td><td>13. b</td></tr>
<tr><td>4. F</td><td>9. F</td><td>14. F</td><td>4. a</td><td>9. n</td><td>14. e</td></tr>
<tr><td>5. T</td><td>10. T</td><td>15. T</td><td>5. k</td><td>10. j</td><td>15. g</td></tr>
</table>

Part 3 ■ Multiple Choice

1. d Process costing accumulates costs by production process or department. It is used when units are not separately distinguishable from one another during one or more manufacturing processes.

2. b Job order costing would be appropriate for printing because costs would be accumulated per job. The other three processes lend themselves to process costing because they produce units that are not separately distinguishable.

3. b In job order costing, specific materials and labor costs are identified by job, and no averaging occurs.

4. a In an historical cost system, the presentation of results is delayed until all manufacturing operations of the accounting period have been performed. The other three answers apply only to a standard cost system.

5. d Drug production usually consists of manufacturing long runs of homogeneous products for which process costing is used. The other three industries would utilize job order costing.

6. c Job order costing is used when the products manufactured within a department or cost center are heterogeneous.

7. a A flexible manufacturing system consists of an integrated collection of automated production processes, automated materials movement, and computerized systems controls.

8. b A fixed automation manufacturing system is characterized by one kind of product, a large range of viable production volumes, and tightly constrained production quality.

9. a A manual manufacturing system is characterized by many kinds of products, a substantial learning curve effect, and long lead times.

10. d Backflush costing is characterized by no detailed accounting for work in process inventories.

Part 4 ■ Problem

	Beginning	Ending
1. Direct materials:		
Materials inventory, beginning	$20,000	
Purchases	75,000	
Materials available for use	$95,000	
Less raw materials inventory, ending	17,000	
Direct materials consumed		$ 78,000
Direct labor		180,000
Factory overhead		90,000
Total manufacturing costs		$348,000
2. Total manufacturing costs [from (1)]		$348,000
Add work in process inventory, beginning		55,000
		$403,000
Less work in process inventory, ending		45,000
Cost of goods manufactured		$358,000
3. Cost of goods manufactured [from (2)]		$358,000
Add finishing goods inventory, beginning		30,000
Cost of goods available for sale		$388,000
Less finishing goods inventory, ending		25,000
Cost of goods sold		$363,000

Part 5 ■ Problem

Description	Debit	Credit
(a)		
Materials...	70,000	
Accounts Payable.....................................		70,000
(b)		
Work in Process.......................................	52,000	
Factory Overhead Control.............................	6,300	
Materials...		58,300
(c)		
Payroll...	180,000	
Accrued Payroll.....................................		180,000
Accrued Payroll......................................	180,000	
Cash...		180,000
(d)		
Work in Process.......................................	75,000	
Factory Overhead Control.............................	40,000	
Marketing Expenses Control...........................	30,000	
Administrative Expenses Control.......................	35,000	
Payroll...		180,000
(e)		
Factory Overhead Control.............................	27,500	
Accumulated Depreciation...........................		25,000
Prepaid Expenses...................................		2,500
(f)		
Factory Overhead Control.............................	12,500	
Accounts Payable...................................		12,500
(g)		
Accounts Payable.....................................	76,000	
Cash...		76,000
(h)		
Cash...	315,000	
Accounts Receivable.................................		315,000
(i)		
Finished Goods.......................................	151,000	
Work in Process.....................................		151,000
(j)		
Accounts Receivable..................................	285,000	
Sales...		285,000
Cost of Goods Sold...................................	140,000	
Finished Goods......................................		140,000

CHAPTER 5

Part 1 ■ True/False			Part 2 ■ Matching		
1. T	6. T	11. F	1. o	8. q	15. l
2. T	7. F	12. T	2. k	9. m	16. e
3. F	8. F	13. T	3. h	10. t	17. p
4. T	9. F	14. F	4. c	11. a	18. b
5. F	10. T	15. T	5. s	12. i	19. d
			6. j	13. r	20. g
			7. f	14. n	

Part 3 ■ Multiple Choice

1. d   The cost of each order produced for a given customer or the cost of each lot to be placed in stock is recorded on a job cost sheet. An invoice is a document used to record the sale of goods or services to a customer. A purchase order is used to order goods from a supplier. A materials requisition sheet is prepared to issue materials from the storeroom to a job.

2. a   Details about a job are recorded on a job cost sheet, which may be in paper or electronic form.

3. d   Accumulated Depreciation is a general account; whereas, the other three are cost accounts and would be a part of a factory ledger if one were maintained.

4. c   When completed goods are sold, Cost of Goods Sold is debited and Finished Goods is credited in manufacturing accounting.

5. b   Factory Overhead Control is debited and Materials is credited for the issuance of indirect materials into production.

6. c   Work in Process is debited and Payroll is credited for distributing the direct labor charges in the payroll.

7. d   The activity chosen, such as direct labor hours or machine hours, is called the base or overhead allocation base and should be closely related to the costs being allocated.

8. c   Work in Process is debited and Applied Factory Overhead is credited to charge all jobs worked on during the period with their fair share of estimated overhead.

9. b   In a highly automated manufacturing environment, the amount of overhead costs incurred probably would be most highly correlated with the number of machine hours worked.

10. a   In service businesses, direct labor and labor-related costs are usually larger than any other costs, so the predetermined overhead rate typically is based on direct labor cost.

Obermyer Office Supply, Inc.
313 Oak Street, Cincinnati, OH 45227

Job Order No. **1215**

For:	Engleman Engineering
Product:	Executive Chairs
Specifications:	Attached
Quantity:	20

DATE ORDERED: 3/5/19--
DATE STARTED: 3/7/19--
DATE WANTED: 3/23/19--
DATE COMPLETED: 3/19/19--

Direct Materials

Date	Department	Req. No.	Cost	Total
3/12	Cutting	6281	$3,600	
3/12	Assembly	6288	240	
3/19	Cutting	6299	1,800	
3/19	Assembly	6308	360	$ 6,000

Direct Labor

Date	Department	Hours	Hourly Rate	Cost	Total
3/12	Cutting	400	$10.80	$4,320	
3/12	Assembly	200	9.50	1,900	
3/19	Cutting	220	10.80	2,376	
3/19	Assembly	300	9.50	2,850	$11,446

Factory Overhead Applied

Date	Department	Rate of Application	Hours	Cost	Total
3/12	Cutting	$7.50 per machine hour	300	$2,250	
3/12	Assembly	$6.00 per direct labor hour	200	1,200	
3/19	Cutting	$7.50 per machine hour	160	1,200	
3/19	Assembly	$6.00 per direct labor hour	300	1,800	$ 6,450

Direct Materials	$ 6,000	Sales Price	$40,000
Direct Labor	11,446	Factory Cost	$23,896
Factory Overhead Applied	6,450	Marketing and Administrative Expenses	9,558
Total Factory Cost	$23,896	Cost to Make and Sell	33,454
		Profit	$ 6,546

Part 5 ■ Problem

Work in Process	
March 1 Bal:	To finished goods
	100,000
Job 101 15,000	
Job 103 5,300	
Materials 25,000	
Direct labor ... 30,000	
Factory	
overhead ... 30,000	
March 31 Bal:	
Job 110 5,300	

Finished Goods	
From work in process	To cost of goods sold
100,000	91,000
March 31 Bal:	
Job 107 9,000	

Cost of Goods Sold	
From fininshed goods	1,500
91,000	
89,500	

Factory Overhead Control	
28,500	30,000
1,500	
30,000	

Applied Factory Overhead	
30,000	30,000

Part 6 ■ Problem

	Description	Debit	Credit
1.	Materials	25,000	
	Accounts Payable		25,000
2.	Payroll	33,000	
	Accrued Payroll		33,000
3.	Accrued Payroll	33,000	
	Cash		33,000
4.	Factory Overhead Control	5,500	
	Work in Process...	27,500	
	Payroll		33,000
5.	Factory Overhead Control	2,500	
	Work in Process...	29,000	
	Materials..		31,500
6.	Factory Overhead Control	1,000	
	Accumulated Depreciation		1,000
7.	Factory Overhead Control	15,000	
	Accounts Payable		15,000
8.	Work in Process...	27,500	
	Applied Factory Overhead		27,500
9.	Finished Goods	52,000	
	Work in Process		52,000
10.	Cash	40,000	
	Sales..		40,000
11.	Cost of Goods Sold.......................................	28,000	
	Finished Goods		28,000
12.	Applied Factory Overhead.................................	27,500	
	Factory Overhead Control		27,500
13.	Factory Overhead Control	3,500	
	Cost of Goods Sold		3,500

CHAPTER 6

Part 1 ■ True/False

1. T	6. T	11. T
2. F	7. F	12. T
3. T	8. F	13. F
4. T	9. T	14. F
5. T	10. F	15. F

Part 2 ■ Matching

1. a	6. e	11. d
2. j	7. f	
3. k	8. h	
4. c	9. i	
5. b	10. g	

Part 3 ■ Multiple Choice

1. a   In the selective product flow format, the product moves to different departments within the plant depending upon what final product is to be produced.

2. d   In highly automated factories, the distinction between direct and indirect labor often is blurred, and as a result the labor and overhead costs are combined and applied as a single conversion cost to departments.

3. d   All of the statements are features of process costing.

4. b   The cost per job would appear on a job order cost sheet. Answers a, c, and d would appear on a cost of production report.

5. c $14,000 + (80\% \times 7,000) = 19,600$.

6. a   Answer a is a characteristic of process costing; b and c relate to job order costing; and d would not be true for either process or job order costing.

7. c   If the percentage of completion of the ending work in process inventory were overstated, then the equivalent units would also be overstated. If equivalent units were overstated, then the cost per unit would be understated. If the cost per unit were understated, then the total cost of the completed goods would also be understated.

8. b   Transferred-in cost is the cost of the production of a previous internal process that is subsequently used in a succeeding internal process.

9. e   Quantity schedule:

	Units
Work in process, October 1	6,000
Units started	50,000
	56,000
Transferred out	44,000
Work in process, October 31	12,000
	56,000

Materials cost of work in process, October 31:

$$\frac{\$3,000 + \$25,560}{56,000} = \$.51 \times 12,000 = \$6,120$$

10. d   The correct answer is:

Let x = units started during the month:

$$3,000 + x = 10,000 + 4,000$$
$$x = 11,000$$

Part 4 ■ Problem

	Materials Units	Conversion Units
Department A:		
Transferred out	2,500	2,500
Ending inventory	1,000	250
Equivalent production	3,500	2,750

	Units from Preceding Department	Conversion Units
Department B:		
Transferred out	2,600	2,600
Ending inventory	500	250
Equivalent production	3,100	2,850

Part 5 ■ Problem

Materials (7,500 x $3)	....	$22,500
Conversion (3,750 x $2.30)	....	8,625
Work in process inventory	....	$31,125

Computations:

$$\text{Materials:} \quad \frac{\$7,500 + \$120,000}{35,000 + (15,000 \times .50)} = \$3.00$$

$$\text{Conversion:} \quad \frac{\$9,125 + \$80,000}{35,000 + (15,000 \times .25)} = \$2.30$$

Part 6 ■ Problem

Happy Valley Company
Department B
Cost of Production Report
For the Month of June, 19--

Quantity Schedule	Materials	Labor	Overhead	Quantity
Beginning inventory				5,000
Received from Department A				45,000
				50,000
Transferred to Department C				38,000
Completed and on hand				2,000
Ending inventory	--	50%	50%	10,000
				50,000

Cost Charged to Department	Total Cost	Equivalent Units	Unit Cost
Beginning inventory:			
Cost from preceding department	$ 30,000		
Labor	2,000		
Factory overhead	1,000		
Total cost in beginning inventory	$ 33,000		
Cost added during period:			
Cost from preceding department	$225,000	50,000	$ 5.10
Labor	25,000	45,000	.60
Factory overhead	12,500	45,000	.30
Total cost added during period	$262,500		
Total cost charged to the department	$295,500		$ 6.00

Cost Accounted for as Follows	Units	Percent Complete	Unit Cost	Total Cost
Transferred to Department C	38,000	100 %	$6.00	$228,000
Completed and on hand	2,000	100	6.00	12,000
Work in process, ending inventory:				
Cost from preceding department	10,000	100	5.10	51,000
Labor	10,000	50	.60	3,000
Factory overhead	10,000	50	.30	1,500
Total cost accounted for				$295,500

Part 7 ■ Problem

Cochrane Chemical Company
Refining Department
Cost of Production Report
For the Month of May, 19--

Quantity Schedule	Conversion Costs	Quantity
Beginning inventory	50%	10,000
Received from Mixing Department		35,000
		45,000
Transferred to Finishing Department		40,000
Ending inventory	75%	5,000
		45,000

Cost Charged to Department	Total Cost	Equivalent Units	Unit Cost
Beginning inventory:			
Cost from preceding department	$ 7,500		
Conversion	2,500		
Total cost in beginning inventory	$ 10,000		
Cost added during current period:			
Cost from preceding department	$120,050	35,000	$3.43
Conversion	89,900	38,750	2.32
Total cost added this period	$209,950		
Total cost charged to the department	$219,950		$5.75

Cost Accounted for as Follows	Units	Percent Complete	Unit Cost	Total Cost
Transferred to finished goods inventory:				
From beginning inventory				$ 10,000
Cost to complete this period:				
Conversion	10,000	50%	$2.32	11,600
Started and completed this period	30,000	100	5.75	172,500
Total cost transferred to finished goods				$194,100
Work in process, ending inventory:				
Cost from preceding department	5,000	100%	$3.43	$ 17,150
Conversion	5,000	75	2.32	8,700
Total cost in ending inventory				$ 25,850
Total cost accounted for				$219,950

* rounding error

CHAPTER 7

Part 1 ■ True/False

1. T	6. T	11. F
2. F	7. T	12. T
3. F	8. F	13. T
4. T	9. T	14. F
5. F	10. T	15. T

Part 2 ■ Matching

1. h	6. j	11. o
2. d	7. g	12. b
3. i	8. l	13. k
4. a	9. e	14. c
5. f	10. m	15. n

Part 3 ■ Multiple Choice

1. d **Internal failure** costs occur during the manufacturing or production process such as scrap, spoilage, rework, and downtime.

2. c **Appraisal costs** are the costs incurred to detect product failure, such as inspecting and testing materials, inspecting products, and obtaining information on customer satisfaction.

3. c All employees, including new employees, should be actively involved in quality improvement.

4. b If spoilage is caused by exacting specifications, customer changes, or other unusual and unexpected factors, the spoilage cost should be charged to that order.

5. d The cost of spoilage caused by internal failure cannot be passed on to the customer and results in lower profits.

6. a **Spoiled goods** are units of the final product or units of component parts that are either not technically correctable or not economically feasible to correct.

7. d When spoilage is caused by internal failure, the unrecoverable cost of the spoiled goods should be charged to **Factory Overhead Control**.

8. a If the rework is caused by the customer, the cost of the rework should be charged to the job by a debit to **Work in Process**.

9. e The correct answer is 12,000 + 6,000 = 18,000, because the cost of the lost units is spread over the remaining good units when the loss is due to normal production shrinkage.

10. d

Equivalent units transferred out...................	12,000
Equivalent units in ending inventory (6,000 x .40)....	2,400
Equivalent units in of spoilage (2,000 x .75).........	1,500
Total equivalent units............................	15,900

Part 4 ■ Problem

	Description	Debit	Credit
1.	Accounts Receivable................................	4,300	
	Scrap Sales (or Other Income)		4,300
2.	Accounts Receivable................................	4,300	
	Cost of Goods Sold		4,300
3.	Accounts Receivable................................	4,300	
	Factory Overhead Control...........................		4,300
4.	Accounts Receivable................................	4,300	
	Work in Process		4,300

Part 5 ▪ Problem

Description	Debit	Credit
1. Spoiled Goods Inventory (20 units x $10 salvage).........	200	
Factory Overhead Control	163	
Work in Process (20 units x $18.16 cost)		363
Cost of Goods Sold....................................	8,717	
Work in Process ($9,080 - 363)		8,717
Accounts Receivable ($8,717 x 200%)	17,434	
Sales		17,434
2. Spoiled Goods Inventory (20 units x $10 salvage)..........	200	
Work in Process...................................		200
Cost of Goods Sold....................................	8,880	
Work in Process ($9,080 - 200)		8,880
Accounts Receivable (8,880 x 200%)	17,760	
Sales		17,760

$$\frac{\$9,080 \text{ total job cost}}{500 \text{ units on job}} = \$18.16 \text{ per unit}$$

Part 6 ▪ Problem

Description	Debit	Credit
1. Factory Overhead Control ($25 x 50)	1,250	
Materials		250
Payroll..		500
Applied Factory Overhead..........................		500
Finished Goods.......................................	60,000	
Work in Process.....................................		60,000
2. Work in Process......................................	1,250	
Materials		250
Payroll..		500
Applied Factory Overhead..........................		500
Finished Goods.......................................	61,250	
Work in Process.....................................		61,250

Part 7 ■ Problem

Laurel Corporation
Finishing Department
Cost of Production Report
For September, 19--

Quantity Schedule	Materials	Labor	Overhead	Quantity
Beginning inventory				1,000
Received from Cutting Department				7,500
				8,500
Transferred to finished goods				5,000
Ending inventory.....................................	50%	25%	25%	2,000
Spoiled in process	100%	100%	100%	1,500
				8,500

Cost Charged to Department		Total Cost	Equivalent Units*	Unit Cost
Beginning inventory:				
Cost from preceding department		$ 8,850		
Materials.......................................		4,625		
Labor		3,150		
Factory overhead................................		5,250		
Total cost in beginning inventory		$ 21,875		
Cost added during period:				
Cost from preceding department		$122,900	8,500	$15.50
Materials.......................................		53,500	7,500	7.75
Labor		33,600	7,000	5.25
Factory overhead................................		42,000	7,000	6.75
Total cost added during period		$252,000		
Total cost charged to the department.................		$273,875		$35.25

Cost Accounted for as Follows	Units	Percent Complete	Unit Cost		Total Cost
Transferred to finished goods	5,000	100%	$35.25		$176,250
Transferred to spoiled goods inventory at salvage value	1,500		$25.00		37,500
Charge to factory overhead for spoilage:					
Cost of completed spoiled units	1,500	100%	$35.25	$52,875	
Less salvage value of spoiled units......	1,500		25.00	37,500	15,375
Work in process, ending inventory:					
Cost from preceding department	2,000	100%	$15.50	$31,000	
Materials.............................	2,000	50	7.75	7,750	
Labor	2,000	25	5.25	2,625	
Factory overhead.....................	2,000	25	6.75	3,375	44,750
Total cost accounted for					$273,875

* Total number of equivalent units required in the cost accounted for section determined as follows:

	Prior Dept. Cost	Materials	Labor	Overhead
Equivalent units transferred out............	5,000	5,000	5,000	5,000
Equivalent units in ending inventory	2,000	1,000	500	500
Equivalent units of spoilage...............	1,500	1,500	1,500	1,500
	8,500	7,500	7,000	7,000

2.

Description	Debit	Credit
Fininshed Goods Inventory	176,250	
Spoiled Goods Inventory	37,500	
Factory Overhead Control	15,375	
Work in Process—Finishing Department		229,125

CHAPTER 8

Part 1 ■ True/False

1. F	6. T	11. T	
2. T	7. F	12. T	
3. T	8. T	13. T	
4. T	9. T	14. F	
5. T	10. T	15. F	

Part 2 ■ Matching

1. k	6. b	11. c
2. f	7. l	12. e
3. d	8. i	13. g
4. n	9. a	14. m
5. h	10. j	15. o

Part 3 ■ Multiple Choice

1. **a** The market value method enjoys great popularity because of the argument that the market value of any product is a manifestation of the cost incurred in its production.

2. **a** Whenever two or more different joint products or by-products are created from a single cost factor, a joint cost results. By-products and joint products are difficult to cost because a true joint cost is indivisible.

3. **d** This method is called the market value (reversal cost) method, and it reduces the manufacturing cost of the main product by an estimate of the by-product's value at the time of recovery. The by-product account is charged with this estimated amount and the manufacturing cost of the main product is credited. Any additional costs of materials, labor, or factory overhead incurred after the by-product is separated from the main product are charged to the by-product.

4. **a** All manufacturing costs (materials, labor, and overhead) should be allocable as joint costs.

5. **a** Joint costs should be allocated in a manner that assigns a proportionate amount of the total cost to each product by means of a quantitative basis such as the market value method, the quantitative or physical unit method, the average unit cost method, or the weighted average method.

6. **e** Answers a, b, c, and d are all methods of allocating joint costs.

7. **a**

$$\frac{\$60,000}{10,000} = \$6 \text{ per unit}$$

Product C: $8,000 \times \$6 = \$48,000$

Product R: $2,000 \times \$6 = \$12,000$

8. **c**

Oar: $\dfrac{\$9,000 - \$3,000}{\$15,000 - \$6,000} \times \$6,600 = \$4,400$

Wade: $\dfrac{\$6,000 - \$3,000}{\$15,000 - \$6,000} \times \$6,600 = \$2,200$

9. **c**

Product	Market Value at Split-Off (Per Gallon)	Gallons	Market Value at Split-Off	Apportionment of Joint Production Cost
A	$10	500	$ 5,000	$1,200
B	14	1,000	14,000	3,360
			$ 19,000	$4,560

$3,360 + ($2 x 1,000) = $5,360 cost to produce 1,000 gallons of B.

10. d   Integrity and objectivity are the two standards most closely related to considerations of joint cost allocation
         methods.

Part 4 ■ Problem

1.   Sales.. $15,000
      Cost of goods sold:
      Beginning inventory .... $ 3,750
      Total production cost   6,750
      Cost of goods available for sale $10,500
      Ending inventory (4,000 units $.75)   3,000   7,500
      (a) Gross profit.. $7,500
          Marketing and administrative expense   3,000
          Operating income $4,500
          Revenue from sale of by-product   750
      (b) Income before income tax................................... $5,250

2.   (a) $ 7,500 + $750 = $8,250

      (b) $ 8,250 - $3,000 = $5,250

3.   (a) $15,000 - ($7,500 - $750) = $8,250
      (b) $ 8,250 - $3,000 = $5,250

4.   (a) Beginning inventory $3,750
           Total production cost .... $ 6,750
           Less revenue from by-product........................   750   6,000
           Cost of goods available for sale $9,750

           New average unit cost for main product: $9,750 ÷ 14,000 = $.696

      (b) 4,000 units x $.696 = $2,784

Part 5 ■ Problem

Greek Products Inc.
Income Statement
For the Month of July, 19--

	Main Product	By-Product Chi	By-Product Phi	Total
Sales...............................	$80,000	$12,000	$6,000	$98,000
Cost of goods sold:				
Manufacturing cost before separation:				
Cost assigned:				
Operating profit...................		$ 3,000	$1,200	
Marketing and administrative expense		2,000	750	
Manufacturing cost after separation......		5,000	2,500	
Total...............................		$10,000	$4,450	
Cost before separation	$ 36,450*	$ 2,000	$1,550	$40,000
Manufacturing cost after separation.....................	15,000	5,000	2,500	22,500
Cost of goods sold.................	$51,450	$ 7,000	$4,050	$62,500
Gross profit.......................	$28,550	$ 5,000	$1,950	$35,500
Marketing and administrative expense	8,000	2,000	750	10,750
Operating profit...................	$20,550	$ 3,000	$1,200	$24,750

Part 6 ■ Problem

Waste Products Inc.
Allocation of Joint Cost
For January, 19--

Chemical	Units Produced (1)	Units Sold	Units in Ending Inventory	Unit Sales Price at Split-Off (2)	Market Value of Production	Joint Cost Allocated (3)	Cost of Sales (4)	Ending Inventory
Gunk	2,000	1,500	500	$10	$ 20,000	$ 15,000	$11,250	$ 3,750
Sledge	6,000	5,000	1,000	12	72,000	54,000	45,000	9,000
Grunge	10,000	8,000	2,000	7	70,000	52,500	42,000	10,500
					$162,000	$121,500	$98,250	$23,250

Computations:

(1) Sledge:
  Gunk: 1/5 x 10,000 = 2,000
  Sledge: 3/5 x 10,000 = 6,000
  Grunge: 5/5 x 10,000 = 10,000

(2) Gunk: $15,000 ÷ 1,500 = $10
  Sledge: $60,000 ÷ 5,000 = $12
  Grunge: $56,000 ÷ 8,000 = $7

$$\frac{\text{Joint processing cost}}{\text{Market value of production}} = \frac{\$60.75 \times (10,000 \div 5)}{\$162,000} = \frac{\$121,500}{\$162,000} = \$.75$$

(3) Gunk: $20,000 x .75 = $15,000
  Sledge: $72,000 x .75 = $54,000
  Grunge: $70,000 x .75 = $52,500

(4) Gunk: 1,500 x $10 x .75 = $11,250
  Sledge: 5,000 x $12 x .75 = $45,000
  Grunge: 8,000 x $7 x .75 = $42,000

Part 7 ■ Problem

1.

Space Products Inc.
Quantitative Unit Method
For April, 19-

	Units Produced and Sold	Joint Cost Allocated	Unit Market Value	Unit Cost of Sales	Unit Gross Profit
Star	225,000	$ 759,375	$10	$3.375	$ 6.625
Trek	75,000	253,125	15	3.375	11.625
	300,000	$1,012,500			

Computations:

Star: $\dfrac{225,000}{300,000} \times \$1,012,500 = \$759,375$

Trek: $\dfrac{75,000}{300,000} \times \$1,012,500 = \$253,125$

2.

Space Products Inc.
Market Value Method
For April, 19--

	Units Produced and Sold	Unit Market Value	Total Market Value	Joint Cost Allocation	Unit Cost of Sales	Unit Gross Profit
Star..................	225,000	$10	$2,250,000	$ 675,000	$3.00	$ 7.00
Trek	75,000	15	1,125,000	337,500	4.50	10.50
	300,000		$3,375,000	$1,012,500		

Computations:

$$\frac{\text{*Cost of sales}}{\text{Total market value}} = \frac{\$1,012,500}{\$3,375,000} = \$.30$$

Star: $2,250,000 × .30 = $675,000

Trek: $1,125,000 × .30 = $337,500

CHAPTER 9

Part 1 ■ True/False

1.	T	6.	T	11.	F
2.	T	7.	T	12.	T
3.	F	8.	F	13.	F
4.	T	9.	T	14.	T
5.	T	10.	T	15.	T

Part 2 ■ Matching

1.	o	8.	b	15.	n
2.	k	9.	i	16.	c
3.	a	10.	q	17.	l
4.	j	11.	f	18.	r
5.	t	12.	e	19.	d
6.	g	13.	p	20.	m
7.	s	14.	h		

Part 3 ■ Multiple Choice

1. d   All withdrawals of materials from the storeroom are evidenced by a materials requisition form and result in debits to Work in Process, Factory Overhead, or Marketing and Administration Expense.

2. d $$\sqrt{\frac{2 \times RU \times CO}{CU \times CC}} = \sqrt{\frac{2 \times 40,000 \times \$60}{\$10}} = \sqrt{480,000} = 693$$

3. a

$$EOQ = \sqrt{\frac{2 \times RU \times CO}{CU \times CC}}$$

$$200 = \sqrt{\frac{2 \times 6,000 \times \text{Setup cost}}{\$.60}}$$

$$\$.60(40,000) = (2 \times 6,000 \times \text{Setup cost})$$

$$\$24,000 = 12,000(\text{Setup cost})$$

Setup cost = $2

4. c   In determining EOQ, only the variable ordering costs, such as preparing the purchase order, handling the incoming shipment, and preparing the receiving report, should be considered.

5. a   The three items needed to compute the EOQ are the annual demand, the cost of placing an order, and the annual cost of carrying one unit in stock.

6. c   The EOQ is that point where carrying costs equal ordering costs. If a quantity greater than the EOQ is ordered, carrying costs will exceed ordering costs.

7. a   The economic order quantity is that point where ordering costs and carrying costs are minimized.

8. c   If safety stocks are ignored, the only factor relevant for determining the order point is the anticipated demand during the lead time.

9. c   The purchase requisition informs the purchasing agent of the quantity and kind of materials needed.

10. a If materials cost is to include acquisition costs, an applied rate can be added to each invoice and to each item, and the journal entry credit would be to Applied Purchasing Department Costs.

Part 4 ■ Problem

1. Freight allocated to materials based on cost:

$$\frac{\$950}{\$50,000} = \$.019 \text{ per dollar of cost}$$

Part 001:	$22,500	x $.019	= $427.50
Part 002:	16,000	x .019	= 304.00
Part 003:	11,500	x .019	= 218.50
	$50,000		$950.00

2. Freight allocated to materials based on volume:

$$\frac{\$950}{3,800 \text{ gallons}} = \$.25 \text{ per gallon}$$

Part 001:	1,600	gallons	x $.25	=	$400
Part 002:	1,400	gallons	x .25	=	350
Part 003:	800	gallons	x .25	=	200
	3,800	gallons			$950

Part 5 ■ Problem

$$EOQ = \sqrt{\frac{2 \times RU \times CO}{CU \times CC}} = \sqrt{\frac{2 \times 180,000 \times \$80}{\$400 \times .20}} = \sqrt{360,000} = 600$$

$$\frac{RU \times CO}{EOQ} = \frac{180,000 \times \$80}{600} = \$24,000 \text{ Order cost}$$

$$\frac{CU \times CC \times EOQ}{2} = \frac{\$400 \times .20 \times 600}{2} = \$24,000 \text{ Carrying cost}$$

Part 6 ■ Problem

Safety Stock Level	Expected Annual Stockouts	Total Stockout Cost	Total Carrying Cost	Total Stockout and Carrying Cost
0	50	$5,000	0	$5,000
200	30	3,000	$ 400	3,400
400	10	1,000	800	1,800
800	5	500	1,600	2,100

The optimum level of safety stock is 400 units, because that is the level at which total stockout cost and carrying cost are minimized.

Part 7 ■ Problem

1. $$EOQ = \sqrt{\frac{2 \times (250 \times 100) \times \$25}{\$5}} = \sqrt{250,000} = 500$$

2. Maximum use per day . . . .   150 units
    Normal use per day   100
    Safety stock (maximum) . . . .   50 units x 10 days lead time=500 units

3. Normal use per day [100 x days of lead time (10)] . . . .   1,000 units
    Safety stock   500
    Order point . . . .   1,500 units

4. Order point . . . .   1,500 units
    Normal use during lead time (100 x 10)   1,000
    On hand at time order received . . . .   500 units
    Quantity received   500
    Maximum inventory . . . .   1,000 units

CHAPTER 10

Part 1 ■ True/False

1. F	6. F	11. F
2. T	7. T	12. T
3. F	8. T	13. F
4. T	9. F	14. F
5. F	10. T	15. T

Part 2 ■ Matching

1. j	4. h	8. c
2. f	5. e	9. g
3. b	6. a	10. d
	7. i	

Part 3 ■ Multiple Choice

1. b   JIT is a philosophy centered on the reduction of costs through the elimination of inventory.

2. c   One of the dangers of JIT is that it eliminates the cushion against production orders and imbalances that inventories provide.

3. d   JIT is least applicable where each customer order is unique and demand is uncertain.

4. e   All of the other items are appropriate for describing the JIT effort to reduce inventories.

5. c   The JIT production ideal is a batch size of one that is produced only when it is ordered.

6. c   All of the changes except c enhance the objective of reducing inventory to zero.

7. e   All of the steps in a through d aid in the continuing reduction in inventories.

8. d   The speed with which units or tasks are processed in a system is called the velocity, and it is inversely related to throughput time.

9. b   Backflush costing is used in a mature JIT system in which velocity is so high that the usefulness of tracking the cost of WIP is questionable.

10. a   The cost of completed work is subtracted from the balance of the work in process account in a step called postdeduction.

Part 4 ■ Problem

1. Carrying cost savings = 25% × reduction in average cost of WIP

    = 25% × 40% past average cost of WIP

    = .25× .4 × 5 × 100 × 60

    = $3,000

2.   Savings in cost of defects = $15 × reduction in number of defective units produced per undiscovered out-of-control conditions × number of out-of-control conditions not discovered immediately

$$= \$15 \times (40\% \times 100 \times 10\%) \times \left(\frac{1}{4} \times 300\right)$$

$$= \$4,500$$

Part 5 ■ Problem

Journal entries involving RIP and/or Finished Goods are:

Description	Debit	Credit
Raw and In Process	325,000	
Accounts Payable		325,000
Finished Goods	327,500	
Raw and In Process		327,500

To backflush material cost from RIP to Finished Goods. This is the postdeduction. The calculation is:

Material in March 1 RIP balance	$ 15,000
Material received during March	325,000
	$340,000
Material in March 31 RIP, per physical count	12,500
Amount to be backflushed	$327,500

Description	Debit	Credit
Cost of Goods Sold	331,500	
Finished Goods		331,500

To backflush material cost from Finished Goods to Cost of Goods Sold. This is a postdeduction. The calculation is:

Material in March 1 Finished Goods	$ 11,500
Material backflushed to Finished Goods	327,500
	$339,000
Material in March 31 Finished Goods, per physical count	7,500
Amount to be backflushed	$331,500

Description	Debit	Credit
Cost of Goods Sold	3,000	
Raw and In Process		1,000
Finished Goods		2,000

Conversion cost in RIP is adjusted from the $2,500 of March 1 to the $1,500 estimate at March 31. Conversion cost in Finished Goods is adjusted from the $7,500 of March 1 to the $5,500 estimate at March 31. The offsetting entry is made to the cost of goods sold account, where all conversion costs were charged during March.

Part 6 ■ Problem

1.   (a) Equivalent production = 5,000 + (.25 x 40) = 5,010 units

$$\frac{\$200,550}{5,010} = \$40.030 \text{ per unit}$$

(b)

$$\frac{\$200,000}{5,000} = 40 \text{ per unit}$$

(c) Units started = 5,000 + 40 - 50 = 4,990

$$\frac{\$200,000}{4,990} = \$40.080 \text{ per unit}$$

2.   400, because 40 x .25 x $40.030 = $400.30
     400, because 40 x .25 x $40.000 = $400.00
     400, because 40 x .25 x $40.080 = $400.80

3. Processing speed is very fast, with the result that work in process inventory levels are kept to a very low level—both in absolute terms and in relation to total production activity for the month. Therefore, the backflush method used in 1(b) would be preferable for computing costs because it is the simplest.

CHAPTER 11

Part 1 ■ True/False

1. T	6. T	11. T
2. T	7. F	12. T
3. F	8. F	13. T
4. T	9. T	14. T
5. T	10. T	15. F

Part 2 ■ Matching

1. o	8. j	15. h
2. t	9. f	16. p
3. k	10. i	17. g
4. a	11. b	18. n
5. s	12. d	19. l
6. q	13. r	20. m
7. c	14. e	

Part 3 ■ Multiple Choice

1. d   Before the daily time tickets are sent to the payroll department, the total time reported on each time ticket is compared with the total hours on each employee's time clock card. If there is any difference, an adjustment is made after having identified the reasons for the difference.

2. c

Times	Cumulative Average Required Labor Hours per Time
1	100 minutes
2	80 (100 x 8)
4	64 (80 x 8)

3. d   4 x 64 = 256

4. c   The clock card (or time card) is needed to provide evidence of the employee's presence in the plant from the time of entry to departure.

5. d   In the 100% group bonus plan, each worker in the group receives an hourly rate for production up to the standard output. Units produced in excess of the standard are regarded as time saved by the group, and each worker is in effect paid a bonus for time saved.

6. a   The pace at which an observed employee is working is referred to as a rating or performance rating.

7. d   Fringe costs form a substantial element of labor cost and include such items as the employer portion of the FICA tax, holiday pay, overtime premium pay, and pension costs.

8. b   Advance manufacturing technologies enhance productivity and competitiveness, but few firms reconfigure human resource needs to reap the benefits of technological innovation.

9. a   To curtail the wage-price spiral requires increases that do not exceed the unit cost reduction resulting from increased productivity.

10. c   The cost department is responsible for recording the direct and indirect labor costs on the job cost sheets and departmental cost analysis sheets, respectively.

Part 4 ■ Problem

Worker	Hours Worked	Output Units	Standard Units	Efficiency Ratio	Base Rate	Base x Efficiency Ratio	Total Earned	Labor Cost per Unit	Overhead per Hour	Overhead per Unit	Conversion Cost per Unit
Allen	40	840	800	1.05	$15.00	$15.75	$630.00	$.75	$20.00	$ .95	$1.70
Birge	40	800	800	1.00	15.00	15.00	600.00	.75	20.00	1.00	1.75
Cole	40	880	800	1.10	15.00	16.50	660.00	.75	20.00	.91	1.66
Duffy	36	750	720	1.04	10.00	10.40	374.40	.50	20.00	.96	1.46
Easton	40	720	800	.90	7.50	--	300.00	.42	20.00	1.11	1.53

Part 5 ■ Problem

Day	Units Produced	Daily Earnings	Labor Cost per Unit Produced Each Day
Monday	30	$ 96.00	$3.20
Tuesday	32	96.00	3.00
Wednesday	46	138.00	3.00
Thursday	28	96.00	3.43
Friday	34	102.00	3.00

Part 6 ■ Problem

1.

Cumulative Lots x	Cumulative Average Time per Lot =	Cumulative Time (Total Hours)
1	150.00	150.00
2	120.00 (150 x .8)	240.00 (120 x 2)
4	96.00 (120 x .8)	384.00 (96 x 4)
8	76.80 (96 x .8)	614.40 (76.80 x 8)

2.   614.40 x $17.50 = $10,752

3. $10,752 cost of eight lots
     - 2,625 cost of first lot
     $ 8,127 cost of Lots 2-8

Part 7 ■ Problem

Description	Debit	Credit
1. Work in Process [(50 x $14) + (10 x $7)]	770	
Payroll		770
2. Work in Process ($50 x $14)	700	
Factory Overhead Control (10 x $7)	70	
Payroll		770

Part 8 ■ Problem

Description	Subsidiary Record	Debit	Credit
Work in Process		3,300	
Factory Overhead Control		600	
Bonus Pay ($3,300 ÷ 11)	300		
Vacation Pay $3,300 ÷ 11)	300		
Accrued Payroll			3,300
Liability for Bonus			300
Liability for Vacation Pay			300

CHAPTER 12

Part 1 ■ True/False

1. T	6. T	11. T
2. F	7. F	12. T
3. F	8. F	13. F
4. F	9. F	14. T
5. T	10. T	15. F

Part 2 ■ Matching

1. f	8. n	15. t
2. l	9. g	16. a
3. b	10. h	17. q
4. m	11. p	18. o
5. e	12. s	19. i
6. c	13. j	20. d
7. r	14. k	

Part 3 ■ Multiple Choice

1. d When the overhead applied to jobs or products during the period is more than the actual overhead incurred, overhead is said to be overapplied.

2. b Since the expected actual capacity concept calculates an overhead rate by basing its numerator and denominator on the expected actual output for the period, it minimizes the difference between actual factory overhead and applied factory overhead.

3. c The fixed cost per unit would be more because the same dollar amount of fixed cost is being spread over fewer units. The per-unit variable cost should be unchanged because the fewer units produced should result in less variable cost.

4. c Direct manufacturing costs consist of direct materials and direct labor, whereas the other terms are synonymous with factory overhead.

5. a There should be a high correlation between the base being used and the type of overhead cost incurred. Answers b through d are examples of bases that are frequently used.

6. e If factory overhead is overapplied, more units were produced than the number used to compute the predetermined factory overhead rate, thus resulting in more fixed factory overhead being charged to products than was actually incurred.

7. a If factory overhead costs are mostly variable, changes in the level of production should have little effect on the amount of overhead cost applied to products.

8. a The direct labor hour method is considered the most accurate method of applying overhead when the overhead cost is comprised predominantly of labor-related costs and the employees earn varying wage rates.

9. d Internal Revenue Service regulations require that inventories include an allocated portion of significant annual overhead variances.

10. a All are examples of factory overhead, except for the punch press operators who are direct laborers.

Part 4 ■ Problem

1. $20 per unit ($500,000 ÷ 25,000)
     $10 per direct labor hour ($500,000 ÷ 50,000)
     125% of direct labor cost ($500,000 ÷ $400,000)
     $50 per machine hour ($500,000 ÷ 10,000)

2. $20 per hour variable ($200,000 ÷ 10,000)
     $30 per hour fixed ($300,000 ÷ 10,000)
     $50 per hour ($20 + $30)

Description	Debit	Credit
3. Work in Process	500,000	
Applied Factory Overhead		500,000

4.   Factory Overhead Control

5.   (a)

Work in Process		Factory Overhead Control	
520,000		550,000	520,000

(b) Underapplied; $30,000

(c)

Overhead Rate	March Overhead Applied
$4 (200,000 ÷ 50,000)	$208,000
6 ($300,000 ÷ 50,000)	312,000
10	520,000

Part 5 ■ Problem

Factory Expense Category	Budget Rate	Level of Activity (Machine Hours)			
		45,000	50,000	55,000	60,000
Variable costs (per machine hour):					
Indirect labor	$2.00	$ 90,000	$100,000	$110,000	$120,000
Indirect materials	0.80	36,000	40,000	44,000	48,000
Repairs	0.60	27,000	30,000	33,000	36,000
Total variable cost	$3.40	$153,000	$170,000	$187,000	$204,000
Fixed costs (total):					
Depreciation—					
factory and machinery	$200,000	$200,000	$200,000	$200,000	$200,000
Insurance—factory and machinery	50,000	50,000	50,000	50,000	50,000
Total fixed cost	$250,000	$250,000	$250,000	$250,000	$250,000
Total overhead budget		$403,000	$420,000	$437,000	$454,000
Factory overhead rate per hour		$8.96	$8.40	$7.95	$7.57
Fixed overhead rate per hour		$5.56	$5.00	$4.55	$4.17
Variable overhead rate per hour		$3.40	$3.40	$3.40	$3.40

Part 6 ■ Problem

	Description	Debit	Credit
1.	Work in Process	1,100	
	Finished Goods	2,750	
	Cost of Goods Sold	7,150	
	Factory Overhead Control		11,000

	Description	Debit	Credit
2.	Work in Process	1,151	
	Finished Goods	2,686	
	Cost of Goods Sold	7,163	
	Factory Overhead Control		11,000

	Requirement (1)		Requirement (2)	
	Account Balance	Percentage of Total	Applied Overhead	Percentage of Total
Work in Process	$ 10,000	10%	$ 4,500	10.46%
Finished Goods	25,000	25%	10,500	24.42%
Cost of Goods Sold	65,000	65%	28,000	65.12%
Total	$ 100,000	100%	$ 43,000	100.00%

CHAPTER 13

Part 1 ■ True/False

1.	F	6.	F	11.	T
2.	T	7.	T	12.	F
3.	T	8.	T	13.	T
4.	T	9.	F	14.	T
5.	T	10.	T	15.	T

Part 2 ■ Matching

1.	j	7.	g	13.	m
2.	p	8.	i	14.	o
3.	k	9.	q	15.	c
4.	l	10.	a	16.	h
5.	n	11.	b	17.	e
6.	d	12.	f		

Part 3 ■ Multiple Choice

1. b A producing department contributes directly to the manufacture of the product by changing the shape, form, or nature of the material that is converted into the finished product.

2. b All of the other departments listed are service departments.

3. d All of the other departments listed are producing departments.

4. c

		P1	P2	S1	S2*
Beginning		$400,000	$300,000	$ 52,640	$ 105,280
Allocation of S2:	30%	31,584			
	50%		52,640		
	20%			21,056	(105,280)
				$ 73,696	$ 0
Allocation of S1:	4/7	42,112			
	3/7		31,584	(73,696)	
Ending		$473,696	$384,224	$ 0	

*Note that S2 is distributed before S1 because it has higher costs to be distributed, and they each service the same number of other departments.

5. a To charge each department with its fair share of an expense, a base using some factor common to all departments must be found. Therefore, the number of employees would be a good basis to use for charging supervision.

6. d The direct labor method allocates service department costs to producing departments only.

7. a
Direct labor	$ 100,000
Other	190,000
	$ 290,000
Percentage of employees	x .25
Payroll department costs chargeable to Department B	$ 72,500

8. c All of the items listed except for the number of employees in each department are factors to be considered.

9. a All of the items listed are direct departmental overhead costs except for the expenses associated with the factory building, which would have to be allocated to the individual departments.

10. c A better case for allocating the variable portion of electricity expense would be the number of kilowatt hours.

Part 4 ■ Problem

1. Using the step method of allocation:

	Service Departments			Producing Departments		Total
	X	**Y**	**Z**	**A**	**B**	
Total	$ 40,000	$ 30,000	$ 25,000	$100,000	$150,000	$345,000
Dept. X distribution	$(40,000)	16,000	12,000	8,000	4,000	
Dept. Y distribution		$(46,000)	18,400	16,100	11,500	
Dept. Z distribution			$(55,400)	38,780	16,620	
Total				$162,880	$182,120	$345,000

2. Using the direct method of allocation:

	Service Departments			Producing Departments		Total
	X	**Y**	**Z**	**A**	**B**	
Total	$ 40,000	$ 30,000	$ 25,000	$100,000	$150,000	$345,000
Dept. X distribution	$(40,000)	--	--	26,667	13,333	
Dept. Y distribution		$(30,000)	--	17,500	12,500	
Dept. Z distribution			$(25,000)	17,500	7,500	
Total				$161,667	$183,333	$345,000

Part 5 ■ Problem

		Producing Departments			Service Departments			
	Total	Preparation	Mixing	Packaging	Utilities	Maintenance	Materials Handling	Factory Office
Distribution of service departments costs:	$35,500	$ 6,000	$ 5,700	$ 6,950	$ 7,200	$4,200	$2,875	$2,575
Utilities:								
70% metered hours		(30%) 1,512	(36%) 1,814	(14%) 706	(5,040)	(10%) 504	(6%) 302	(4%) 202
30% sq. footage		(36%) 778	(26%) 562	(24%) 518	(2,160)	(4%) 86	(2%) 43	(8%) 173
					$ 7,200	$4,790		
Maintenance		(50%) 2,395	(25%) 1,198	(10%) 479		($4,790)	(10%) 479	(5%) 239
							$3,699	$3,189
Materials handling		(45%) 1,664	(35%) 1,295	(20%) 740			($3,699)	
Factory office		(40%) 1,276	(40%) 1,276	(20%) 637				($3,189)
	$35,500	$ 13,625	$ 11,845	$ 10,030				
Bases:								
Pounds handled		300,000	500,000					
Direct labor cost				$ 20,000				
Rates		$.0454 per pound handled	$.0237 per pound handled	50.15% of direct labor cost				

Part 6 ■ Problem

1. Equations: Utilities   = $25,000 + 25% Maintenance

                Maintenance = $40,000 + 10% Utilities

Substitutions: U = $25,000 + .25 ($40,000 + .10U)

                  U = $25,000 + $10,000 + .025U

        .975 U = 35,000

            U = 35,897

            M = $40,000 + .10 ($35,897)

            M = $43,590

2.

	Total	Milling	Planing	Utilities	Maintenance
Primary Overhead	$215,000	$ 90,000	$60,000	$ 25,000	$ 40,000
Distribution of:					
Utilities		17,948	14,359	(35,897)	3,590
Maintenance		17,436	15,257	10,897	(43,590)
	$215,000	$125,384	$89,616	$ 0	$ 0

CHAPTER 14

Part 1 ■ True/False

1. T	6. T	11. T
2. T	7. T	12. F
3. F	8. F	13. T
4. T	9. T	14. F
5. F	10. F	15. T

Part 2 ■ Matching

1. l	6. n	11. k
2. f	7. b	12. g
3. o	8. m	13. d
4. a	9. i	14. j
5. h	10. c	15. e

Part 3 ■ Multiple Choice

1. a   Unit-level activities include direct labor tasks such as, cutting, soldering, painting, assembling, and packaging.

2. b   Examples of batch-level costs include salaries of schedulers, setup personnel, and material handlers.

3. c   Examples of product-level activity drivers include number of products, design changes, and design hours.

4. d   Examples of plant-level activities include heating, lighting, cooling, and providing security.

5. a   Traditional costing systems are characterized by their exclusive use of unit-level measures as bases for allocating overhead to output.

6. e   ABC systems are characterized by their use of all four of the activity drivers listed.

7. b   The number of allocation bases used in ABC systems tends to be higher than in traditional costing systems.

8. d   It is not necessary to ever replace the traditional accounting system with ABC to get ABC's benefits.

9. e   Choices a through d are all ways in which activities may be managed to achieve improvements in a process.

10. a   Materials conversion is a value-added activity that converts the raw material into a finished product.

Part 4 ■ Problem

Item	Unit-Level Driver	Batch-Level Driver	Product-Level Driver	Plant-Level Driver
1. Number of setups		✓		
2. Number of design changes			✓	
3. Units of output	✓			
4. Square footage occupied				✓
5. Number of part numbers			✓	
6. Loads of materials moved		✓		
7. Machine hours	✓			
8. Marketing promotions			✓	
9. Number of production orders		✓		
10. Direct material cost	✓			

Part 5 ■ Problem

1.

$$\frac{\$700,000}{40,000 \text{ direct labor hours}} \times 400 \text{ direct labor hours} = \$7,000$$

$$\frac{\$7,000}{200 \text{ units of Product \#747}} = \$35 \text{ per unit}$$

2.

$$\frac{\$150,000}{240 \text{ setups}} \times 12 \text{ setups} = \$7,500 \text{ of batch-level costs}$$

$$\frac{\$250,000}{2,000 \text{ design hours}} \times 140 \text{ design hours} = \$17,500 \text{ of product-level cost}$$

$$\frac{\$100,000 + \$200,000}{40,000 \text{ direct labor hours}} \times 400 \text{ direct labor hours} = \$3,000 \text{ of unit- and plant-level cost}$$

So the overhead allocated to a unit of Product #747 is:
($7,500 + $17,500 + $3,000) ÷ 200 units = $140/unit

Part 6 ■ Problem

1.

Herold Company
Product Costs from Existing Cost System

Overhead Rate: $2,000,000 of overhead divided by $2,000,000 direct labor cost = 100% of direct labor cost

	Standard	Custom	Total
Direct material	$ 390,000	$ 80,000	$ 470,000
Direct labor	1,900,000	100,000	2,000,000
Overhead:			
100% x $1,900,000	1,900,000		
100% x $100,000		100,000	2,000,000
Total cost	$4,190,000	$280,000	$4,470,000
Units produced	39,000	1,000	
Cost per unit	$ 107.44	$ 280.00	

2.

Herold Company
Product Costs from Existing Cost System

Overhead Rate:

$250,000 setup-related costs divided by 25 setups = 10,000 per setup

$700,000 design-related costs divided by 3,500 design hours = $200 per design hour

$1,050,000 of other overhead divided by $2,000,000 direct labor cost = 52.5% of direct labor cost

	Standard	Custom	Total
Direct material	$ 390,000	$ 80,000	$ 470,000
Direct labor	1,900,000	100,000	2,000,000
Overhead:			
$10,000 x 15 setups	150,000		
$10,000 x 10 setups		100,000	250,000
$200 x 2,000 design hours	400,000		
$200 x 1,500 design hours		300,000	700,000
52.5% x $1,900,000	997,500		
52.5% x $100,000		52,500	1,050,000
Total cost	$3,837,500	$632,500	$4,470,000
Units produced	39,000	1,000	
Cost per unit	$ 98.40	$ 632.50	

CHAPTER 15

Part 1 ■ True/False		
1. F	6. T	11. T
2. F	7. F	12. F
3. T	8. T	13. T
4. T	9. T	14. F
5. F	10. T	15. T

Part 2 ■ Matching		
1. s	8. t	15. j
2. m	9. i	16. c
3. a	10. q	17. n
4. k	11. d	18. f
5. o	12. p	19. l
6. b	13. e	20. g
7. r	14. h	

Part 3 ■ Multiple Choice

1. a   Some organizations use a continuous budget, in which a month or quarter in the future is added as the month or quarter just ended is dropped; also, the budget for the entire period is revised and updated as needed.

2. d   When applied to the consideration of general business conditions, the industry's prospects, the company's potential market share, and the plans of competitive companies, probability analysis helps provide a sound basis for estimating future sales.

3. a   In the *a priori* method, the profit objectives take precedence over the planning process. In the *a posteriori* method, the profit objectives emerge as the product of the planning process. In the pragmatic method, management uses a profit standard that has been tested empirically and sanctioned by experience.

4. d   Profit planning is the process of developing a well-thought-out operational plan that includes the attributes in the question.

5. a   Market trends and economic factors, inflation, population growth, personal consumption expenditures, and indexes of industrial production form the background for long-range planning.

6. c The principal functions of the budget committee are to (1) decide on general policies, (2) request, receive, and review individual budget estimates, (3) suggest revisions to budget estimates, (4) approve budgets and later revisions, (5) receive and analyze budget reports, and (6) recommend actions designed to improve efficiency where necessary.

7. d The budgeted balance sheet discloses unfavorable ratios and serves as a check on the accuracy of all other budgets.

8. d All of the items in a through c are limitations of profit planning.

9. a The sales variable is usually the most difficult to predict because the demand for an entity's products or services normally depends on forces and factors largely beyond the scope of management's control.

10. c Production = Sales + Ending Inventory - Beginning Inventory

54,000 = 60,000 + <u>12,000</u> - 18,000

Part 4 ■ Problem

1.

VCR Model No.	Predicted Unit Sales	Less: Beginning Inventory	Plus: Ending Inventory	Production Required
007	500	40	50	510
2525	800	20	80	860
1984	1,300	110	130	1,320

2.

VCR Model No.	Unit Sales	Unit Price	Total Sales
007	500	$500	$ 250,000
2525	800	450	360,000
1984	1,300	400	520,000
Total Sales			$1,130,000

3.

VCR Model No.	Units Produced	Production Cost
007	510	$153,000 (510 x $500 x .60)
2525	860	232,200 (860 x $450 x .60)
1984	1,320	316,800 (1,320 x $400 x .60)
Total production cost		$702,000

Working capital required: $702,000 x 20% = $140,400.

Part 5 ■ Problem

1.

	Ravioli	Tortellini	Cavatelli
Units required to meet sales budget	40,000	20,000	50,000
Add desired ending inventories	3,000	1,000	4,000
Total units required	43,000	21,000	54,000
Less estimated beginning inventories	2,500	2,000	5,000
Planned production	40,500	19,000	49,000

2.

	Flour		Cheese
Ravioli	40,500 x 4 lbs. = 162,000		40,500 x 2 lbs. = 81,000
Tortellini	19,000 x 5 lbs. = 95,000		0
Cavatelli	0		49,000 x 3 lbs. = 147,000
	257,000		228,000
Add desired ending inventories ..	6,000		7,500
	263,000		235,500
Less estimated beginning inventories	5,000		6,000
Budgeted quantities of materials purchased	258,000		229,500
Budgeted price per pound	$.50		$1.00
Budgeted dollar amounts of materials purchased	$129,000		$229,500

3.

	Ravioli	Tortellini	Cavatelli	Total
Materials:				
Flour: 40,500 x 4 x $.50	$ 81,000			$ 81,000
19,000 x 5 x $.50		$ 47,500		47,500
Cheese: 40,500 x 2 x $1.00	81,000			81,000
49,000 x 3 x $1.00			$147,000	147,000
	$162,000	$ 47,500	$147,000	$ 356,500
Direct labor:				
40.5 x 200 x $20..................	$162,000			$ 162,000
19 x 400 x $20		$152,000		152,000
49 x 50 x $20			$ 49,000	49,000
	$162,000	$152,000	$ 49,000	$ 363,000
Factory overhead—variable:				
40.5 x 200 x $10..................	$ 81,000			$ 81,000
19 x 400 x $10		$ 76,000		76,000
49 x 50 x $10			$ 24,500	24,500
	$ 81,000	$ 76,000	$ 24,500	$ 181,500
Total variable manufacturing cost	$405,000	$275,500	$220,500	$ 901,000
Fixed manufacturing cost....................				100,000
Total manufacturing cost				$1,001,000

Part 6 ■ Problem

1.

L. H. Herold Company
Budgeted Cost of Goods Manufactured and Sold Statement
For the Year Ending December 31, 19C

Materials:		
Beginning inventory	$ 87,500	
Add purchases...	568,663	
Total materials available for use	$656,163	
Less ending inventory..................................	107,125	
Cost of materials used		$ 549,038
Direct labor		2,161,680
Factory overhead		226,503
Total manufacturing cost...............................		$2,937,221
Add beginning inventory of finished goods		84,745
Cost of goods available for sale		$3,021,966
Less ending inventory of finished goods......................		60,895
Cost of goods sold		$2,961,071

2.

L. H. Herold Company
Budgeted Income Statement
For the Year Ending December 31, 19C

	Amount
Sales	$3,650,000
Cost of goods sold	2,961,071
Gross profit	$ 688,929
Commercial expenses:	
Marketing expenses	$300,000
Administrative expenses	200,000 500,000
Income from operations	$ 188,929
Less provision for income tax	66,125
Net income	$ 122,804

Part 7 ■ Problem

1.

Gabriel Corporation
Prospective Statement of Income and Retained Earnings
For the Year Ending December 31, 19D
(000s omitted)

Revenue:			
Sales		$900,000	
Other income		15,000	$915,000
Costs of goods manufactured and sold:			
Materials	$225,000		
Direct labor	270,000		
Variable factory overhead	140,000		
Fixed factory overhead	24,000		
	$659,000		
Beginning inventory	60,000		
	$719,000		
Ending inventory	98,850 *	$620,150	
Marketing:			
Salaries	$21,000		
Commissions	25,000		
Promotion and advertising	55,000	101,000	
General and administrative:			
Salaries	$ 25,000		
Travel	4,000		
Office costs	11,000	40,000	761,150
Income before tax			$153,850
Income tax			46,155
Net income			$107,695
Beginning retained earnings			197,900
Subtotal			$305,595
Less dividends			7,500
Ending retained earnings			$298,095
*Inventory			
Units:			
Beginning inventory			50,000
Added to inventory (500,000 - 475,000)			25,000
Ending inventory			75,000
Cost:			
19D Manufacturing costs			$659,000
Units manufactured			500,000
Cost per unit			$1.318
Ending units			75,000
Cost of ending inventory			$ 98,850

2.

Gabriel Corporation
Prospective Balance Sheet
December 31, 19D
(000s omitted)

Assets

Current assets

Cash	$ 2,400	
Accounts receivable	120,000	
Inventory	98,850	$221,250
Plant and equipment	$480,000	
Less accumulated depreciation	82,000	398,000
Total assets		$619,250

Liabilities and Shareholders' Equity

Current liabilities:

Accounts payable	$ 65,000	
Accrued payables	40,000	
Income tax payable	46,155	
Notes payable	75,000	$226,155
Shareholders' equity:		
Common stock	$ 95,000	
Retained earnings	298,095	393,095
Total liabilities and shareholders' equity		$619,250

CHAPTER 16

Part 1 ■ True/False

1.	T	6.	T	11.	T
2.	F	7.	T	12.	F
3.	T	8.	F	13.	T
4.	F	9.	F	14.	T
5.	T	10.	F	15.	T

Part 2 ■ Matching

1.	i	8.	b	15.	h
2.	q	9.	n	16.	j
3.	d	10.	r	17.	o
4.	a	11.	s	18.	e
5.	l	12.	c	19.	g
6.	k	13.	t	20.	f
7.	p	14.	m		

Part 3 ■ Multiple Choice

1. c PPBS (Planning, Programming, Budgeting System) is an analytical tool that is closely related to cost-benefit analysis, focusing on the final results rather than the initial dollars expended.

2. d The longest path through a network is known as the critical path.

3. b Cash flows based on projected sales.

4. d Zero-base budgeting (ZBB) requires managers to start over each budget period and to justify each proposed expenditure.

5. c The major burden of PERT is the determination of the longest time duration for the completion of an entire project.

6. c $120,000 - $35,000 - $25,000 + $65,000 + $80,000 + $45,000 = $250,000

7. c

Estimated cost of goods sold for November	$ 900,000
Estimated inventories at end of November	160,000
	$1,060,000
Estimated inventories at beginning of November	180,000
Estimated November purchases	$ 880,000
Estimated percentage of payments in November for purchases in November	x 80%
Estimated payments in November for purchases in November	$ 704,000
Estimated payments in November for purchases prior to November	210,000
Estimated cash disbursements for inventories in November	$ 914,000

8. c $t_e = \dfrac{t_o + 4t_m + t_p}{6} = \dfrac{4 + 4(8) + 18}{6} = 9$

9. e $1,350,000 - $1,200,000 - $90,000 - $400,000 + $500,000 + $100,000 - $50,000 = $210,000

10. e   All of the choices are requirements for the successful implementation of zero-base budgeting.

Part 4 ■ Problem

Cleaver Candy Co.
Cash Budget
For March-June, 19X

Receipts From:	March	April	May	June
Cash sales	$20,000	$12,000	$16,000	$ 22,000
January credit sales (35% x $24,000)	8,400	--	--	--
February credit sales:				
60% x $18,000	10,800	--	--	--
35% x $18,000	--	6,300	--	--
March credit sales	--	6,000	3,500	--
April credit sales	--	--	2,400	1,400
May credit sales	--	--	--	7,200
Total Receipts	$39,200	$24,300	$21,900	$ 30,600
Disbursements for:				
Payroll	$ 4,000	$ 3,000	$ 5,000	$ 6,000
Other expenses	5,000	4,800	5,200	5,600
February purchases	5,000	--	--	--
March purchases	3,000	3,000	--	--
April purchases	--	2,600	2,600	--
May purchases	--	--	2,800	2,800
June purchases	--	--	--	4,000
Tax payment	--	--	--	35,000
Total disbursements	$17,000	$13,400	$15,600	$ 53,400
Net increase (decrease) in cash:				
Receipts less disbursements	$22,200	$10,900	$ 6,300	$(22,800)
Cash balances:				
Beginning	5,000	27,200	38,100	44,400
Ending	$27,200	$38,100	$44,400	$ 21,600

Part 5 ■ Problem

1.

Activity	t_e
A-B	$\dfrac{4 + 4(6) + 8}{6} = 6$
A-C	$\dfrac{16 + 4(18) + 20}{6} = 18$
A-D	$\dfrac{6 + 4(9) + 12}{6} = 9$
B-E	$\dfrac{6 + 4(10) + 14}{6} = 10$
C-F	$\dfrac{5 + 4(9) + 19}{6} = 10$
D-F	$\dfrac{3 + 4(5) + 7}{6} = 5$
E-H	$\dfrac{10 + 4(16) + 22}{6} = 16$
F-E	$\dfrac{3 + 4(7) + 11}{6} = 7$
F-G	$\dfrac{4 + 4(6) + 14}{6} = 7$
G-H	$\dfrac{7 + 4(11) + 15}{6} = 11$

2.

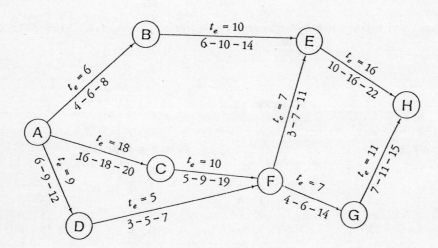

3. Path

1. A-B-E-H   6 + 10 + 16 = 32
2. A-C-F-E-H 18 + 10 + 7 + 16 = 51 (critical path)
3. A-C-F-G-H 18 + 10 + 7 + 11 = 46
4. A-D-F-E-H 9 + 5 + 7 + 16 = 37
5. A-D-F-G-H 9 + 5 + 7 + 11 = 32

Part 6 ■ Problem

1.

Hickok Company
Cash Budget
For July

Cash balance, July 1		$ 10,000
Cash receipts:		
June sales ($50,000 x 70%)	$35,000	
July sales ($55,000 x 25%)	13,750	48,750
Cash available		$ 58,750
Cash disbursements:		
June purchases ($20,000 x 50%)	$10,000	
July purchases ($23,000 x 50%)	11,500	
Other marketing and administrative expenses	14,500	
Income tax	1,350	
Dividends	25,000	62,350
Cash balance, July 31		$ (3,600)
Calculation of June income tax:		
Sales		$ 50,000
Cost of goods sold		25,000
Gross profit		$ 25,000
Commercial expenses:		
Depreciation	$ 7,500	
Other marketing and administrative	13,000	20,500
Taxable income		$ 4,500
Income tax ($4,500 x 30%)		$ 1,350

2. Since the desired minimum cash balance is $10,000, arrangements should be made to borrow $13,600 ($10,000 + $3,600).

CHAPTER 17

Part 1 ■ True/False

1. T		6. F		11. T	
2. T		7. T		12. F	
3. T		8. T		13. F	
4. T		9. F		14. T	
5. F		10. T		15. F	

Part 2 ■ Matching

1. l		6. g		11. m	
2. o		7. f		12. n	
3. h		8. e		13. i	
4. j		9. b		14. c	
5. a		10. k		15. d	

Part 3 ■ Multiple Choice

1. c   Since the department manager did not have the authority to make the decision regarding his or her compensation, he or she should not be held accountable for the related salary charges.

2. c   Any overhead charges shown on a responsibility report should be limited to those expenses over which the supervisor has control.

3. b   The purpose of a flexible budget is to provide a budget for any level of activity within the relevant range.

4. c   A cost should be assigned to a responsibility center if its incurrence is controllable by the manager of that center.

5. c   The spending variance is a result of the prices paid for overhead items or the quantities used of overhead items being more or less than was budgeted for a given level of production.

6. a   The department manager should be measured on the basis of the revenue generated by the department less the department expenses over which the manager had control.

7. a   Responsibility accounting is based on a classification of managerial responsibilities at every level in the organization for the purpose of establishing a budget for each.

8. a   The idle capacity variance is due to volume or activity factors and results from the under- or overutilization of plant and equipment.

9. b   The costs would be controllable by the production vice president who decided to lease the production equipment.

10. d   Inefficiencies in a service department should not be allocated to producing departments, but rather should be reported on the service department's performance report as an unfavorable variance from budget.

Part 4 ■ Problem

1. Budgeted variable cost at capacity/Capacity available = $48,000/150,000 kwh = $.32/kwh

2.

	Fabricating	Assembly
Fixed cost distribution:		
$25,000 x (100,000/150,000)....................	$16,667	
$25,000 x (50,000/150,000).....................		$ 8,333
Variable cost distribution:		
$.32 x 85,000 kwh	27,200	
$.32 x 45,000 kwh		14,400
Total cost distributed	$43,867	$22,733

3.

	Fabricating	Assembly
Total variable cost		$40,000
Costs distributed:		
Fabricating.................................	$27,200	
Assembly	14,400	41,600
Over- or underdistributed cost		$ (1,600)

Part 5 ■ Problem

1. General Maintenance: $100,000/10,000 hours = $10 per service hour
    Machine Repairs: $40,000/2,000 hours = $20 per service hour

2.

	Department Machining	Assembling	Finishing	Total
General Maintenance	$46,000	$25,000	$16,000	$ 87,000
Machine Repairs	26,000	13,000	5,000	44,000
Total......................................	$72,000	$38,000	$21,000	$131,000

3.

	Monthly Budget	Fixed Cost Percentage	Fixed Cost	Variable Cost	Variable Rate per Hour
General Maintenance	$100,000	75%	$75,000	$25,000	$2.50
Machine Repairs	$ 40,000	60%	$24,000	$16,000	$8.00

	General Maintenance		Machine Repairs	
Actual overhead		$ 94,000		$45,000
Budget allowance:				
Fixed overhead.	$75,000		$24,000	
Variable overhead:				
($2.50 x 8,700 hrs.)	21,750	96,750		
($8.00 x 2,200 hrs.)			17,600	41,600
Spending variance		$(2,750) Fav.		$ 3,400 Unfav.

4.

	General Maintenance	Machine Repairs
Budget allowance (from (3) above)	$96,750	$ 41,600
Costs charged out:		
($10 x 8,700 hrs.)	87,000	
($20 x 2,200 hrs.)		44,000
Idle capacity variance	$ 9,750 Unfav.	$ (2,400) Fav.

Part 6 ■ Problem

	60% of Capacity	80% of Capacity	100% of Capacity
Units	3,000	4,000	5,000
Direct labor hours	2,880	3,840	4,800
Direct materials	$12,000	$16,000	$ 20,000
Direct labor.	34,560	46,080	57,600
Variable factory overhead:			
Supplies.	1,440	1,920	2,400
Indirect labor	8,640	11,520	14,400
Other charges	2,880	3,840	4,800
Fixed factory overhead	2,500	2,500	2,500
Total manufacturing cost	$62,020	$81,860	$101,700
Manufacturing cost per unit	$ 20.67	$ 20.47	$ 20.34
Factory overhead rate per direct labor hour	$ 5.37	$ 5.15	$ 5.02

CHAPTER 18

Part 1 ■ True/False

1. T	6. F	11. T
2. F	7. T	12. F
3. T	8. T	13. T
4. T	9. T	14. F
5. T	10. T	15. T

Part 2 ■ Matching

1. c	8. b	15. l
2. g	9. j	16. k
3. e	10. d	17. s
4. i	11. t	18. q
5. a	12. n	19. o
6. h	13. r	20. m
7. f	14. p	

Part 3 ■ Multiple Choice

1. c Normal standards are set for a normal level of operation and efficiency and are intended to represent challenging yet attainable results. Theoretical standards are set for an ideal or maximum level of operation and efficiency. Expected actual standards are set for an expected level of operation and efficiency. Practical capacity is theoretical capacity less allowance for unavoidable interruptions.

2. d The volume variance indicates the cost of capacity available but not utilized.

3. d

Actual factory overhead		$232,000
Budget allowance based on standard hours allowed:		
Fixed overhead budgeted........................	$ 66,000	
Variable overhead (32,000 standard hours allowed		
x $5 variable overhead rate)	160,000	226,000
Controllable variance		$ 6,000

4. a Labor rate variance = Actual hours (Actual rate - Standard rate)

5. e Standard rate x (Actual quantity - Standard quantity) = $1.30 x [5800 - (1,000 x 6)] = $260 favorable

6. b Total factory overhead variance = Actual factory overhead ($86,000) - Applied factory overhead ($80,000) = $6,000 unfavorable

7. d $\dfrac{\$44,000}{20,000 \text{ units}} = \$2.20$

   $2.20 - $2.10 = $.10 x 20,000 units = $2,000 unfavorable

8. c If actual materials used exceeds standard materials, then the usage variance must be unfavorable. If actual cost is less than standard cost, however, the favorable materials price variance must more than offset the unfavorable materials usage variance.

9. c If the materials price variance is isolated at the time of use, it is known as the materials price usage variance.

10. a The higher paid, more experienced workers had a higher wage rate, but they were more efficient.

Part 4 ■ Problem

1.

	Pounds	Unit Cost	Amount	
Actual quantity used................	29,200	$ 1.10 actual	$ 32,120	
Actual quantity used................	29,200	1.00 standard	29,200	
Materials price usage variance........		$ .10	$ 2,920	unfavorable
Actual quantity used................	29,200	$ 1.00 standard	$ 29,200	
Standard quantity allowed (9,500 x 3) .	28,500	1.00 standard	28,500	
Materials quantity variance...........	700		$ 700	unfavorable

2.

	Hours	Rate	Amount	
Actual hours worked	19,500	$14.50 actual	$282,750	
Actual hours worked	19,500	15.00 standard	292,500	
Labor rate variance................		$ (.50)	$ (9,750)	favorable
Actual hours worked	19,500	$15.00 standard	$292,500	
Standard hours allowed (9,500 x 2) ...	19,000	15.00 standard	285,000	
Labor efficiency variance	500		$ 7,500	unfavorable

3.

Actual factory overhead		$112,000	
Budget allowance based on standard hours allowed:			
Fixed overhead budgeted..........................	$ 20,000		
Variable overhead (9,500 x 2 x $5)	95,000	115,000	
Controllable variance................................		$ (3,000)	favorable
Budget allowance based on standard hours allowed........		$115,000	
Overhead charged to production			
(9,500 x 2)($1 fixed + $5 variable)...................		114,000	
Volume variance		$ 1,000	unfavorable

4.

Actual factory overhead...............................		$112,000
Budget allowance based on actual hours worked:		
Fixed overhead budgeted	$ 20,000	
Variable overhead (19,500 x $5)...................	97,500	117,500
Spending variance		$ (5,500) favorable
Budget allowance based on actual hours worked..........		$117,500
Budget allowance based on standard hours worked		115,000
Variable efficiency variance............................		$ 2,500 unfavorable
Budget allowance based on standard hours allowed		$115,000
Overhead charged to production		114,000
Volume variance.....................................		$ 1,000 unfavorable

This part is based on material in the Appendix to the chapter.

5.

Actual factory overhead................................	$112,000
Budget allowance based on actual hours worked..........	117,500
Spending variance	$ (5,500) favorable
Budget allowance based on actual hours worked..........	$117,500
Budget allowance based on standard hours allowed	115,000
Variable efficiency variance............................	$ 2,500 unfavorable
Actual hours x fixed overhead rate	$ 19,500
Standard hours allowed x fixed overhead rate	19,000
Fixed efficiency variance..............................	$ 500 unfavorable
Normal capacity hours x fixed overhead rate (20,000 x $1)	$ 20,000
Actual hours worked x fixed overhead rate (19,500 x $1)	19,500
Idle capacity variance	$ 500 unfavorable

Part 5 ■ Problem

1.

Material	Pounds	Actual Cost per Pound	Amount	
X	220,000	$2.00	$440,000	
Y	60,000	1.00	60,000	
Z	170,000	3.00	510,000	$1,010,000

Material	Pounds	Standard Cost per Pound	Amount	
X	220,000	$1.75	$385,000	
Y	60,000	.85	51,000	
Z	170,000	3.25	552,500	$ 988,500
Materials price usage variance.................................				$ 21,500 unfavorable

2.

Actual input quantities at individual standard materials cost	$ 988,500
Actual input quantities at weighted average standard materials cost (450,000 x $2.20)	990,000
Materials mix variance	$ (1,500) favorable

3.

Actual input quantities at weighted average standard materials cost.....	$ 990,000
Actual output quantities at standard materials cost (375,000 x $2.75) ...	1,031,250
Materials yield variance	$ (41,250) favorable

CHAPTER 19

Part 1 ■ True/False

1. F	6. T	11. T
2. F	7. F	12. F
3. F	8. T	13. T
4. T	9. T	14. F
5. T	10. T	15. F

Part 2 ■ Matching

1. h	6. i	11. o
2. b	7. c	12. k
3. j	8. d	13. n
4. f	9. g	14. l
5. a	10. e	15. m

Part 3 ■ Multiple Choice

1. a Unfavorable variances are recorded as debits and favorable variances as credits. If the variance account has a credit balance, standard hours allowed exceed actual hours worked.

2. b Materials price variances indicate the difference between the purchase price and the standard price. If they are isolated at the time of purchase, they are known as materials purchase price variances.

3. b If significant variances exist, inventory and cost of goods sold figures are not stated at actual cost in a standard cost system unless these variances are allocated prior to the preparation of the financial statements.

4. c Immaterial variances appear as part of Cost of Goods Sold on the income statement or as additions or subtractions to gross profit in the period in which they arose.

5. b A credit balance in Labor Efficiency Variance indicates that direct labor was overapplied because the standard hours allowed were greater than the actual hours worked.

6. b Current IRS regulations require that significant standard cost variances be allocated among inventories and cost of goods sold. Also, the taxpayer must treat both favorable and unfavorable variances consistently.

7. b

Actual rate	$ 7.00	($241,500 ÷ 34,500)
Standard rate	6.40	($3,200 ÷ 500)
	$ .60	
	x 34,500	hours
Rate variance	$ 20,700	unfavorable

8. d The three-variance method is used because there is a factory overhead variable efficiency variance, and the variance is unfavorable because it is recorded as a debit.

9. e Even not-for-profit organizations and relatively small organizations can utilize many aspects of standard costing.

10. d If the new standard costs reflect conditions that affected the actual cost of the goods in the ending inventory, most firms adjust the ending inventory to the new standard cost. Ending inventories are costed at the old standards if the new standards have not affected costs in the past period.

Part 4 ■ Problem

Materials.	90,000	
Materials Purchase Price Variance		900
Accounts Payable		89,100
Work in Process	75,000	
Materials Quantity Variance	750	
Materials.		75,750
Work in Process	81,600	
Labor Efficiency Variance		1,000
Labor Rate Variance		600
Payroll		80,000
Factory Overhead Control	60,000	
Various Credits		60,000

Work in Process..................................   59,750
    Factory Overhead Control   59,750

Volume Variance   1,500
    Variable Efficiency Variance   750
    Spending Variance   500
    Factory Overhead Control   250

Part 5 ■ Problem

1.

	Square Yards	Unit Cost	Amount
Actual quantity purchased	15,000	$ 5.20 actual	$ 78,000
Actual quantity purchased	15,000	4.95 standard	74,250
Materials purchase price variance	15,000	$ .25	$ 3,750 unfavorable
Actual quantity used	12,500	$ 4.95 standard	$ 61,875
Standard quantity allowed (4,000 x 3)	12,000	4.95 standard	59,400
Materials quantity variance	500		$ 2,475 unfavorable

	Time	Rate	Amount
Actual hours worked	8,500	$ 8.25 actual	$ 70,125
Actual hours worked	8,500	8.00 standard	68,000
Labor rate variance	8,500	$ .25	$ 2,125 unfavorable
Actual hours worked	8,500	$ 8.00 standard	$ 68,000
Standard hours allowed	8,000	8.00 standard	64,000
Labor efficiency variance............	500		$ 4,000 unfavorable

Actual factory overhead............................... $ 32,100
Budget allowance based on actual hours worked:
    Fixed overhead budgeted (5,000 x $4) .... $ 20,000
    Variable overhead (8,500 x $1.50)   12,750   32,750
Spending variance .... $ (650) favorable
Budget allowance based on actual hours worked.......... $ 32,750

Budget allowance based on standard hours allowed:
    Fixed overhead budgeted .... $ 20,000
    Variable overhead (4,000 x 2 x $1.50)................   12,000   32,000
    Variable efficiency variance........................ $ 750 unfavorable

Actual hours x fixed overhead rate (8,500 x $2) .... $ 17,000
Standard hours allowed x fixed overhead rate (4,000 x 2 x $2)   16,000
Fixed efficiency variance... $ 1,000 unfavorable

Budget allowance based on actual hours worked......................... $ 32,750
Actual hours worked x factory overhead rate (8,500 x $3.50)   29,750
Idle capacity variance .... $ 3,000 unfavorable

2.

Materials (15,000 x $4.95)   74,250
Materials Purchase Price Variance..................   3,750
    Accounts Payable   78,000

Work in Process (4,000 x 3 x $4.95)...............   59,400
Materials Quantity Variance.......................   2,475
    Materials (12,500 x $4.95)   61,875

Payroll (8,500 x $8.25)   70,125
    Accrued Payroll...............................   70,125

Work in Process (4,000 x 2 x $8.00)	64,000	
Labor Rate Variance	2,125	
Labor Efficiency Variance.	4,000	
Payroll		70,125
Factory Overhead Control	32,100	
Various Credits		32,100
Work in Process (8,000 x $3.50).	28,000	
Factory Overhead Control.		28,000
Factory Overhead Idle Capacity Variance	3,000	
Factory Overhead Variable Efficiency Variance	750	
Factory Overhead Fixed Efficiency Variance.	1,000	
Factory Overhead Spending Variance		650
Factory Overhead Control.		4,100
Finished Goods (4,000 x $37.85).	151,400	
Work in Process		151,400
Accounts Receivable (3,000 x $50)	150,000	
Sales.		150,000
Cost of Goods Sold (3,000 x $37.85)	113,550	
Finished Goods		113,550
Cost of Goods Sold	16,450	
Factory Overhead Spending Variance	650	
Materials Quantity Variance		2,475
Labor Rate Variance		2,125
Factory Overhead Idle Capacity Variance		3,000
Materials Purchase Price Variance		3,750
Labor Efficiency Variance		4,000
Factory Overhead Variable Efficiency Variance		750
Factory Overhead Fixed Efficiency Variance.		1,000

Part 6 ■ Problem

1.

Materials purchase price variance to:

Materials.	($25,000 ÷ $400,000) x ($7,000) =	$ (437.50)
Work in process	($40,000 ÷ $400,000) x ($7,000) =	(700.00)
Finished goods	($35,000 ÷ $400,000) x ($7,000) =	(612.50)
Cost of goods sold	($300,000 ÷ $400,000) x ($7,000) =	(5,250.00)
Total.		$ (7,000.00)

Materials price usage variance to:

Work in process	($40,000 ÷ $375,000) x $9,240 =	$ 985.60
Finished goods	($35,000 ÷ $375,000) x $9,240 =	862.40
Cost of goods sold	($300,000 ÷ $375,000) x $9,240 =	7,392.00
Total.		$ 9,240.00

(Note that inventories are already stated at actual cost when the price usage variance is used, therefore none of the variance is allocated to materials.)

Labor rate variance to:

Work in process	($35,000 ÷ $750,000) x $(12,160) =	$ (567.47)
Finished goods	($35,000 ÷ $750,000) x $(12,160) =	(567.47)
Cost of goods sold	($680,000 ÷ $750,000) x $(12,160) =	(11,025.06)
Total.		$(12,160.00)

Labor efficiency variance to:

Work in process..................	($35,000 ÷ $750,000) x $6,340 =	$ 295.87
Finished goods	($35,000 ÷ $750,000) x $6,340 =	295.87
Cost of goods sold.............	($680,000 ÷ $750,000) x $6,340 =	5,748.27
Total...		$ 6,340.01

Overhead variances to:

Work in process..................	($62,000 ÷ $600,000) x $9,790 =	$ 1,011.63
Finished goods	($88,000 ÷ $600,000) x $9,790 =	1,435.87
Cost of goods sold.............	($450,000 ÷ $600,000) x $9,790 =	7,342.50
Total...		$ 9,790.00

2.

Standard:

Materials		$ 300,000
Labor		680,000
Overhead..		450,000
Standard cost of goods sold		$ 1,430,000

Add unfavorable variances:

Material price usage variance	$ 7,392.00	
Labor efficiency variance	5,748.26	
Overhead variances	7,342.50	20,482.76
		$ 1,450,482.76

Less favorable variances:

Materials purchase price variance	$ (5,250.00)	
Labor rate variance...........................	(11,025.06)	(16,275.06)
Actual cost of goods sold		$ 1,434,207.70

CHAPTER 20

Part 1 ■ True/False

1.	T	8.	T	15.	T	
2.	T	9.	T	16.	T	
3.	T	10.	T	17.	T	
4.	T	11.	F	18.	F	
5.	F	12.	T	19.	F	
6.	T	13.	F	20.	T	
7.	F	14.	T			

Part 2 ■ Matching

1.	c	8.	j	15.	m
2.	a	9.	n	16.	l
3.	e	10.	p	17.	i
4.	b	11.	q	18.	t
5.	d	12.	f	19.	s
6.	k	13.	o	20.	r
7.	h	14.	g		

Part 3 ■ Multiple Choice

1. a The use of direct costing for financial reporting is not accepted by the accounting profession, the IRS, or the SEC. The position of these groups is generally based on their opposition to excluding fixed costs from inventories.

2. d Proponents of direct costing argue that period costs, such as depreciation, property taxes, and insurance, are a function of time rather than of production and should be excluded from the cost of the product.

3. d In absorption costing, fixed manufacturing expenses form part of the predetermined factory overhead rate and are included in inventories. The exclusion of this overhead from inventories under direct costing and its offsetting effect on periodic income determination has been criticized by opponents of direct costing.

4. e Since direct costing excludes fixed manufacturing costs from inventory, the differences would be 400 units x $2 fixed manufacturing cost per unit = $800 decrease in inventory using direct costing.

5. d

Operating income (direct costing)	$50,000
Cost released in inventory decline (5,000 units x $4)	-20,000
Operating income (absorption costing)	$30,000

6. b Break-even sales $400,000
     Sales beyond break-even:
     Operating income for 19A ($200,000) ÷ contribution margin (40%)   500,000
     Total sales for 19A $900,000

7. a Contribution margin per unit:
     Alt   = $4 x .3 = $1.20
     Tude = $3 x .2 = $.60
     Break-even units = $250,000 ÷ [(.3333 x $1.20) + (.6667 x $.60)] =312,500
     ($104,167 Alt and $208,333 Tude)

8. c Contribution margin per unit:
     Y = $120 - $70 = $50
     Z = $500 - $200 = $300
     Break-even units $300,000 ÷ [(.6 x $50) + (.4 x $300)] = <u>2,000</u> (1,200 Y and 800 Z)

9. a The contribution margin as a percentage of sales will decrease because the variable cost as a percentage of sales increases. If the fixed cost increases and the contribution margin ratio decreases, both of these factors will cause the break-even point to increase.

10. d The contribution per unit is needed to compute break-even sales units; it is obtained by subtracting the variable cost per unit from the sales price per unit.

Part 4 ■ Problem

1.   Ending inventory: 5,000 x $15 = $75,000

2.   Fixed manufacturing cost ($60,000 total ÷ 30,000) . . . . $ 2
     Variable manufacturing cost per unit   15
       Total cost per unit $17
     Ending inventory: 5,000 x $17 = $85,000

3.   Variable manufacturing cost (25,000 x $15) $375,000
     Variable administrative cost (30,000 x $5) 150,000
       Total $525,000

4.   Fixed manufacturing cost (25,000 x $2) $50,000
     Fixed marketing and administrative expenses 25,000
       Total $75,000

5.   Fixed manufacturing cost $60,000
     Fixed marketing and administrative expense 25,000
       Total $85,000

Part 5 ■ Problem

Franchi Corporation
Income Statement—Absorption Costing
For Quarter Ended June 30, 19--

1.   Sales (4,000 x $25) $1,000,000
     Cost of goods manufactured:
       Materials $100,000
       Direct labor 250,000
       Factory overhead—variable 125,000
       Factory overhead—fixed 150,000
         Cost of goods manufactured $625,000
         Finished goods inventory (10,000 x ($625,000 ÷ 50,000)) . . 125,000
     Cost of goods sold   500,000
     Gross profit . . . . $ 500,000
     Marketing and administrative expenses   350,000
     Operating income . . . . $ 150,000

Franchi Corporation
Income Statement—Direct Costing
For Quarter Ended June 30, 19--

2.

Sales		$1,000,000
Variable cost of goods manufactured:		
Materials	$100,000	
Direct labor	250,000	
Factory overhead—variable	125,000	
Variable cost of goods manufactured	$475,000	
Finished goods inventory (10,000 x (475,000@ 50,000))	95,000	
Variable cost of goods sold		380,000
Gross contribution margin		$ 620,000
Variable marketing and administrative expense		100,000
Contribution margin		$ 520,000
Fixed expenses:		
Factory overhead	$150,000	
Marketing and administrative expenses	250,000	400,000
Operating income		$ 120,000

Part 6 ■ Problem

1.

	October	November	December
Sales	$5,000	$2,000	$20,000
Beginning inventory	0	$1,500	$ 3,900
Variable cost of goods manufactured (variable costs)	$3,000	3,000	3,000
Variable cost of goods available for sale	$3,000	$4,500	$ 6,900
Ending inventory (Ending units x $3 variable cost/unit)	1,500	3,900	900
Variable cost of goods sold	$1,500	$ 600	$ 6,000
Gross contribution margin	$3,500	$1,400	$14,000
Less fixed factory overhead	2,000	2,000	2,000
Gross profit (loss)	$1,500	$ (600)	$12,000

2.

	October	November	December
Gross profit—absorption costing	$2,500	$1,000	$10,000
Gross profit—direct costing	1,500	(600)	12,000
Difference	$1,000	$1,600	$ (2,000)
Inventory change—absorption costing	$2,500	$4,000	$ (5,000)
Less inventory change—direct costing	1,500	2,400	(3,000)
Difference	$1,000	$1,600	$ (2,000)

Part 7 ■ Problem

1.
$$\frac{\$80,000}{1 - \frac{90}{150}} = \frac{\$80,000}{.40} = \$200,000$$

2.
$$\frac{\$80,000}{(\$150 - \$90)} = 1,333 \ or \ \$200,000 \div \$150 = 1,333$$

3.

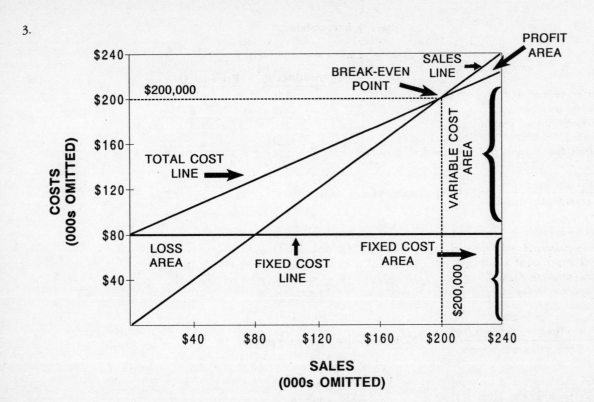

Part 8 ■ Problem

1. (a) $\dfrac{\$600,000}{1 - \dfrac{\$140}{\$400}} = \dfrac{\$600,000}{1 - .35} = \dfrac{\$600,000}{.65} = \$923,077$

   (b) $\dfrac{\$600,000}{\$400 - \$140} = 2,308 \text{ units}$

2. (a) $\$1,200,000 - \$923,077 = \$276,923$

   (b) $\dfrac{\$1,200,000 - \$923,077}{\$1,200,000} = 23.08\%$

3. $\dfrac{\$600,000}{1 - \dfrac{\$140}{\$350}} = \dfrac{\$600,000}{.60} = \$1,000,000$

4. (a) $\dfrac{\$600,000 + \$100,000}{.65} = \$1,076,923$

   (b) $\dfrac{\$600,000 + \$100,000}{.60} = \$1,166,667$

5.

Sales (3,000 units x $400)	$1,200,000
Variable cost (3,000 units x $140)	420,000
Contribution margin	$ 780,000
Fixed cost	600,000
Expected profit	$ 180,000*

or

C/M x M/S x Budgeted Sales = 65% x 23.08% x $1,200,000 = $180,024*

*Rounding difference

Part 9 ■ Problem

1.

	Product P		Product Q	
Sales price per unit	$25		$10	
Variable cost per unit	18		6	
Unit contribution margin	$ 7		$ 4	
Expected sales mix	3		2	
Contribution margin per hypothetical package	$21	+	$ 8	= $29

2.

$$\frac{\$435,000 \text{ fixed cost}}{\$29 \text{ contribution margin}} = 15,000 \text{ packages to break even}$$

15,000 packages x 3 units of P =	45,000 units of P
15,000 packages x 2 units of Q =	30,000 units of Q
45,000 units of P x $25 =	$1,125,000 sales of P
30,000 units of Q x $10 =	300,000 sales of Q
Break-even sales	$1,425,000

3.

$$\frac{\$435,000 \text{ fixed cost} + \$75,000 \text{ profit}}{\$29 \text{ contribution margin}} = 17,586 \text{ packages to achieve profit}$$

17,586 packages x 3 units of P =	52,758 units of P
17,586 packages x 2 units of Q =	35,172 units of Q
52,758 units of P x $25 =	$1,318,950 sales of P
35,172 units of Q x $10 =	351,720 sales of Q
Sales to achieve profit	$1,670,670

CHAPTER 21

Part 1 ■ True/False

1.	F	6.	T	11.	T
2.	T	7.	F	12.	T
3.	T	8.	T	13.	T
4.	T	9.	T	14.	F
5.	T	10.	F	15.	F

Part 2 ■ Matching

1.	e	6.	d	11.	o
2.	a	7.	b	12.	k
3.	c	8.	h	13.	n
4.	g	9.	j	14.	m
5.	f	10.	i	15.	l

Part 3 ■ Multiple Choice

1. e The opportunity cost is zero when there is no alternative use of the facility.

2. c Because sunk costs have already been incurred, they are not relevant to an alternative choice decision problem.

3. d Imputed costs include interest on invested capital, rental value of company-owned properties, and salaries of owner-operators of proprietorships and partnerships. These costs are not considered in a company's regular cost and profit calculations, but they are relevant in deciding between alternative courses of action.

4. b Depreciation is a fixed factory overhead cost that will be incurred whether or not the idle capacity is used. Direct materials, direct labor, and variable factory overhead are variable costs that will not be incurred unless the capacity is used.

5. b

Selling price		$18
Less:		
Variable costs	$16	
Overtime	3	19
Loss		$ (1) x 40,000 units = $(40,000)

6. e

Variable costs	$6
Income ($10,000 ÷ 10,000)	1
Selling price	$7

7. d

Direct materials...............................	$ 2
Direct labor.................................	8
Variable overhead............................	4
Applied fixed overhead that would not continue ($\frac{1}{3}$ x $6) ..	2
	$16

$16 x 5,000 units = $80,000 + $4,000 opportunity cost = $84,000

8. b Differential cost, also known as marginal cost or incremental cost, is the added cost incurred when a project or an undertaking is extended beyond its originally intended goal.

9. e All of the considerations listed should be examined when faced with a make-or-buy decision.

10. e Contribution margin:
Product Q : $20 - $13 = $7
Product P : $17 - $12 = $5
Contribution margin maximization objective function is 7Q + 5P.

Part 4 ■ Problem

1. The company should accept the special order because the proposed $9.50 sales price more than covers all variable manufacturing costs per unit, which are:

Direct materials.......................................	$4.00
Direct labor..	$2.50
Variable factory overhead................................	$2.00
Total..	$8.50

Note: Even if the variable marketing expense of $.50 per unit is incurred for this order, there will still be a positive contribution margin of $.50 per unit.

2. The company would be willing to pay an outside supplier as much as the variable manufacturing cost of $8.50 per unit plus the $.25 per unit ($2,500 ÷ 10,000) of fixed cost that would be saved, or $8.75 per unit.

Part 5 ■ Problem

Variable cost to make [($5 + $17 + $10) x 1,000]	$32,000
Fixed factory overhead eliminated ($8 x 1,000)	8,000
Contribution from alternate use of facilities................	10,000
	$50,000
Cost to buy ($45 x 1,000)................................	45,000
Savings from buying....................................	$ 5,000

Part 6 ■ Problem

1. $\dfrac{\text{Added cost}}{\text{Units produced}} = \dfrac{\$10,000}{5,000} = \$2.00$ per unit

2.

	Anthony	Brutus	Cassius
Sales value if processed further	$90,000	$72,000	$58,000
Sales value at split-off	75,000	60,000	43,000
Added sales value	$15,000	$12,000	$15,000
Added cost	15,000	20,000	10,000
Difference in favor (against) processing further ..	$ 0	$(8,000)	$ 5,000

Note that the joint production cost of $100,000 is irrelevant to the decision to sell or process further.

Part 7 ■ Problem

1.

	Cassette	Disk
Sales price per unit	$ 25	$ 26
Standard cost per unit	17	28
Profit (loss) per unit	$ 8	$ (2)
Total profit (loss)	$400,000	$ (50,000)

2. Both products have a positive contribution margin and should be continued unless there is a more profitable alternative.

3.

	Disk	Super Disk
Sales price	$ 26	$ 50
Variable cost per unit	18	20
Contribution margin per unit	$ 8	$ 30
Total contribution margin	$200,000	$375,000

4. Produce Super Disk due to higher contribution margin. The opportunity cost of Disk is the $200,000 in contribution margin that will be foregone if Super Disk is produced.

Part 8 ■ Problem

1.

Department	Hours Available	Hours Required Per Apollo	Hours Required Per Lunar	Maximum Units Apollo	Maximum Units Lunar
Mixing	80	2	1	80÷2= 40	80÷1=80
Holding	60	.5	1	60÷.5=120	60÷1=60

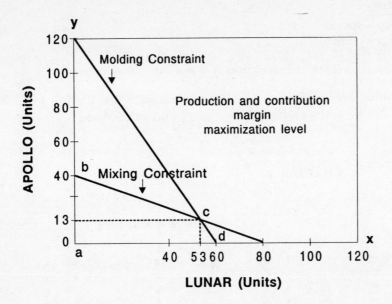

2.
a(Apollo = 0; Lunar = 0); $100,000(0) + $80,000(0) = $0 CM
b(Apollo = 40; Lunar = 0); $100,000(40) + $80,000(0) = $4,000,000 CM
*c(Apollo = 13; Lunar = 53); $100,000(13) + $80,000(53) = $5,540,000 CM
d(Apollo = 0; Lunar = 60); $100,000(0) + $80,000(60) = $4,800,000 CM
13 units of Apollo and 53 units of Lunar maximize the CM with $5,540,000
*Corner point "c" values:

$$1x + 2y = 80 \qquad\qquad 1x + 2y = 80$$
$$-1x - .5y = -60 \qquad 1x + 2(13,333) = 80$$
$$1.5y = 20 \qquad\qquad 1x + 26.67 = 80$$
$$y = 13.33 \text{ or } 13 \qquad\qquad x = 53.33 \text{ or } 53$$

Part 9 ■ Problem

6,000 ravioli and 6,000 ziti packages

Mixing   (3 x 6,000) + (4 x 6,000) = 42,000
Stuffing (4 x 6,000) + (3 x 6,000) = 42,000
Cooking (3 x 6,000) + (2 x 6,000) = 30,000
No constraints are violated;
    CM = $1(6,000) + $.50(6,000) = $9,000

7,200 ravioli and 4,800 ziti packages

Mixing   (3 x 7,200) + (4 x 4,800) = 40,800
Stuffing (4 x 7,200) + (3 x 4,800) = 43,200
Cooking (3 x 7,200) + (2 x 4,800) = 31,200
No constraints are violated;
    CM = $1(7,200) + $.50(4,800) = $9,600

8,400 ravioli and 3,600 ziti packages

Mixing   (3 x 8,400) + (4 x 3,600) = 39,600
Stuffing (4 x 8,400) + (3 x 3,600) = 44,400
Cooking (3 x 8,400) + (2 x 3,600) = 32,400
No constraints are violated;
    CM = $1(8,400) + $.50(3,600) = $10,200

9,600 ravioli and 2,400 ziti packages

Mixing   (3 x 9,600) + (4 x 2,400) = 38,400
Stuffing (4 x 9,600) + (3 x 2,400) = 45,600
Cooking (3 x 9,600) + (2 x 2,400) = 33,600
The Stuffing Department constraint is violated; therefore, this is not a feasible solution.

Conclusion: The feasible solution that will maximize the contribution margin is 8,400 ravioli and 3,600 ziti packages.

CHAPTER 22

Part 1 ■ True/False

1.	T	6.	F	11.	F
2.	F	7.	T	12.	T
3.	T	8.	T	13.	T
4.	T	9.	F	14.	F
5.	F	10.	T	15.	T

Part 2 ■ Matching

1.	h	6.	j	11.	c
2.	b	7.	n	12.	i
3.	f	8.	m	13.	d
4.	k	9.	a	14.	g
5.	o	10.	l	15.	e

Part 3 ■ Multiple Choice

1. c   Future costs that differ between alternatives are the relevant costs. Historical costs are not relevant costs, and b and d are incorrect because variable costs alone or fixed costs alone are not relevant costs.

2. d   The accountant should go to the accounting supervisor before discussing the ethical problem with the individuals involved.

3. a   Replacement expenditures include the acquisition of new machinery and/or buildings to replace worn-out or obsolete assets.

4. c   Expansion expenditures include plant enlargement for the purpose of expanding existing markets or invading new markets.

5. d   Improvement expenditures include the improvements for product quality or design to counter competitors' actions.

6. c   Although cost savings may occur the primary motivation for CIM, robotics, and FMS is strategic considerations such as a, b, and d.

7. b   Computer programming and fine tuning are common cash *outflows* related to capital expenditure proposals.

8. c   The Accelerated Cost Recovery System (ACRS) was required for tangible, depreciable property placed in service after 1980.

9. a   Cost of new machine................................. $150,000
        Less: After-tax inflow from old machine ($25,000 x 70%) ...   17,500
                                                               $132,500

10. c   Cost of new machine.................................. $150,000
        Trade-in allowance....................................   25,000
                                                               $125,000

Part 4 ■ Problem

Year	Estimated Demand in Units	Unit Sales Price	Unit Variable Cost	Unit Contribution Margin	Net Pretax Cash Inflows From Sales
1	15,000	$50	$25	$25	$ 375,000
2	15,000	$50	$25	$25	375,000
3	15,000	$50	$25	$25	375,000
4	15,000	$50	$25	$25	375,000
5	15,000	$50	$25	$25	375,000

Total net pretax cash inflows from sales $1,875,000

Initial cash outflow (cost of asset) $1,000,000

Less pretax estimated salvage value . . . .   (200,000)   800,000

Excess of net pretax cash inflows over cost $1,075,000

Part 5 ■ Problem

Year	Estimated Net Pretax Cash Inflows	6% Annual Price-level Adjustment	Price-level Adjusted Net Cash Inflows
1	$20,000	$(1 + .06)^1 = 1.060$	$ 21,200
2	25,000	$(1 + .06)^2 = 1.124$	28,100
3	25,000	$(1 + .06)^3 = 1.191$	29,775
4	25,000	$(1 + .06)^4 = 1.262$	31,550
5	15,000	$(1 + .06)^5 = 1.338$	20,070

Total price-level adjusted net pretax cash inflows from operations. . . $130,695

Plus cash inflow from salvage. $10,000

Price-level adjustment. 1.338   13,380

Total price level adjusted net pretax cash inflows over initial cash

    outflow. $144,075

Less initial cash outflow.   100,000

Excess of net pretax cash inflows over initial cash outflow . . . . $ 44,075

Part 6 ■ Problem

	(1)	(2)	(3)	(4)	(5)
Year	Estimated Inflation Adjusted Net Cash Inflows	Tax Depreciation*	Taxable Income (Loss) (1)-(2)	Tax Liability With 40% Tax Rate 40% x (3)	Net After-tax Cash Inflows (1) - (4)
1	$50,000	$60,000	$(10,000)	$(4,000)	$ 54,000
2	60,000	96,000	(36,000)	(14,400)	74,400
3	70,000	57,600	12,400	4,960	65,040
4	80,000	34,500	45,500	18,200	61,800
5	50,000	34,500	15,500	6,200	43,800
6	35,000	17,400	17,600	7,040	27,960
7	20,000	0	20,000	8,000	12,000

Total net after-tax cash inflows. $339,000

Less initial cash outflow to purchase system.   300,000

Excess of net after-tax cash inflows over initial cash outflow. . . . . $ 39,000

*

Year	MACRS 5-year Recovery Rate	Depreciable Basis	Tax Depreciation
1	0.200	$300,000	$ 60,000
2	0.320	300,000	96,000
3	0.192	300,000	57,600
4	0.115	300,000	34,500
5	0.115	300,000	34,500
6	0.058	300,000	17,400
	1.000		$300,000

CHAPTER 23

Part 1 ■ True/False

1.	F	6.	T	11.	T
2.	T	7.	T	12.	F
3.	F	8.	T	13.	F
4.	T	9.	T	14.	F
5.	T	10.	T	15.	T

Part 2 ■ Matching

1.	h	6.	j	11.	c
2.	b	7.	n	12.	i
3.	f	8.	m	13.	d
4.	k	9.	a	14.	g
5.	o	10.	l	15.	e

Part 3 ■ Multiple Choice

1. b The specific cost of financing a specific project often is called the marginal cost of capital.

2. d The cost of capital represents the expected return that investors demand for a given level of risk; a, b, and c are capital expenditure evaluation techniques.

3. a Payback is the point where cumulative net cash inflow equals the cost of the investment.
$2,000 x 3 yrs. = $ 6,000
$3,000 x 3 yrs. =   9,000
                  $15,000

4. b Advantages of using the payback method include:
   1. It is simple to compute and easy to understand.
   2. It may be used to select those investments yielding a quick return of cash.
   3. It permits a company to determine the length of time required to recapture its original investment.
   4. It is a widely used method that is an improvement over an intuitive method.

5. b The advantages of the net present value method and internal rate of return methods include: (1) consideration of the time value of money and (2) consideration of cash flows over the entire life of the project.

6. c The internal rate of return is the rate at which the sum of positive present values (inflows) exactly equals the sum of negative present values (outflows): $843,000 = $800,000 + $43,000.

7. a Let x = original investment.
NPV = PV of cash flows - Investment
$2,000 = ($8,000 x .91) + ($9,000 x .83) + ($10,000 x .75) - x
x = $20,250

8. a Disadvantages of the present value method include:
   1. It is difficult to compute and to understand.
   2. Management must determine a discount rate to be used.
   3. It does not consider the relative size of competing investments.
   4. It does not account for differences due to projects having unequal lives.

9. d $\dfrac{\text{Net cash inflow} - \text{depreciation}}{\text{Initial investment}} = \text{Accounting rate of return}$

$\dfrac{\text{Net cash inflow} - (\$28,000 / 8)}{\$28,000} = 15\%$

Net cash inflow − $3,500 = $4,200

Net cash inflow = $7,700

10. **a** The answer is the interest rate that causes the present value of the cash flows to equal the amount of the investment; in this case, 14%:

200 (.8772) + 200 (.7695) + 248 (.6750) = $497

Part 4 ■ Problem

Funds - Source	Proportion of Funds	After-Tax Cost	Weighted Cost
Bonds	.333	.105[1]	.035
Preferred Stock	.167	.125[2]	.021
Common stock and retained earnings	.500	.162[3]	.081
	1.000		.137 or 13.7%

[1]15% x (1 - 30%)
[2](12% x $100 par) ÷ $96 = .125
[3]($121,500 ÷ 50,000) ÷ $15 = .162

Part 5 ■ Problem

1.

Year	Pretax Cash Benefit	Annual Depreciation*	Taxable Income	(3) x 30% Federal Income Tax	(1) - (4) Net After-tax Cash Inflow
1	$45,000	$20,000	$25,000	$7,500	$ 37,500
2	50,000	32,000	18,000	5,400	44,600
3	44,000	19,200	24,800	7,440	36,560
4	38,000	11,500	26,500	7,950	30,050
5	34,000	11,500	22,500	6,750	27,250
6	10,000	5,800	4,200	1,260	8,740
					$184,700

*Year	Depreciable Base	MACRS Rate	Annual Depreciation
1	$100,000	20.0 %	$20,000
2	100,000	32.0	32,000
3	100,000	19.2	19,200
4	100,000	11.5	11,500
5	100,000	11.5	11,500
6	100,000	5.8	5,800

2. (a)

Year	Cash Flow	Needed	Balance	Payback Years Required
1	$37,500	$100,000	$62,500	1.00
2	44,600	62,500	17,900	1.00
3	36,560	17,900	17,900	.49
4	--	--	--	--
5	--	--	--	--
6	--	--	--	--
Total payback period in years				2.49 or 2.5 years

(b)

$$\text{Average annual return on original investment} = \frac{\text{Net income}}{\text{Economic life}} \div \text{Original investment} = \frac{\$84,700^*}{6 \text{ years}} \div \$100,000 = 14.1\%$$

*Net after-tax cash inflow $184,700
Less depreciation............................. 100,000
Net income .... $ 84,700

(c)

$$\text{Average annual return on original investment} = \frac{\text{Net income}}{\text{Economic life}} \div \text{Average investment} = \frac{\$84,700}{6 \text{ years}} \div \$50,000^* = 28.2\%$$

*Original investment........................ $100,000
Salvage value at end of life 0
Average investment ($100,000 ÷ 2) .... $ 50,000

(d)

Year	Cash (Outflow) Inflow	Present Value of $1 @ 12%	Net Present Value of Cash Flow
0	$(100,000)	1.000	$(100,000)
1	37,500	.893	33,488
2	44,600	.797	35,546
3	36,560	.712	26,031
4	30,050	.636	19,112
5	27,250	.567	15,451
6	8,740	.507	4,431
Net present value			$ 34,059

(e) The internal rate of return

Year	Cash (Outflow) Inflow	Present Value of $1 @ 25%	Net Present Value of Cash Flow @ 25%	Present Value of $1 @ 26%	Net Present Value of Cash Flow @ 26%
0	$(100,000)	1.000	$(100,000)	1.00	$(100,000)
1	37,500	.800	30,000	.794	29,775
2	44,600	.640	28,544	.630	28,098
3	36,560	.512	18,719	.500	18,280
4	30,050	.410	12,321	.397	11,930
5	27,250	.328	8,938	.315	8,584
6	8,740	.262	2,290	.250	2,185
			$ 812		$ (1,148)

Internal rate of return: 25% + {1% x [812 ÷ (812 + 1,148)]} = 25.4%

Part 6 ■ Problem

1. (a)

Purchase:

Investment.......................................			$(300,000)
Annual net cash inflow	$100,000	$100,000	
Less depreciation	30,000		
Taxable income	$ 70,000		
Income tax		28,000	
Annual net cash inflow, after income tax		$ 72,000	
Present value of annual after-tax cash inflow			$ 406,800 [1]
Present value of salvage value			9,660 [2]
Net present value.................................			$ 116,460

[1]$72,000 x 5.650 = $406,800
[2]$30,000 x .322 = $9,660

(b)

Lease:

Annual net cash inflow, before lease payment	$100,000
Less annual lease payment	70,000
Annual net cash inflow	$ 30,000
Income tax	12,000
Annual net cash inflow, after income tax	$ 18,000
Net present value.................................	$101,700 *

*$18,000 x 5.650 = $101,700

2. Decision: The purchase alternative is preferable by $14,760.

CHAPTER 24

Part 1 ■ True/False

1. F	6. F	11. F	
2. T	7. F	12. T	
3. T	8. T	13. F	
4. T	9. T	14. T	
5. T	10. T	15. F	

Part 2 ■ Matching

1. e	6. k	11. h
2. d	7. g	12. j
3. c	8. f	13. i
4. b	9. m	14. l
5. a	10. n	15. o

Part 3 ■ Multiple Choice

1. c In capital budgeting analysis, the standard deviation is generally viewed as a measure of investment risk.

2. a Perfectly correlated cash flows might occur because consumer acceptance of the product in one period might have a direct bearing on the level of sales in the following period.

3. e Because the normal distribution is symmetrical and has only one mode, the expected value is not only the mean of the probability distribution, but it is also the mode.

4. a The net present value of the expected cash flows would be the same when a normal probability distribution is used in capital expenditure analysis as it would when the probability distribution of future cash flows is ignored.

5. d If the cash flows in each period are independent, the standard deviation of the expected net present value is computed by taking the square root of the sum of the discounted period variances.

6. c Sometimes it may be necessary to construct a nonnormal probability distribution because not all future events that affect cash flows follow the pattern of random variables drawn from a normal distribution.

7. d In decision-tree analysis, a process referred to as "backward induction" is used to determine the best course of action.

8. b Monte Carlo simulations are especially valuable in evaluating problems that contain numerous stochastic variables because such problems are difficult to evaluate analytically.

9. b
Variance of NPV for dependent cash flows	$500,000
Variance of NPV for independent cash flows	150,000
Variance of total NPV of investment	$650,000

10. c Standard deviation of total net present value = $\sqrt{\text{Variance of total net present value}}$
$$= \sqrt{650,000} = \$806$$

Part 4 ■ Problem

1.

Units Demanded	Probability of Unit Demand	Total Contribution Margin of Units Demanded	Expected Contribution Margin
0	.05	0	$ 0
5	.10	$1,500	150
10	.40	3,000	1,200
15	.20	4,500	900
20	.15	6,000	900
25	.10	7,500	750
			$3,900

2.

(1) Contribution Margin (Conditional Value)	(2) Difference From Expected Value ($3,900)	(3) (2) Squared	(4) Probability	(5) Variance (3) x (4)
$0	$ - 3,900	15,210,000	.05	$ 760,500
1,500	- 2,400	5,760,000	.10	576,000
3,000	- 900	810,000	.40	324,000
4,500	+ 600	360,000	.20	72,000
6,000	+ 2,100	4,410,000	.15	661,500
7,500	+ 3,600	12,960,000	.10	1,296,000
				$3,690,000

Standard deviation = $\sqrt{\$3,690,000}$ = $1,921

3.   Coefficient of variation = $\dfrac{\text{Standard deviation}}{\text{Expected contribution margin}}$ = $\dfrac{\$1,921}{\$3,900}$ = .4926

Part 5 ■ Problem

1.

(1) Year	(2) Periodic Standard Deviation	(3) Periodic Variance (2)²	(4) Present Value of $1 @10%	(5) Present Value of $1 @10% Squared (4)²	(6) Present Value of Variance (3) x (5)
0	$0	0	1.000	1.000000	$0
1	1,000	$1,000,000	.909	.826281	826,281
2	1,000	1,000,000	.826	.682276	682,276
3	1,000	1,000,000	.751	.564001	564,001
4	1,000	1,000,000	.683	.466489	466,489
5	1,000	1,000,000	.621	.385641	385,641
Variance of the net present value for the independent cash flows					$2,924,688

2.

(1) Year	(2) Periodic Standard Deviation	(3) Present Value of $1 at 10%	(4) PresentValue of Standard Deviation (2) x (3)
0	$0	1.000	0
1	2,000	.909	$1,818
2	2,000	.826	1,652
3	2,000	.751	1,502
4	2,000	.683	1,366
5	2,000	.621	1,242
Standard deviation of the net present value for dependent cash flows			$7,580

3.

Variance of net present value for dependent cash flows............................ $57,456,400

Variance of net present value for independent cash flows 2,924,688

Variance of total net present value of investment $60,381,088

4. $\sqrt{60,381,088} = \$7,771$

Part 6 ■ Problem

1.

Potential Action (Racquetball Facility Capacity to be Built	Annual After-Tax Net Cash Inflows From Different Levels of Demand				Expected Value of After-Tax Net Cash Inflows
	60,000	80,000	100,000	120,000	
60,000	$200,000	$200,000	$200,000	$200,000	$200,000
80,000	200,000	300,000	300,000	300,000	270,000
100,000	200,000	300,000	400,000	400,000	300,000
120,000	200,000	300,000	400,000	500,000	310,000
	.30	.40	.20	.10	

2.

(1) Possible Action (Racquetball Facility Capacity to be Built)	(2) Expected Value of Annual After-Tax Net Cash Inflows	(3) Present Value of 20-Year Annuity of $1@10%	(4) Present Value of Annual After-Tax Net Cash Inflows (2)x(3)	(5) Initial Cash Outflow	(6) Expected Net Present Value (4) - (5)
60,000	$200,000	8.514	$1,702,800	$1,500,000	$202,800
80,000	270,000	8.514	2,298,780	2,000,000	298,780
100,000	300,000	8.514	2,554,200	2,500,000	54,200
120,000	310,000	8.514	2,639,340	3,000,000	(360,660)

Wallbanger should build the racquetball facility with the 80,000 one-hour time slot capacity because it has the largest expected net present value.

CHAPTER 25

Part 1 ■ True/False

1. F	6. F	11. F
2. T	7. T	12. T
3. T	8. T	13. T
4. F	9. T	14. F
5. T	10. T	15. F

Part 2 ■ Matching

1. o	8. q	15. d
2. b	9. m	16. p
3. t	10. a	17. i
4. l	11. c	18. g
5. s	12. n	19. e
6. j	13. r	20. f
7. h	14. k	

Part 3 ■ Multiple Choice

1. d   Order-getting costs are the costs of activities carried on to bring in the sales orders; whereas, warehousing is an order-filling cost.

2. a   Flexible budgets should be used for the control of marketing costs, such as order-filling costs, because a comparison of actual costs with predetermined fixed budget figures does not always give a fair evaluation of the activities of a function, due to the influence of volume and capacity.

3. a   Actual 19X4 sales.. $ 750,000
     19X4 sales at 19X3 prices (150,000 x $4)........................   600,000
     Favorable sales price variance.................................. $ 150,000

     Actual 19X4 sales at 19X3 prices................................ $ 600,000
     Total 19X3 sales..   720,000
       Unfavorable sales volume variance......................... $(120,000)

4. c

$$\text{Price} = \frac{\text{Total cost} + (\text{Desired rate of return} \times \text{Total capital employed})}{\text{Sales volume in units}}$$

$$= \frac{\$200,000 + (15\% \times \$500,000)}{50,000 \text{ units}} = \frac{\$275,000}{50,000 \text{ units}} = \$5.50$$

5. d   Activity based management is the process of analyzing marketing activities and expenses created by those activities to produce a basis for controlling and improving efficiency.

6. c   Life cycle costs include all the costs that the manufacturer will incur over the life of the product.

7. c   Budget allowance:
     Fixed overhead budget... $ 3,000
     Variable overhead ($.30 x 32,000 invoice lines).................   9,600
                                         $12,600

8. b   Spending variance:
     Actual expenses... $12,700
     Budget allowance.. 12,600
     Unfavorable spending variance................................. $ 100

9. d   Idle capacity variance:
     Budget allowance.. $12,600
     Standard cost charged in ($.40 x 32,000 lines)................. 12,800
     Favorable idle capacity variance.............................. $ (200)

10. a   Contribution margin or differential pricing is a short-run approach, usually used only for special orders, that accepts any price over and above total differential cost.

Part 4 ■ Problem

	Total	Territory	
		Indianapolis	Fort Wayne
Sales salaries................................	$108,000	$ 72,000	$36,000
Salespersons' expenses.......................	50,000	32,000	18,000
Advertising	63,000	50,000	13,000
Delivery expense	33,000	27,500	5,500
Credit investigation expense	5,000	4,000	1,000
Collection expense...........................	12,000	9,600	2,400
Total	$271,000	$195,100	$75,900

Part 5 ■ Problem

1. $50,000 ÷ $400,000 = .125
     $7,500 x .125 = $938

2.   Actual cost $4,100
     Budget allowance................................... 4,300
     Spending variance .... $ (200) fav.

3.   Budget allowance................................... $4,300
     Standard selling cost ($35,000 x .125) 4,375
     Idle capacity variance .... $ (75) fav.

Part 6 ■ Problem

ACR
Income Statement
For the Year Ended December 31, 19#

	Department Stores	Retail Appliance Stores	Wholesalers	Total
Sales	$280,000	$525,000	$300,000	$1,105,000
Cost of goods sold	180,000	325,000	225,000	730,000
Gross profit	$100,000	$200,000	$ 75,000	$ 375,000
Less marketing expenses:				
Selling	$ 28,800	$ 38,400	$ 48,000	$ 115,200
Packing and shipping	1,920	9,280	4,800	16,000
Advertising	12,670	23,756	13,574	50,000
Credit and collection	4,200	9,200	6,600	20,000
General accounting	2,640	12,760	6,600	22,000
Total	$ 50,230	$ 93,396	$ 79,574	$ 223,200
Operating income (loss)	$ 49,770	$106,604	$ (4,574)	$ 151,800

Part 7 ■ Problem

1.

	Product Delta	Product Gamma	Total
Sales	$550,000	$100,000	$650,000
Less variable costs and expenses:			
Cost of goods sold (at 15%)	$82,500	--	$82,500
(at 25%)	--	$25,000	25,000
Advertising	24,000	--	24,000
Commissions (at 5%)	27,500	5,000	32,500
Shipping and packing	16,000	4,000	20,000
General and administrative expenses (15% of gross profit)	52,500	5,700	58,200
Total variable costs and expenses	$202,500	$39,700	$242,200
Contribution margin	$347,500	$60,300	$407,800
Fixed costs and expenses (not allocated):			
Manufacturing costs			$154,500
Administrative sales salaries			16,000
General and administrative expenses			13,800
Total fixed costs and expenses			$184,300
Net income			$223,500

2. Net income would decrease by $60,300 with the elimination of Product Gamma, since Product Gamma's contribution margin would be eliminated and the fixed costs allocated to Product Gamma in the original income statements would continue if Product Gamma were not produced.

Additional Computations:
Allocation of shipping and packing costs—

$$\frac{\text{Shipping and packing expenses}}{\text{Number of orders processed}} = \frac{\$20,000}{1,250} = \$16 \text{ per order}$$

To Product Delta . . . .   1,000 orders x $16 = $16,000
To Product Gamma . . . .   250 orders x $16 = $4,000

Fixed costs and expenses:

Manufacturing costs	=	Total costs - Variable costs
	=	$262,000 - $82,500 - 25,000
	=	$154,500
Marketing costs	=	Administrative sales salaries
	=	$16,000
General and administrative expense	=	Total costs - Variable costs
	=	$72,000 - $58,200
	=	$13,800

Part 8 ■ Problem

1.

(a)
Actual sales....................................		$568,000
Actual sales at budgeted prices		
X (50,000 x $8.25)............................	$412,500	
Y (24,000 x $7.50)............................	180,000	592,500
Sales price variance		$ 24,500 unfav.

(b)
Actual sales at budgeted prices		$592,500
Budgeted sales		517,500
Sales volume variance		$ 75,000 fav.

(c)
Cost of goods sold—actual		$480,000
Budgeted cost of actual units sold:		
X (50,000 x $7)	$350,000	
Y (24,000 x $6)	144,000	494,000
Cost price variance		$ 14,000 fav.

(d)
Budgeted cost of actual units sold....................		$494,000
Budgeted cost of budgeted units sold.................		430,000
Cost volume variance............................		$ 64,000 unfav.
Sales volume variance		$ 75,000 fav.
Cost volume variance............................		64,000 unfav.
Net volume variance		$ 11,000 fav.

2.

Actual sales at budgeted prices		$592,500
Budgeted cost of actual units sold....................		494,000
Difference		$ 98,500
Budgeted gross profit of actual units sold		
[($517,500 - $430,000) ÷ 65,000] x 74,000		99,615
Sales mix variance		$ 1,115 unfav.
Budgeted gross profit of actual units sold		$ 99,615
Budgeted sales	$517,500	
Budgeted cost of budgeted units sold	430,000	
Budgeted gross profit		87,500
Final sales volume variance		$ 12,115 fav.

Part 9 ■ Problem

Alternate Sales Price	Variable Manufacturing Cost per Unit	Contribution Margin per Unit	Unit Sales	Total Contribution Margin	Additional Advertising and Promotion Expenditures	Contribution to Other Fixed Costs
19A:						
$20.00	$15	$5.00	225,000	$1,125,000	$550,000	$575,000
22.50	15	7.50	210,000	1,575,000	700,000	875,000
25.00	15	10.00	200,000	2,000,000	750,000	1,250,000
27.50	15	12.50	190,000	2,375,000	800,000	1,575,000
30.00	15	15.00	175,000	2,625,000	1,000,000	1,625,000

The recommended sales price would be $30.

19B:						
$20.00	$17	$3.00	245,000	$735,000	$600,000	$135,000
22.50	17	5.50	230,000	1,265,000	725,000	540,000
25.00	17	8.00	220,000	1,760,000	750,000	1,010,000
27.50	17	10.50	210,000	2,205,000	825,000	1,380,000
30.00	17	13.00	195,000	2,535,000	1,200,000	1,335,000

The recommended sales price would be $27.50.

Part 10 ■ Problem

1.

$$\text{Price} = \frac{\text{Total cost} + \left(\text{Desired rate of return} \times \text{Total capital employed}\right)}{\text{Sales volume in units}}$$

$$\$25 = \frac{(\$20 \times 200,000) + \left(\text{Desired rate of return} \times \$5,000,000\right)}{200,000}$$

$$\$5,000,000 = \$4,000,000 + (\$5,000,000 \times \text{Desired rate of return})$$

Desired rate of return = 20%

2.

$$\text{Price} = \frac{(\$20 \times \$220,000) + (.20 \times \$5,000,000)}{220,000} = \$24.55$$

CHAPTER 26

Part 1 ■ True/False

1. T	6. T	11. T
2. T	7. F	12. T
3. F	8. T	13. T
4. T	9. T	14. F
5. T	10. F	15. F

Part 2 ■ Matching

1. g	6. f	11. m
2. e	7. c	12. h
3. a	8. n	13. i
4. l	9. d	14. j
5. b	10. k	15. o

Part 3 ■ Multiple Choice

1. c The use of different accounting methods by companies makes comparisons difficult without first adjusting the financial statements.

2. a Return on investment = Capital-employed turnover rate x Profit margin on sales

3. a Market-based transfer prices are the best transfer prices to use for evaluating departmental performance.

4. a Suboptimization means that the decision made by the individual segment manager did not maximize the profits for the company as a whole.

5. d If Y's facilities would otherwise remain idle, it would be more profitable for X to buy inside because there would be a positive contribution margin of $5 per unit ($75 - $70) to contribute to the recovery of the fixed costs of $15,000.

6. c Return on investment (ROI) is affected by both profit as a percentage of sales and by capital turnover. If one decreases while the other remains the same, ROI will decrease.

7. d In a decentralized company, the transfer pricing system should be designed so that division managers have the freedom to sell/buy outside if it enhances division profit. The appraisal of managerial performance is meaningful only if division managers are given this autonomy.

8. d Rate of return on capital employed =

$$\frac{Profit}{Capital\ Employed} \quad x \quad \frac{\$25,000}{\$100,000} \quad = \quad 25\%$$

$$\frac{Profit}{Sales} \quad x \quad \frac{Sales}{Capital\ Employed}$$

$$\frac{\$25,000}{\$150,000} \quad x \quad \frac{\$150,000}{\$100,000} \quad = \quad 25\%$$

9. a Capital-employed turnover rate =

$$\frac{Sales}{Capital\ Employed} \quad x \quad \frac{\$100,000}{\$100,000} \quad = \quad 1$$

10. c Residual income = Income - (Capital charge x Assets employed)

Part 4 ■ Problem

1.

Product	(1) Capital-Employed Turnover Rate	(2) Percentage of Profit to Sales	(3) Rate of Return on Capital Employed
Orville	$\frac{\$1,500,000}{\$750,000} = 2$	$\frac{\$75,000}{\$1,500,000} = 5\%$	5% × 2 = 10%
Wilbur	$\frac{\$1,000,000}{\$500,000} = 2$	$\frac{\$200,000}{\$1,000,000} = 20\%$	20% × 2 = 40%
Amelia	$\frac{\$6,000,000}{\$12,000,000} = .5$	$\frac{\$12,000,000}{\$6,000,000} = 20\%$	20% × .5 = 10%

2.   No, they do not have the same problems. Orville's profit as a percentage of sales is too low, whereas Amelia's capital-employed turnover rate is too low. Assuming that sales are currently maximized, Orville must concentrate on cost-cutting measures; while Amelia must reduce its investment in assets such as receivables, inventory, and property, plant and equipment.

Part 5 ■ Problem

1.

System	Cannes	Paris	Corporation as a Whole
Market-based transfer pricing:			
Sales to outsiders	$600,000	$500,000	$1,100,000
Cost of goods sold	560,000 [1]	400,000	960,000
Gross profit	$ 40,000	$100,000	$ 140,000
Standard costing (using 25,000 gallons as a basis for allocating fixed costs):			
Sales to outsiders	$600,000	$500,000	$1,100,000
Intracompany sales	130,000	(130,000) [3]	--
Cost of goods sold	(650,000) [2]	(265,000) [4]	(915,000)
Gross profit	$ 80,000	$105,000	$ 185,000

[1]($18 x 20,000 gals.) + $200,000 = $560,000
[2]($18 x 25,000 gals.) + $200,000 = $650,000

$$^3\left(\$18 + \frac{\$200,000}{25,000}\right) \times 5,000 \text{ gals.} = \$130,000$$

$$^4\left(\$40 - \frac{\$27}{2}\right) \times 10,000 \text{ bags} = \$265,000$$

2.   The transfer either should be made at the standard cost of $26.50 per gallon or at the $27 market price that Paris pays to outside suppliers. These prices will promote internal transfer.

Part 6 ■ Problem

1.

$$\text{Average invested capital} = \frac{\$500,000 + \$700,000}{2} = \$600,000$$

Net income:

Sales	$600,000
Less: Variable costs	450,000
Contribution margin	$150,000
Less: Fixed costs	90,000
Operating income	$ 60,000

$$\text{Return on investment} = \frac{\$60,000}{\$600,000} = 10\%$$

2.   Residual income (loss) = $60,000 - (8% x $600,000) = $12,000

3.

Sales	$600,000
Less: Variable costs	450,000
Contribution margin	$150,000